Praise for **Conflict across Cultures**
and Michelle LeBaron

"**Conflict across Cultures** is a rare _____ and
practice, real-life stories and m_____ _istic
approaches. The end result is a book that is remarkably readable, and even
more valuable for its contribution to understanding the problems that
underpin virtually every major conflict in the world today.

This is one of the few works on culture and conflict resolution that actually
practices what it preaches. The authors have drawn on their own cultural
diversity to produce a framework that can be used by conflict resolution
practitioners and laypeople from all walks of life."

—Ambassador John W. McDonald,
Chairman, The Institute for Multi-Track Diplomacy

"Learning to handle cross-cultural conflict is emerging as a central problem
in human relations. And no one is better qualified to describe the intricate
ins and outs of that learning process than the extraordinary—and
extraordinarily honest—team that has written *Conflict across Cultures*."

—Christopher Honeyman
Conflict Management Consultant and Co-Editor, *The Negotiator's Fieldbook*

"LeBaron and colleagues fused, with elegance, their substantial knowledge
in the fields of peace, conflict and culture with stories and experiences, and
artistic imagination which made reading this book like a walk in a terrain,
or a swim in a river … with pleasant friends."

—Amr Abdalla, Ph.D.
Professor and Dean for Academic Programmes
University for Peace
United Nations Affiliated University

"**Conflict across Cultures** teaches how each of us can build bridges across
the chasms that separate different cultures. With insights born of rich
experiences, the authors explore metaphor, ritual and storytelling to help
people understand one another, and by helping us to recognize what is
sacred to others, they help us to find our own sacred ground."

—Dr. Mary-Wynne Ashford
International Physicians for the Prevention of Nuclear War

CONFLICT
ACROSS CULTURES

CONFLICT ACROSS CULTURES

A Unique Experience of Bridging Differences

*Michelle LeBaron
and Venashri Pillay*

INTERCULTURAL PRESS
A Nicholas Brealey Publishing Company

BOSTON • LONDON

First published by Intercultural Press, a division of Nicholas Brealey Publishing, in 2006.

Intercultural Press, a division of
Nicholas Brealey Publishing
53 State Street, 9th Floor
Boston, MA 02109, USA
Tel: 617-263-1823
Fax: 617-263-2856

Nicholas Brealey Publishing
3-5 Spafield Street, Clerkenwell
London, EC1R 4QB, UK
Tel: +44-(0)-207-239-0360
Fax: +44-(0)-207-239-0370

www.nicholasbrealey.com

Printed in the United States of America

20 19 18 17 16 15   8 9 10 11 12 13 14 15

ISBN-13: 978-1-931930-22-2
ISBN-10: 1-931930-22-8

Library of Congress Cataloging-in-Publication Data

Conflict across cultures: a unique experience of bridging differences / [edited by] Michelle LeBaron and Venashri Pillay.
        p. cm.
     Includes bibliographical references and index.
     ISBN-13: 978-1-931930-22-2
     ISBN-10: 1-931930-22-8
        1. Culture conflict.   2. Conflict management.   3. Multiculturalism.   4. Intercultural communication.   5. Cross-cultural orientation.   I. LeBaron, Michelle, 1956-   II. Pillay, Venashri.

HM1121.C66453 2006

305.8—dc22

2006020995

To those who share the possible
dream of celebrating differences
in all their richness.

Contents

Acknowledgments

We appreciate the efforts of the team at Intercultural Press to shepherd this book to completion in a time of change and transition. The book would not have come into being without Patricia O'Hare's enthusiastic support, Judy Carl-Hendrick's thorough and insightful suggestions, and Erika Heilman's thoughtful input. We appreciate their work and their belief in this project, and the assistance of the many other committed people at Nicolas Brealey Publishing who helped bring this work to fruition.

The Institute for Conflict Analysis and Resolution at George Mason University brought us together as a community of scholars and practitioners. We are thankful for the opportunities we had to teach and study there, and to create this book together. Many of the ideas we express are richer for our experiences at George Mason. The University of British Columbia Faculty of Law and the Social Sciences and Humanities Research Council of Canada also contributed resources essential to the completion of the book, and we appreciate their support. We also appreciate the help of Emily MacAdams, who lent her talent with computer graphics.

We thank all our wonderful friends and colleagues who have shared their insights and stories with us over the years and whose experiences have enriched our own. And we appreciate the patience and care of our family members as we wrote and completed this book. To Matthew, Yu Chun, and Alex, our deep thanks. Finally, this book is richer for the life of Jang Singh Bhangoo, for whom we share deep respect and appreciation.

Preface

"...the world which seems to lie before us
like a land of dreams,
So various, so beautiful, so new,
Hath really neither joy, nor love, nor light,
Nor certitude, nor peace, nor help for pain;
And we are here as on a darkling plain
Swept with confused alarms of struggle and flight,
Where ignorant armies clash by night."
—Matthew Arnold (1822–1888)

Shared concerns and dreams brought our group together to write this book. Each of us had made individual decisions to come to the United States, to a place outside Washington, DC, to teach, practice, and study conflict resolution. We brought experiences from around the world. We were hungry to learn, while we were also mindful of the wisdom of the places from which we had traveled. What drew us together was a shared concern to find ways through the "darkling plain"—ways that would help ameliorate the confusion and destruction of intercultural conflict and illuminate paths to resilience and resolution.

We often found ourselves meeting between and after classes, talking about our lives—Tatsushi, a Japanese man married to a Taiwanese woman whose experience included work in Rwanda, former Yugoslavia, and the United States; Nike, a German-born woman raised in Texas who, with her partner, a composer, was soon to move to Barcelona, Spain, and whose work ranged from Northern Ireland to Eastern Europe; Venashri, a South African woman of South Asian descent who had met her Alaskan husband while studying social work in Boston, and who had worked in South African townships amidst the transition from apartheid; Karenjot, a first-generation Canadian Sikh woman who grew up in coastal British Columbia, Canada, in a town where racism and religious conflict surrounded her, and whose work centered on India; and Michelle, a Euro-Canadian lawyer, scholar, and parent of four who had written about cross-cultural conflict resolution in earlier books and who had worked in Switzerland, Japan, and China.

Looking around the table during our first meetings, we realized that we had tremendous diversity among us—diversity that would make our process richer, and also more difficult. We brought different disciplinary backgrounds—law, social work, community development, business, sociology, intercultural communication—as well as different languages, generations, and ideas about conflict to the table. We knew that others had tried and given up on the kind of journey we were about to undertake, weaving together not only our disciplines and diverse ideas but also our cultural stories and understandings into a coherent, practical product.

We were encouraged as we realized that we shared several concerns that mattered to us very deeply. Our concerns arose from our experiences of working in diverse contexts, and then coming from different parts of the world to the United States to study, teach, and practice conflict resolution. We each had lived and worked outside our birth cultures, feeling pulled between cultures of origin and local ways of responding to conflict, and learning code-switching as a coping skill. Each of us had experienced cross-cultural conflicts along the way, and had sought guidance that was not easy to locate. The models we encountered in academic settings arose primarily from Western perspectives that did not always reflect our lived experiences. All these experiences contributed to our central concern: to develop and share approaches to conflict resolution applicable across cultures.

We realized that writing such a book was a dream. Dreams are ephemeral and intangible until concrete steps are taken to materialize them. During those early talks, we tried to anticipate challenges and barriers that might arise and develop ways of meeting those challenges so they would not derail our progress. We knew that it would be challenging to write a book that honored each of our voices, yet was an integrated whole. We sensed that we would encounter disagreement and discouragement along the way, though it was hard to know how these would manifest, captured as we were with the excitement of our dream. We hoped that the process of conceiving and writing the book would deepen and grow our relationships, some of which were new, while others had been growing for a few years. We anchored our writing in a shared vision that included all of us—our stories, our "common sense" of conflict, and our experiences of resolving it.

At the same time, we were only too aware of the barriers we faced: over-stretched calendars and workloads; group members traveling and moving from one side of the earth to the other; the challenges of English that, while a common language for all of us, had limitations born of its structure and rules that were only compounded by our diverse ways of using it; individual differences among us that led some to find the uncertainty and enormity of what we had set out to do exhilarating, while for others it was overwhelming. We were also vulnerable to challenges arising from different starting-points and ways of making sense of ideas. We aspired to balance our different ways of expression, striving for specificity and generalizability; normalizing ambiguity, while addressing our desires for certainty. We sought to be neither universalistic nor reductionistic, believing that one-size-fits-all formulas are unattainable and preferring the nuanced richness of stories.

We were also acutely aware of the urgency of our subject matter. We live in the midst of worldwide devastation resulting from misunderstood and poorly addressed cross-cultural conflicts, and a general sense of resignation from those who believe that the causes are too buried in time and the factors too complex for cross-cultural conflict resolution approaches to work.

We did not want to believe in such a discouraging picture. We wanted to see what would happen when we explored stories, hunches, theories, and experiences over a sustained period of collaborative work. From the beginning, we sought to bring hope; to inspire others from a range of cultures with practical strategies to work together and prevent destructive conflict.

None of us knew when we began how long or difficult the process would be. Cross-cultural collaboration is not for the faint of heart! Yet none of us knew, either, how rewarding it would be to create this book. Together, we realized the wisdom of the African proverb: "the market is not attended from a single road." The diversity of routes from which we came to the journey made the experience richer in the end.

This book arises from the journey. We invite you to share it with us, the jewels and the storms, the struggles and the discoveries. It has contributed richly to our research and practice but, more than that, it has contributed to our capacities to relate well across all kinds of boundaries and differences. As we share our journey of becoming a well-functioning multicultural team while writing practically and accessibly about conflict and culture, we hope it will spark ideas and help you develop effective skills and approaches.

Tatsushi Arai, Fairfax, Virginia
Karenjot Bhangoo, Surrey, Canada
Nike Carstarphen, Washington, DC
Michelle LeBaron, Vancouver, Canada
Venashri Pillay, Durban, South Africa
April 2006

CHAPTER ONE

Crossing Boundaries

*Venashri Pillay and
Michelle LeBaron*

This book is written with a spirit of inquiry, posing questions and offering answers from our collective resources. We are acutely aware of the limitations of our vision and committed to honoring the wisdom of others: readers, people in conflict with whom we work, and those whose understandings of conflict and conflict resolution may be very different from our own. Our resources include

- the experiences we have collected around the world as family members, as participants in teams and communities; and as scholars, teachers, and practitioners of conflict analysis and resolution;
- our intuitions that whisper ways forward;
- our imaginations that help us dream of new and more constructive ways to invest in the relationships and creations that give meaning to our lives; and
- the work of many others who have shared their stories with us, and have thought long and carefully about the human condition and its manifestations in cultures and conflicts.

We draw on our love of stories, stories that carry the wisdom of the past and remind us of our potential to create and to hope even amidst violence and destruction. We weave together the places from which we come—Canada, South Africa, Japan, Germany, the United States—with the people and stories

1

we have encountered around the world. In dozens of places, we have worked in partnership with local people to contribute to positive change and hope in societies ravaged by war and poverty, organizations scarred by painful pasts, and families stretched by divisive differences.

When we first thought of writing this book, the United States was reeling from the horror and pain of September 11, 2001. All of us lived in the U.S. at that time, studying, teaching, and mediating. The pain of September 11 is present still—and will be—and yet it lives, hand-in-hand, with the hope that fuels our need to write this book. Our aim is to present ways of understanding and navigating human relationships across cultural and worldview boundaries in ways that are both readable and practical. We share the boldness to imagine a different world and the sanguinity to acknowledge the totality of the human condition, complete as it is with capacities to love and to hate, to build and to destroy.

We begin with some images—word pictures of our collective senses of selves drawn from our home cultures. These word pictures reveal the optimism that lives in our traditions, our legacies from ancestors who themselves sought ways to balance the age-old poles of belonging and autonomy. Each of the images is a window into cultural ways of seeing ourselves and others. These images speak to us, guiding us when complexity and conflict challenge us. Within them are vision, hope, and strength, as well as struggle, stress, and strain. They are windows into our experiences of diversity and community, coming together and maintaining separateness.

When we embarked on writing this book, these images were the first things we shared. They were our answers to the question: Who are we and what do we bring to the challenge of understanding and bridging conflicts and cultures? They showed us something of our values, our dreams, and our identities, giving us a base from which to develop and articulate ways of bridging the differences that divide us. The common threads among them— threads of community and connection, of stress and stretching—helped us talk about our starting points and uncover both commonalities and differences. We offer them here as introductions to us—a multicultural group of writers—and our subject, resolving conflict across cultures.

Images of Ourselves: Differences and Connections

The first image, which reminds us that we are never completely separate from those around us, comes from South Africa. The rainbow is the image most closely associated with post-apartheid South Africa. Different colors make up the rainbow, representing the coming together of races in a new national community. Like a rainbow, this new vision spans the entire nation and encompasses all. It represents hope, brightness, life, and freedom. A rainbow's beauty does not come from complete unification or blending of the different colors; instead, its magnificence is revealed in the way that the colors complement and harmonize with each other. The different colors come together and create a beautiful rainbow, yet each color's individuality, uniqueness, and brightness is not lost. In fact, it is the complete rainbow that makes the individual colors more visible. This image of the rainbow intro-duces the South African idea of *ubuntu,* which means "I am because we are." From this image, we remember that unity is not uniformity or sameness, but harmony in the midst of diversity. Since diversity involves differences and some of those differences bring us into conflict, our shared goal is not the elimination of conflict, but finding ways to live well with it.

For a clue about how to live well with conflict, we turn to an image from Western Europe, Canada, and the United States: the symphony orchestra. Individuals in an orchestra are all different, yet they have a common interest— playing beautiful music together. The music is most beautiful when everyone is working together, playing diverse instruments that contrast with and complement each other. Sometimes in orchestral music there is discord and tension, but eventually all the performers come back together in harmony and synchronicity. The conductor helps interpret the music and facilitates communication between all the performers in order to achieve their desired results. This image shows that structure, leadership, and shared goals can help resolve conflict. It also reminds us that diversity is the richness that makes music beautiful. Our lives would be impoverished if we were all of the same minds and hearts.

An image from Japan speaks to the importance of maintaining an open mind as we relate across differences. The image Shima-guni Kon-Jou refers to the Japanese mindset of insularity. It is generally considered an insulting expression in Japanese. In literal translation, *shima-guni* means "an island nation" and *kon-jou* refers to fundamental human character. The image illus-trates narrow-mindedness and a poor capacity to understand others due to a lack of experience in interacting with foreign influences. Despite global eco-nomic expansion during the last few decades, there remains an inward-looking habit in the Japanese collective mindset. This inward-looking orientation makes it difficult to be fluent with a variety of cultural starting points and to navigate conflict in global and local multicultural contexts.

As the Shima-guni Kon-Jou image reminds us, not all images of community are positive or supportive of creative approaches to bridging differences. A Canadian image of shifting sands demonstrates that the human tendencies to include and exclude can operate in hurtful ways in our communities. Canada has one of the longest coastlines in the world, a coastline that has marked arrival for waves of immigrants from many parts of the world. Shifting sands conjures a landscape in flux, still inventing itself and its relationships to these diverse immigrants. The image represents the paradox of a nation that sees itself as celebrating diversity while still presenting racist experiences to newcomers and those outside dominant groups including indigenous peoples. Sand is attractive—it can be soft and warm, a home for many different creatures from the ocean and land. At the same time, sand is affected by tides and can be unstable when storms, winds, and other influences are present. Conflict over resources or ways of constructing identities can bring a sting to those whose differences threaten emerging norms.

The Challenge

As these diverse images reflect, the authors of this book came together with different ideas of ourselves and each other, shaped by cultures that gave us messages about identity and how cultural differences leading to conflict can be addressed. Coming together was exciting—possibilities danced before us as we imagined the final product of our collaboration. Like every group that seeks to work together over time, we encountered differences. Some of these differences were simply present, residing in our midst like the weather. Others challenged us to find shared language and ideas that spanned our diverse experiences. The stories in our book come not only from our experiences around the world in a variety of settings, but also from our collaboration in writing this book as it tested the mettle of our ideas.

From the beginning, we engaged together in a quest for cohesive ideas, while maintaining healthy receptivity to differences. We preferred disagreement or uncertainty over artificial unanimity. As we wrote our chapters, including stories and developing ideas, we met frequently to dialogue and reflect on our experiences.

Looking back, we recognize that the images with which we began give clues to our different cultural starting points and ways of making meaning. Venashri Pillay, coming from South Africa, thinks of harmony *in* diversity, and how individuality is salient in the collective. Nike Carstarphen emphasizes harmony *through* diversity in the United States, where differences are woven together in a tapestry of voices united by a common goal. Harmony develops as diversity is explored in its ever-changing forms. Karenjot Bhangoo and Michelle LeBaron allude to Canadian dynamism and the challenge of acting on inclusive values in building communities, while Tatsushi Arai contrasts the Japanese habit of insularity with our current age of globalism and integration.

Some of us naturally saw our identities as embedded in communities; others saw our individual selves as the primary units of understanding. Some group members emphasized maintenance of individual distinctness within the whole; others focused on inclusion and collective achievement. These different starting points were felt as we began writing and wrestling with collaborative processes and authorship. For some of us, it was natural to begin working in an isolated way, writing in the first person. For others, ideas came out of extended dialogue and the written voice was a "we."

There were other differences in our starting points as well. For some, it made sense to begin with specific theories and ideas and to look for the commonalities within them. Others wanted to identify broad, abstract themes and to apply them to particular stories as a way of proceeding. Some of us found conversations about how we would proceed protracted and difficult, preferring an action-orientation to extended process-planning. Others saw our process discussions as essential investments in our future success. Because one of us, Michelle LeBaron, was on the faculty and the other group members were completing Ph.D. degrees in the program where she taught, we also encountered different starting points related to hierarchy and status. Some group members were comfortable with horizontal relationships, moving easily into working collaboratively, while others deferred to Michelle because of her position and experience—even when she invited them not to—and found it challenging to work as a collaborative of equals with informality and familiarity.

As we reflected on these different starting points, we recognized that we brought different awareness to the project of understanding conflict and culture. This led to our exploration of awareness itself, summarized in Chapter Four. It also led to explorations of how we each understood and related to the ideas of culture and conflict.

We all agreed that culture is essential to an understanding of conflict, since culture is a part of every relationship and conflict only arises in relationships. Since each of us has multiple cultural identities, all conflicts have cultural components. Culture is one of the most commonly used words around us, and yet one of the hardest to understand. We set out to articulate and deepen our understandings of culture and conflict—how they interact and how they are shifting in our twenty-first-century world. Using ourselves as a laboratory, we devoted three years to learning, reflecting, and integrating the ideas that became this book.

Using the idea of cultural fluency explained in Chapter Four, this book demystifies culture and embraces it for its usefulness in understanding and addressing conflict. We emphasize the importance of culture to any understanding of conflict, and despite culture's complexity, do not believe it need overwhelm us. Mahatma Gandhi's advice is well taken: "I do not want my house to be walled in on all sides and my windows to be stuffed. I want the cultures of all the lands to be blown about my house as freely as possible. But I refuse to be blown off my feet by any"(1995).

In this book, we identify tools to enable understanding of culture-conflict dynamics and develop a range of approaches to working across cultural boundaries and in different intercultural contexts. We give voice to the multidimensional, knowable relationships between culture and conflict.

Forming Our Ideas on Culture and Conflict Resolution

In undertaking this project, we realized that since we ourselves represented such difference and diversity, relationship-building would form the most important part of our collaborative process. In order to work together and give voice to our rich multicultural experiences, we had to first deepen relationships with each other. We had to get to know and understand each other. We believed that when we developed a strong foundation based on relationships and teamwork, the work we engaged in would be more useful and meaningful. When a strong relational base supports processes and products, sustained positive results are more likely. Our experience of relationship-building forms the centerpiece of our approach to conflict resolution across cultures.

Relationship-building as a central focus of intercultural conflict resolution implies a significant investment of time in conflict resolution efforts. Relationships are organic, evolving, and dynamic, and do not automatically follow a linear path. They arise as we work and play together, with a spirit of inquiry about differences, especially those differences that threaten us or our ways of working. Worldview differences—diverse ways of seeing our purpose, values, and relationships—can yield recurrent conflicts in which issues seem to change as conflictual dynamics escalate. These differences can best be resolved in the context of strong, resilient relationships. Our focus in this book will be on interpersonal, intergroup, and community relationships and conflicts. While large-scale international conflicts are very important, the relational dimensions of cultural conflict are easiest to see in interpersonal and community contexts.

A Map through Rough Terrain

The chapters that follow present our approach to resolving conflicts across cultures. Chapter Two begins the exploration of culture and conflict to unearth consistent understandings that will be used throughout the book. We describe the many ways in which culture touches and influences conflict, recognizing that the two are inextricable. The chapter introduces and describes the three dimensions of conflict: material, symbolic, and relational. Each dimension has different implications for conflict and requires different approaches for resolution. Culture connects to all conflict dimensions.

Chapter Three propels us along the river of culture and provides an opportunity to take in its dynamism and unpredictability. We explore what culture is, what role it plays in our lives, and who we see ourselves to be. Chapter Three also presents six guiding lights to help us begin decoding cultural ways of making meaning. These preliminary guides provide us with our first clues toward intercultural understanding and cultural fluency.

Chapter Four immerses us in a deeper understanding of culture as we are introduced to cultural fluency. This chapter explores intercultural understanding anchored in self-awareness and awareness of others. The four key components of cultural fluency—anticipation, embeddedness, expression, and navigation—are unpacked.

In Chapter Five, we come to appreciate how culture and conflict are intertwined in various ways. Culture and conflict constantly shape and reshape each other in an evolving interactive process. This chapter helps us see how culture and conflict continuously influence each other, the interactive dynamics involved, and the consequences for resolution of conflicts.

As we develop awareness and fluency with culture and conflict, we reach out for ways to help us avoid traps, detours, and barriers along the way. Chapter Six introduces several tools we can use in working through intercultural conflict. It offers three capacities for conflict resolution across cultures: flexibility, creative engagement, and momentum. This chapter also lists nine skills through which we can exercise these capacities.

Chapter Seven provides a map through conflict that keeps interdependence and relationships at the center. This map is advisory rather than immutable; suggestive rather than prescriptive. It is a series of guideposts to mark the way, a set of resources to replenish low stocks of ideas, a topographical picture to mirror the shape conflicts may take, and a scattering of stars to inspire creativity. This advisory map illuminates some possible routes through resolving intercultural conflicts.

Finally, Chapter Eight brings our explorations full circle, including reflections on how we applied the ideas in the book to our own multicultural team. Such reflections are perhaps the most useful contribution we can make, for it is only through applying ideas to ourselves that we can speak authoritatively about what has worked, and from which we can begin to speculate about why any given approach is advisable or inadvisable in any particular context. Figure 8.1 provides a visual summary of the key ideas outlined in this book. We conclude with unanswered questions, those queries that we live with every day as we strive to be part of creating a world both more just and generative, a world that welcomes and honors multiple voices.

Deepening the Colors: Expanding Awareness of Conflict and Culture

Look back to the images presented earlier in this chapter and you will realize that some metaphors allude to conflict and dynamic tensions in our worlds, while others refer to harmony and synergy. Tats highlights the dynamic tension between globalism and insularity for people in Japan. Karenjot and Michelle refer to the paradox of official multiculturalism coexisting with racism in Canada. Nike suggests that discord and tension are transformed when diversity becomes synchronized and complementary, and that a conductor as leader and interpreter has a role to play in facilitating this dynamic. Venashri suggests that achieving harmony in South Africa requires some balancing of integration and individualization.

Considering these images prompts many questions: How did our cultural contexts shape our vision of relationships and conflict? Is it coincidence that those of us from Japan and Canada address the struggle between forces, while the South African emphasizes harmony and balancing forces? Is it noteworthy that someone from the United States highlights the leader and third party as important roles in dealing with conflict and tensions? Whatever interpretations or patterns emerge from our images, it is clear that they reveal a range of starting points, illustrating the interconnectedness of culture with perceptions and experiences of harmony and conflict. We explore more of these issues in Chapter Three.

At the same time, we want to be careful not to associate our images with the entire national cultures from which we come. There is too much diversity within our countries, regions, and other identity groups for such associations to work. We offer no specific cultural descriptions of any group, for cultural groups are too dynamic, multifaceted, and variable for generalizations like these to be meaningful. In Chapter Three, we describe some patterns as ways of exploring a range of cultural starting points, but none of them are prescriptions for dealing with any specific group. Just as we do not wish to be seen as exemplars of the groups to which we belong, we also don't want to reify stereotypes of others, or suggest using them as a basis for conflict analysis or intervention.

In writing about conflict and culture, we attempt to explore a whole range of approaches and goals, from resolution to management to appreciation. Conflict does require resolution sometimes—maybe even most times—but there may also be times and contexts where conflict needs to be encouraged, contained, even appreciated. Looking at conflict through an intercultural lens encourages us to question the limited answers and understandings we have of conflict, reminding us that there is no universality or specificity that applies to all situations. It entices us to think of alternative meanings on an ongoing basis, and not to take things for granted. Ultimately, it challenges us to always be mindful of the powerful underground cultural rivers that animate conflict.

This book offers ideas to be used in many cultural and disciplinary settings. Too often, grand theories are created devoid of real-world application. We do not aim for global explanations based on precision and empirical data. Instead, we offer our stories, windows into the rich and fascinating worlds that are beyond measurement, yet affect our every moment. Through stories and anecdotes, culture comes alive. The following pages strive for vitality, connections to real experiences, and a balance of head and heart knowledge. Head and heart, like conflict and culture, are inextricably partnered in the dances of our lives.

We saw the importance of letting head and heart speak together as we worked together on these ideas. We came together with a dream, a dream that it was possible to create a story that would include all of us and hold the keys to deepening our relationships. Along the way, we became an effective intercultural team as our understanding of ourselves and each other grew.

Even as our ideas were developed and took root in the form of this book, we were an immediate test of their validity. We felt conflict emerge among us, sometimes over details and other times over issues of deep importance to one or more of us. When conflict happened, we stretched to see it as a learning opportunity, applying the ideas we were writing about to ourselves. If we had not been able to do this, we could not have continued with the book, for conflict resolution must be alive and real in peoples' lives if it is to live up to its promise of improving our world.

As we engaged our conflicts and challenges, we saw that some gaps are easier to bridge than others; some gaps are shadowy and hard to articulate, living out in the nether world beyond the reach of theories and words. We also experienced joy and energy as we discovered symmetry, synchronicity, and fascinating dissonance in our stories. It was the joy that sustained us, even as we were sometimes slowed by the coordination necessary to collaboratively write a book on this important and difficult subject.

This book comes from the process of learning, reflecting, and becoming, together and separately. We became an extension of the tension between cohesive ideas and meaningful ambiguity. By embracing this tension, our creative energies were given life and momentum, and clarity came to our otherwise opaque visions of culture and conflict. This book is an expression of that vision, in our collective voices.

CHAPTER Two

Conflict, Culture, and Images of Change

*Michelle LeBaron and
Venashri Pillay*

Sojourners, explorers, and boundary-crossers have been with us always. There is something innately human about stretching, uncovering differences, walking to and across the border of the familiar. We do this within ourselves when we reconcile disparate parts of our pasts or inner struggles over decisions. We do it through traveling, trying on new identities as adolescents, and risking uncertainty as adults. Through the course of our lives, we have many opportunities to learn about others—their cultures, their ways of being in the world, and their diverse stories and meanings. We can choose to go toward these opportunities or move away from them. We can live amidst differences and ignore them, or notice the differences that divide us and plumb them for their richness.

The easiest course is to deny differences, moving back into comfort zones and places where the "givens" are clear. But our multicultural world increasingly encroaches into even our remote retreats, as the Internet, global migration, pervasive media, and increased mobility turn each of our communities into McLuhan's global village. The ability to thrive in a multicultural world is now central to our survival; it is a basic life-skill on our shrinking planet. In every land, people from around the world pass through, communicating, coupling, trading, and sometimes fighting. They make things together, share strategies and resources, draw on commonalities to build bridges, and come into conflict over differences. It has been so for centuries, though it has never been so fast or easy to transition from one setting to another as it is in this age of jet travel and high speed communication. It has also never before been possible in the history of the world to so efficiently destroy our human species, and with it, much of life on earth. The need to summon creativity and exercise the choice to cooperate has never been more urgent.

The fault lines that divide us as peoples and nations have become deeper, more raw, and more lethal in our nuclear age. It is essential that we enhance our understanding of conflict and its terrain so that we can navigate the physical, psychological, and spiritual chasms that threaten to swallow us, creative potential and all. Enhancing our understanding of conflict necessarily means building awareness of ourselves—the common sense we share in cultural groups—and coming to know something of those who are different from us by culture and worldview. To do this, we need both conflict fluency and cultural fluency. Conflict fluency means recognizing conflict as a difference that offers us choices and growth. To be fluent with culture is to recognize it as a series of underground rivers that profoundly shape not only who we are, but how we cooperate and engage conflict.

Conflict and Culture: Mapping the Terrain

To begin our work with conflict and culture, we had to agree on working definitions for these terms—no easy task for a group of scholars in conflict resolution! We explored a range of theoretical and philosophical possibilities, opting for simplicity and clarity. Conflict, for our purposes, is a difference within a person or between two or more people that touches them in a significant way. We all constantly encounter differences within and between ourselves and others. Only those differences that that we perceive as challenges to something we believe in or need, or to some aspect of our individual or shared identities, become conflicts. More than a trivial or passing difference, conflict may play out over resources or power, exacerbated by poor communication or negative images of the other. Conflict may also lurk beneath the surface and then become more difficult to address, especially when our core ideas or our shared sense of identity seems threatened through the actions, claims, or the very existence of others.

Conflict is easiest to understand through an example: a Serbian colleague related that she lived in an apartment building in Sarajevo before the war without knowing, or particularly caring, who was Bosnian, Croatian, or Serbian. While people had different religions, languages, and cultural backgrounds, these differences were not generally salient for their everyday lives. Once the conflict began, centuries-old enmities resurfaced, and differences that had existed became conflicts with potentially severe consequences. How these differences became the stuff of conflict is beyond the scope of this book. What is important is to recognize that conflict can occur over resources; over power, status, and hierarchy in relationships; or over deeper issues rooted in worldviews that inform how we organize and make sense of our communities and, ultimately, our lives. Conflicts that touch all three of these dimensions are the hardest to address.

Conflicts are always cultural, since we are all cultural beings. Yet the very definition of conflict is challenging because of our cultural ways of seeing. This became very obvious in a series of interviews conducted as part of the Multiculturalism and Dispute Resolution Project at the University of Victoria, Canada in 1990–1993. One interviewee, an elderly Chinese man who had emigrated after World War II, insisted to a young female interviewer that he had experienced no conflict during his forty-some years in Canada. Was he lying, or was it possible that his way of seeing the world and thinking about his relations led him to pay attention to harmony and the glue of connection rather than discord and conflict episodes? Did his way of understanding conflict include a connotation of cataclysmic events, while his Confucian upbringing led him to seek harmony with others and avoid open confrontation? Discussing this and other examples of how individuals understand conflict, we recognized that our academic bias led us to see conflict as more particularized and episodic than might be perceived by those outside our field of study. We realized that conflict can be defined in multiple ways, and that a central precept for those who work across cultures is to explore how local people think of conflict, and what their "common sense" of conflict tells them to do about it.

John Paul Lederach, an American colleague whose work has advanced our understandings of intercultural conflict considerably, relates his experience of working in Puntarenas, Costa Rica. A participant in a workshop he led there described to him a difficult *clavo,* or nail, that she was experiencing in her neighborhood. Lederach observed in reply that people in Puntarenas did not seem to use the word "conflict" to describe their problems very often. "Ah, no," the woman responded, "here we do not have conflicts. Conflicts are what they have in Nicaragua. In Puntarenas, we have *plietos, lios,* and *enredos* (fights, messes, and entanglements)" (1995, 74). Lederach explains that she meant that the word "conflict" refers to wars, which Nicaragua was experiencing at the time, while Costa Rica was not. Spurred on by this exchange, Lederach went on to collect over two hundred Spanish words that connote conflict—an illustration of the complexity of defining conflict across cultural contexts, and the importance of remaining open to diverse understandings (1995).

Lederach's work also reminds us that conflict always arises in relationship. While much work in the conflict resolution field situates conflict as an individual phenomenon, it is the relational aspect of conflict we wish to emphasize. Conflict happens in relationships, moving across levels from individuals to families to groups and communities. It is about our relationships with self and others, and about the paradoxes and differences that animate our internal worlds and our ways of being together—and apart. Conflict cannot be defined without reference to cultural context, since understandings of conflict vary widely. When a cultural frame for understanding conflict is not articulated, it is generally assumed, and thus may speak to some, but not all, intended audiences.

✳✳✳

And what is culture? This is the million-dollar question, subject of everything from folk tales to academic treatises to talk shows. For our purposes, culture is the shared, often unspoken, understandings in a group. It is the underground rivers of meaning-making, the places where we make choices about what matters and how, that connect us to others in the groups to which we belong. It is the water in which fish swim, unaware of its effect on their vision. It is a series of lenses that shape what we see and don't see, how we perceive and interpret, and where we draw boundaries. Often invisible even to us, culture shapes our ideas of what is important, influences our attitudes and values, and animates our behaviors. Operating largely below the surface, cultures are a shifting, dynamic set of starting points that orient us in particular ways, pointing toward some things and away from others. Each of us belongs to multiple cultures, and so we are experienced in transitioning cultural boundaries within and between us from an early age.

Cultural messages whisper to us from the many groups of which we are part. They come not only from groups that share race, ethnicity, and nationality, but from cleavages of generation, socioeconomic class, sexual orientation, differing abilities, political and religious affiliation, language, gender—the list goes on. They come unheralded and unmarked, initially seeping into our understandings and interpretations of the world with our mothers' milk, turning our heads this way and not that. They tell us what matters and how to pay attention to it without words, but through the beliefs and actions we imitate and incorporate as our own. Cultural messages shape our understandings of relationships and of how to deal with the conflict and harmony that are always present whenever two or more people come together.

It is a challenge to talk about, write about, or work with cultural differences. Among the many reasons are the complexity of culture, its elasticity and constant change; the tendency of individual members of cultural groups to vary considerably from the group norm; and the importance of context and history in shaping behaviors and values. At the same time, culture is so much a part of our identities and the ways we make meaning that it must be taken into account in addressing conflict.

No comprehensive understanding of culture exists, since cultures are never static and they do not exist in isolation. Context shapes how cultures are manifest and nudges them toward change in our continuing dance with each other. Because of the dynamic nature of both conflict and culture, resilience and creativity are called for as we navigate the differences among us. Effectiveness in recognizing and moving among cultural frames or ways of being is part of the idea of cultural fluency, central to effectively addressing conflict. Ways to build cultural fluency will be presented in Chapter Four.

Since culture is potent, it is vital to bring it into conscious awareness, to see it as the lenses that color the world in particular ways. Seeing our lenses, we have the choice at least of trying on others senses', if only temporarily, to realize how others see and experience the same situation so differently. As we become more aware of cultural lenses—our own and others senses'—we recognize that there is no such thing as a culture-free perspective. Given that everyone views the world through their own kaleidoscope of cultural lenses, the only way we can work effectively with the conflicts that are part of cultures in action is to be aware of our standpoints (places from which we look, informed by our experiences and worldviews)—and the ways they frame and exclude certain realities. This awareness is central to effectively addressing cultural conflict.

Culture and Conflict: Intertwined Inextricably

Try as we might to avoid it, conflict is an inevitable part of life. Just recall a recent argument with a loved one, a disagreement with a service provider, or tension with a neighbor or employer to realize that conflict is a normal occurrence in our everyday personal lives. Even when our experience is not direct or personal, we need only turn on the television or page through the newspaper to realize the extent to which conflict and associated violence pervade our lives. By bringing the world to our doorstep no matter where we live, globalization has stretched our attention beyond personal and family conflicts to regional and world conflicts. Conflict and its escalation in the present-day world demands and commands our attention, as well as our commitment to understanding and addressing it.

. ˙ Culture is embedded in every conflict because conflicts arise in human relationships. The ways we name, frame, blame, and attempt to tame conflicts are profoundly influenced by culture. Given its omnipresence, *culture is more than a topic related to conflict and conflict resolution—it is an integral part of all interaction*, harmonious and conflictual. Culture informs how issues are seen, what communication approaches are taken, and how identities and meanings play out in difficult and smooth times. Culture is not the only set of influences—context and individual differences must also be considered—yet it is vitally important because it is so often invisible, out of awareness, and out of our repertoires of conscious choice.

Is culture *always* a factor in conflict? Yes, it is. Culture may play a central role in a conflict, or it might influence a conflict subtly and gently, but for any conflict that touches us where it matters, where we hold precious values and continually construct our identities, there is always a cultural component. For example, the Israeli-Palestinian conflict or the India-Pakistan conflict over Kashmir are not just about territorial, boundary, and sovereignty issues. They are also about the acknowledgement, representation, and legitimization of different identities and ways of living, being, and ordering relationships.

Conflict between a teenager and parent is touched by generational culture, and conflict between spouses or partners is influenced by gender culture. In the workplace, "disciplinary" or departmental culture affects tensions between the professional staff and the administrative staff. Culture permeates conflict no matter what—sometimes it pushes forth with intensity, insisting on being noticed; at other times it quietly snakes along, hardly announcing its presence until people accidentally stumble on it.

Culture is inextricable from conflict, though it does not cause it. When differences surface in families, organizations, or communities, culture is always present, shaping perceptions, attitudes, behaviors, and outcomes.

Even the call of whether a conflict exists is a cultural one—a spirited conversation in an Italian home may be regarded as an unseemly conflict in an English one; Chinese Confucian comfort with harmony may lead to indirect communication and forbearance in place of overt conflict in families, while French Canadian political norms may license robust debate and passionate disagreement.

Conflict and culture are intertwined at every level, arising from pulls of different values within and between us, fueling conflicts between loved ones, coworkers, community groups, and nations. Powerful cultural messages, unseen and subterranean, may be unknown in their course and potency even to those through whom they run.

From within specific cultural groups there is a shared understanding of what is "natural" or "normal." We only notice the effect of cultures that are different from our own, attending to behaviors that we label exotic or strange. For example, at the outset of a U.S. academic seminar, we seldom articulate the norm that we will all stay seated around a table, discussing ideas in civil, calm ways. Only when someone displays anger or frustration, or—more outside the realm of expectations—jumps on a chair and loudly advocates a point of view, do we recognize that our assumptions about how differences are to be handled are not necessarily universal. The more a behavior deviates from collective, often unarticulated expectations, the more likely we are to marginalize that behavior (and the person enacting it) as an abnormal outsider.

Though culture is intertwined with conflict, many analyses of conflict ignore cultural issues and influences. Of the grand theories on conflict that exist, few of them situate cultural dimensions and dynamics in the center, where they belong. Readers should not worry—we do not propose to elucidate these grand theories here. We only want to emphasize that theories, research, or practice addressing conflict that do not take culture into account have missed the largest part of the iceberg, the part beneath the surface. Icebergs unacknowledged can be dangerous, and it is impossible to make choices about them if we don't know their size or location. Acknowledging culture and bringing cultural fluency to conflicts can help all kinds of people make more intentional, adaptive choices, whether they are parents and children, supervisees and supervisors, people on either side of divisive social issues, or people from different identity groups.

For many of those who study or work in the field of conflict resolution, culture often seems like a temperamental child: complicated, elusive, unpredictable, and prone to misbehavior. Rather than get tangled in the net of its complexity or involved in the lifelong process of developing cultural fluency, many writers and practitioners are content to leave culture underground, giving it no more than lip-service. Perhaps it is the combination of complexity and importance that leads to the atomization of culture in attempts to feature it, yet contain it. Countless training programs in leadership, facilitation, and conflict resolution include modules on culture as though it were a separate facet of conflict. In fact, it is not. Conflict and culture are *inseparable* for those who want to understand and effectively prevent and address the conflicts that separate us at the interpersonal, intergroup, and international levels.

There are many ways to think about conflict, and these vary with cultural context, situation, history, and a whole range of personal and group factors. This complexity causes us to question the limited answers and understandings we have of conflict, and reminds us that there are no universal ways of thinking about or responding to conflict. It also entices us to think of alternative meanings on an ongoing basis, recognizing that our common sense is not common. We choose to invoke the Platinum Rule as articulated by Milton Bennett—to treat others as *they* would like to be treated—rather than the Golden Rule, treat others as *you* would like to be treated (1979). Aware of the cultural layers in conflicts, we stop ourselves from taking things for granted, continually learning about the relationship between conflict and culture.

Does culture in all its complexity mean that we are barred from working effectively with conflict? To rest on this belief is to fall into paralysis born of too much analysis. Culture is indeed complex, yet it is possible to develop capacities to navigate it, and even to draw on its richness as a resource in addressing conflicts. As we handle culture in such a way, we avoid the trap of overgeneralizing or ascribing every difference inalienably to culture, while at the same time noticing even the subtle ways culture traces its influence in our relationships. Oliver Mbamara, the Nigerian poet, playwright, and author speaks to the shifting perspectives revealed by diverse cultural lenses in his poem *The Standard of Good and Evil* (2004, 66).

If character is personal to every person
And unique culture strives in a people,
If perspectives differ from one another
And opinions vary by individuals,

Whose 'wrong' shall indeed be a sin?
And whose right shall then be a virtue,
Accepted and taken by all and sundry,
To be the standard of good and evil?

Culture complicates understanding by introducing many ways of knowing and seeing events and relationships. Ideas of truth, relationships to others, and appropriateness of behaviors are all profoundly influenced by culture. Given the many variations in whom we see ourselves to be and how we relate to ideas and each other, the difficulty in finding agreement on major global issues across national and cultural boundaries is hardly surprising. We have northern and southern perspectives, western and eastern perspectives, views of the developed world and the developing world. Perspectives vary with power, historical experiences, leadership, and what conflict resolution specialist Vamik Volkan calls chosen glories and traumas (1997). But very often, cultural views and values are so tightly interwoven into perspectives and choices that they are hard to tease out or analyze effectively, leading to conflicts within conflicts over how to proceed.

Connecting Culture and Conflict Resolution

Connections between culture and conflict are easier to understand if we consider three different dimensions of conflict, as depicted in Figure 2.1. While all three dimensions may be present in any given conflict, conflict dynamics may be most visible in a specific dimension at any given time. Figure 2.1 shows the relational level as the one that both contains and underlies the other two dimensions: symbolic and material. Conflict occurs at

- the material level, or the "what" of the conflict;
- the symbolic level, the meaning of issues to the people involved, especially those meanings that resonate with peoples' identities, values, and worldviews;
- and the relational level, or the dance among the parties, or the way in which conflict plays out.

Effective conflict resolution across cultures must address all three dimensions. Culture contextualizes and shapes all three dimensions, so conflict resolution must also be anchored in cultural fluency.

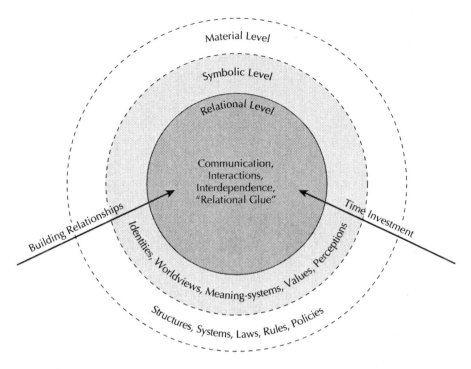

Figure 2.1 Culture and Conflict Resolution (CCR)

Resolution of conflict across cultures is most obvious in the material dimension, situated on the outside of Figure 2.1. This dimension represents the concrete aspects of the conflict. Conflict may point to needed changes in policies, structures, systems, rules, or agreements. To be successful, conflict resolution must result in changes at the material, or concrete, level. These concrete issues are always influenced by symbolic and relational dimensions, and they in turn shape how the concrete issues are perceived.

Culture is most alive and visible in the symbolic and relational dimensions, because it is so powerful in shaping perceptions and meaning-making processes. The symbolic dimension emphasizes how identity and ways of seeing the world shape the way we perceive and act on material issues. Because conflict can seem like a challenge to identity or deeply held meanings, it can touch us to our core. For example, in a conflict over a boundary, it may not be only resources or wealth (material things) at stake, but also national identity, pride, belonging, or security. For such a conflict to be resolved, the meanings people attach to the material issues must be considered.

The relational dimension is closely related to the symbolic dimension. It is the foundation on which sustained progress in conflict can be made. It involves building the capacity to communicate, and—ultimately—recognizing the interdependence that conflict thrusts upon the parties.

Search for Common Ground, a U.S.-based non-governmental organization, uses Figure 2.2 to illustrate the positive change that can happen in relationships when conflict is used as a foundation for discovery.

The symbolic and relational dimensions emphasize the need for relationship-building as a precondition to and a product of conflict resolution. While the material dimension is where conflict is manifest, concrete, and visible, relationship-building, appropriately situated at the center, can create the atmosphere for sustainable change at the material dimension. When relationships between people in conflict remain broken and damaged, changes at the material dimension are likely to be superficial and temporary. Resolving conflict at the material level requires substantive investment of time, effort, and relationship-building to address the deeper symbolic and relational issues below the surface. When relationship-building is seen as a priority in the face of conflict, efforts to solve material problems become more productive. This is illustrated by the South African experience.

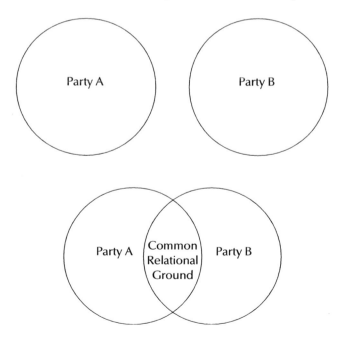

Figure 2.2 Interdependence and Relational Capacity

A decade ago, South Africa began its transition from apartheid. Had conflict resolution merely focused on dismantling racist and discriminatory structures, policies, and laws it would not have been very effective. Relationships had to be built across the races. It was at the symbolic and relational dimensions that the "miracle" of conflict resolution occurred in South Africa. Through large-scale nation-building efforts, the Truth and Reconciliation Commission, the establishment of a racially representative government of National Unity, and various grassroots efforts to support interactions across the racial divides, changes made at the structural level became meaningful. While South Africa is nowhere near being a racially reconciled society, there are significant signs of progress in this direction because conflict resolution efforts at the material dimension were anchored in efforts to build relationships in ways that resonated with people's symbolic meanings and identities.

Another example of these three conflict dimensions is found in a recent Hollywood movie production. The movie was set in Japan, so the sound stage was covered with tatami mats, a tightly woven grass floor-covering typical in Japan. The Japanese members of the production had requested that their U.S. American counterparts remove their boots before walking on the tatami. The Americans intended to do so, but increasingly made "quick adjustments" to lighting, electrical, or set components without taking off their boots. From the material dimension, the issue was clear: Japanese members of the team wanted no outside footwear on tatami, and American members persisted in wearing their boots. Symbolically, this behavior by the Americans communicated disrespect to the Japanese, who became increasingly upset by the Americans' failure to remove their boots. This behavior, with the disrespect it symbolized, led to a deteriorating relationship among the partners in the production, and began to spawn other conflicts and escalate negative impressions.

Positive change in their relationship came after the Japanese members of the production realized that the Americans did not understand the symbolic importance the Japanese attached to respecting tatami. In their next meeting, the Japanese drew an analogy between the place of tatami in their culture, and the place of the U.S. flag in American culture, asking the Americans to please act as they would if a U.S. flag were on the floor of the set. Hearing this, the Americans shifted their perceptions and behavior, rigorously removing their boots before venturing onto the tatami. This example illustrates that relational change often results in progress in the material dimension, and that the symbolic dimension can be a resource from which relational change can be catalyzed. Figure 2.2 shows how common ground comes from recognizing commonalities that pave the way forward, even as differences continue to exist.

Neither the massive transformation still occurring in South Africa, nor the small but important progress experienced on the film set can be understood through conflict analysis alone. Understanding cultural dynamics is necessary to comprehending the issues, relationships, and symbols inherent to the conflicts in each instance. In Chapter Three, we examine the dynamics of culture more deeply, and demonstrate ways it can function as a resource for intercultural conflict resolution.

Culture: Exploring the River

Venashri Pillay

Having being briefly introduced the idea that culture is inextricable from conflict, we are now ready to enter into a deeper exploration of culture in a quest for understanding. Matthew Arnold's poetic words quoted in the preface remind us of the cost of not engaging this exploration: that in our diverse, beautiful world we will remain in the "dark," confused and ignorant about each other, further alienated by conflicts that arise among us. If culture is an underground river that connects us to others and gives meaning to our beliefs, attitudes, and behaviors, it is our inability to know this river and achieve this connection that creates our ignorance. The need to understand *culture* is clear. We need to know what culture is, how it comes to be, how to identify it, what characterizes it, and how to navigate it.

The understanding of culture presented here gives us ways to demystify each other and reduce the confusion that cultural differences bring to relationships by providing starting points to navigate through our world, so beautiful and varied. This chapter explores some of the dynamics of culture and provides a foundation for understanding it. Chapter Four offers some tools for relating constructively across cultural differences.

Dare We Define Culture?

A quick glance back at the first two chapters reminds us that culture has been a mysterious yet robust field of interest and study for as long as humankind has been crossing borders. Scholars, pundits, politicians, and people everywhere have views about culture. Despots have sought to use it to justify atrocities, elders have used it to resist change, and leaders have used it to influence groups of people and to escalate wars and struggles. Yet, despite the many ways culture is open to manipulation and the many struggles in which it has been invoked, culture lives on. It continues: a living, breathing part of our identities and our ways of being in the world. How do we know what is important and worthy if not for the early messages our parents and teachers transmit from "our people?" How can we invent ways forward if not informed by the lessons, hard-won as they may be, from the past?

Culture is never static—its continuously changing nature and shape-shifting form confounds everything it touches. And culture is rich with nuance and humanity. It infuses our stories with meaning; our identities with connections. It gives us an anchor in the flux of a globalizing world. Far from wanting to leave culture at the door lest it cause difficulties, we care about it even more passionately as commodification and homogenization threaten to lessen its impact.

In Chapter Two, we defined culture as the shared, often unspoken, understandings in a group that shape identities and the process of making meaning. We now want to deepen this understanding to provide a foundation for *cultural fluency*—the ability to communicate effectively across cultures. While no comprehensive or perfect definition of culture can be formulated, there are some important aspects about culture that are worth considering. We encourage you to be playful with the ideas we present here—expand them, turn them over, break them down, argue with them, add new perspectives, and stretch your imagination as you remain open and flexible. With a spirit of inquiry, culture and its links to identity and meaning-making can be glimpsed.

Chapter Two paints an introductory picture of culture as an underground river that runs through our lives and relationships connecting us to others in the groups to which we belong. As it twists and turns, this river shapes our ideas and perceptions, influences our attitudes, and gives life to the meanings we express through behaviors. Culture is a flow of meanings and identities that consciously and unconsciously guide us. It is a dynamic channel within which people constantly compose who they are and what they care about in relation to each other.

Culture is, in short, "the way things are done around here." It is embedded in our lives, especially our lives beneath the surface, nurturing our dreams and birthing our legacies. It is important to remember that cultures are more than differences in language, dress, food, and customs. Cultural groups may share ethnicity, race, or nationality, but cultural differences may also arise from socioeconomic class, generational difference, sexual orientation, ability and disability, political and religious affiliation, gender, regional origin, and so on. No taxonomy of a particular group will ever be accurate because cultures are constantly adapting to changing social and physical environments, and because individuals in cultural groups may or may not observe the group's norms and values in any given context.

Because we cannot offer definitive descriptions of culture and its functioning, we look to stories to give us a holistic sense of cultural dynamics. Stories carry context and humanity, two essential elements for understanding culture.

Mourning a Death in Balut-Saranggani

We go first to a remote, rural island community south of Mindanao, Philippines, where our Filipino colleague and friend, Al, experienced a jolting surprise. Through his story we see how meaning-making and identity dance to the beat of cultural values, norms, frames, and symbols.

After a taxing eight-hour pump-boat ride from Mindanao, Al arrived for his first visit to Balut-Saranggani, a rural, agricultural and fishing island community peopled mainly by Indonesians. He was tired, but excited to have an opportunity to learn about the people there and to work with them on local conflicts and challenges. During his visit, Al was honored to be invited to attend a community ritual for an elder who had passed away. Though he had not personally known the elder, he prepared himself to participate in the solemn occasion.

When Al arrived at the community ritual, he was shocked to find the entire community of Balut-Saranggani celebrating. Surely he was in the right place, since the immediate family of the departed was there, in festive and celebratory moods like many others. Children and women sang to music played by male elders. People were enjoying delicacies and special foods. During breaks from the entertainment, joyous words remembering the departed were spoken. (Fuertes 2002).

Al was taken aback. Without realizing it, he had expected the ritual to be similar to those in his own community in another part of the Philippines. Among his people, death is observed in very somber ways, and grieving is done quietly and respectfully. Community members come together to pray for the soul of the departed, and God is called upon to bestow strength and hope for those left behind who are experiencing the tragedy and pain of the loss. During this mourning period, social gatherings and celebrations are put on hold as a sign of respect for the dead person and the bereaved family.

Once he regained his equilibrium, Al had many questions. He wondered how people could be festive about the passing away of a loved one. Were they happy about the tragedy and the loss? From his community's perspective, the Balut-Saranggani people were being disrespectful to their departed loved one. Only after time and reflection did Al realize that he could not find answers in the obvious differences he was observing. In order to understand, he would have to go deeper beneath the surface of the Balut-Saranggani culture to explore the meanings attached to these rituals.

Al's experience points us to an important cue that will help us in unfamiliar settings: surprise. Surprise happens when our expectations are not met. Rather than dismissing or explaining surprises away, it is good to follow them, seeing them as tributaries of the river. It is likely that divergent values or meanings are animating the behavior that surprises us. With a spirit of inquiry, we seek to learn more rather than using our frames of reference to judge the differences that led to our surprise. We take this opportunity to explore new cultural values.

Beneath the surface, waters are influenced by various forms of aquatic life, changing currents, and types of river bed and soil. Similarly, a cultural behavior may appear to be completely visible and explainable to an observer, but this is often only a small part of the larger picture. To understand completely, we need to know more of the context: to dive into the river; to swim among the cultural values, norms, needs, frames, and symbols that influence meaning-making and identity.

Swimming in the cultural waters of the Balut-Saranggani people, we gradually become more familiar with their values, norms, and identities. We slowly come to understand the meaning-making process related to death and grieving. To do this we have to recognize and set aside cultural assumptions that associate death with sadness and endings. We find that the Balut-Saranggani people do not see dying as an end to living. For them, death is not an end—actual or symbolic. Instead, it is seen as the ultimate occasion to celebrate the person's life and to acknowledge the joy of living. Celebration is the ultimate respect that one can pay to the dead and their bereaved family. Adding to the joy is the belief that the ancestor is now able to watch over the living and play a role in their fate.

As Al discovered, views about life, death, living, and grieving are different for the island people of Balut-Saranggani and the Christian Filipinos in his home community. Recognizing this difference is not to make a judgment about which is better; rather, it is to explore beneath the surface with a spirit of inquiry and openness to differences. Using his surprise as a cue to explore the Balut-Sarranganis' beliefs about death, Al was able to suspend judgment and embrace multiple differences by following the surface waters to their underground source.

In his journey to embracing multiple differences, Al saw how his perceptions were culturally shaped by that to which he had been exposed—religious and community teachings. This understanding of how our view of the world is shaped by experience is explored in the following section.

How Culture Works

Many people know the famous tale from the nineteenth century about six blind men encountering an elephant (Saxe 1882). Each man touches a particular part of the large animal and believes his description of that part adequately describes the elephant. The one who touches the elephant's tusk exclaims that the elephant is like a spear, while another who feels the elephant's foot claims that the animal is like a tree trunk. Based on their specific encounters with different elephant body parts, each man offers a completely different description of the animal. While they are all somewhat right in their perception, they are all incorrect too as no one of them has an entirely complete description of the elephant.

A more contemporary example of different experiences leading to diverse perceptions comes from European cities over the past ten years, where increasing tensions have surfaced over multiculturalism and immigration. The Museum of Progress, a Vienna art museum, responding to the decision of the Austrian government to include a far-right freedom party as a coalition partner, commissioned a Canadian artist to mount an exhibit on the theme of "home." The artist created a series of large billboards that were displayed in one of the main traffic hubs of Vienna, depicting people from diverse backgrounds and viewpoints. There was an angry man with a raised fist, with the caption, "Go back to where you came from! Why don't you go home?" and, in another billboard, a dark-skinned girl with a sad face, with the caption, "I don't want to go home, Mommy." Further along is a billboard with an Asian man whose caption rages, "You call this home? This ain't no goddam home." And finally a woman in a headscarf who confesses, "I've never been made to feel at home here." The billboards end with a wide-eyed girl, presumably a tourist, with the caption, "I really like it here. I don't think I ever want to go home!" (Sandercock 2003)

The exhibit raises questions about our cities in the 21st century. To whom do they belong, whose identity is associated with them, and who are outsiders and insiders? Like the blind men and the elephant, the people in the billboards have had very different experiences of the city and have very different feelings about it. Their range of feelings is a product of the interaction between the city, its people, and themselves. This example conveys an important dimension left out by the elephant example: Cultural perspectives are never only one way, but are multidimensional interactions that shape our cultural identities as they affirm, challenge, and jostle them.

Cultural messages are interpreted according to how we are situated and how others welcome or push against our situations. They shape both what we see and what we don't see, our blind spots. Thus, the young tourist in the exhibit saw a city of glamor, excitement, and energy, but missed the hurt flowing to immigrants disliked by earlier inhabitants of the city. The dark-skinned young girl may have been born in Austria, and so the message to "go home" would have been confusing and disorienting. The woman in the headscarf experienced herself as outside of the belonging shared by others in the city, and so felt a loss of home, though she, too, may have lived in Vienna for decades.

By placing these billboards in a public square, the Museum of Progress hoped to provoke people into thinking about home and belonging. The exhibit underlined the ways that people's different identities and historical connections to Vienna changed their experiences of the place and each other. It implicitly raised questions about entitlement in a 21st-century multicultural city. Urban planning scholar Leonie Sandercock suggests that our challenge is to update our conceptions of culture to embrace the complex, dynamic interaction of cultures that surround us.

***

If we accept that cultures are dynamic and ever-changing, we encounter a paradox, for cultures are also robust, with deep roots in the past. Cultural messages are passed on through the stories and tales we fall asleep to as children, they fly to us on the wings of folklore and superstition, they echo in the traditions we uphold, they whisper to us from the poetry we remember and through the music we dance to and the first words we speak.

These early cultural messages are inextricably part of our very identities. Culture completes us as human beings in its ongoing, dynamic process (Geertz 1973). Each of us is a multicultural being with multiple cultural influences. Culture lives in the collective—it is the glue that connects us in social groups providing unwritten rules, codes, and boundaries around communication, perception, and meaning-making. Cultures are the sets of inherited answers to questions posed by life, providing information about whether, how, and when to act. We draw on them for common sense, for what to do, and what not to do.

Pause here a moment and think about the cultural groups to which you belong. How have messages from these groups shaped who you are, what you think, how you perceive and interpret the world, and your actions?

After Al visited Balut-Saranggani, he reflected on the cultural messages he received about death and grieving as a child. These initial messages were conveyed to him indirectly through passed-down rules and customs. He learned that relatives of a deceased person should not wear brightly colored clothes, but dark, plain garments, preferably sackcloth. For him death and mourning were associated with dark colors, a somber mood, and uncomfortable clothing. Dying became internalized as a sorrowful, painful, colorless, and solemn experience. This internalized assumption remained unquestioned common sense until implicitly challenged by a very different way of relating to death.

We can imagine that a Balut-Saranggani child who participated in her first funeral celebration received a different message about death, dying, and grieving. She internalized associations of joy, celebration, music, and brightness with death. For both Al, as a child, and this fictional Balut-Saranggani child we've imagined, these cultural messages became lifelong influences against which later experiences were measured. Of course, contexts and experiences vary and cultures are never static, so there is always the possibility of changing frames, making adjustments, or adding new lenses to our repertoires. Just as rivers deepen, widen, and even change course over time, so is culture constantly formed and transformed from one generation to another.

As we begin to recognize alternative lenses to our own, stereotyping can result. Stereotyping occurs when an assumption is made that a particular cultural group has specific, immutable characteristics shared by all members. In the sweeping generalization of a stereotype, there is no room for nuances, exceptions, or change. Stereotyping functions as a safety and convenience mechanism. It allows us to make judgments about people, provides a basis from which to engage (or not to engage) the other person, and gives us a false sense of knowing others.

For example, I am a South African of Indian origin. Most people I encounter in the United States immediately assume that I am an Indian from India, or perhaps Canada. When I indicate that I am a South African, people often become awkward. The stereotype of me being Indian from South Asia would have provided some general rules for interaction; when they no longer exist there is difficulty with the interaction. For example, people are not sure whether South African Indians eat the same spicy foods as their South Asian counterparts. Faced with this uncertainty, some people freeze or feel over-whelmed. They come face-to-face with the limitations of their stereotypes. This should be a cue to make the necessary adjustments, as discussed further in Chapter Six. It is a time to self-reflect and call on cultural fluency.

Stereotypes are often much more damaging than this example suggests. African Americans, Hispanics, Native Americans, and other members of visible minority groups in the United States and Canada have stories of daily indignities they suffer as a result of stereotypes. It is a paradox that the Horatio Alger vision of individuals achieving their dreams in direct proportion to their goal-setting and effort does not apply to all Americans in the same way. Members of visible minority groups do not see themselves mirrored in elite leadership; they may not be encouraged by teachers to go on to higher education; they may be foreclosed in a million ways from full participation in social and political spaces—all as a result of stereotypes.

Given that differences can be construed in damaging ways, we should not wait for the actual moment of interaction with someone different to gain awareness of our own lenses and our repertoire of other cultural lenses. We need starting points, as well as guiding lights, to ensure that we do not get lost along the way.

Guiding Lights: Cultural Starting Points

The question that arises is, "How do I understand my own cultural starting points, and those of other cultures, especially when it is clear that there can never be any comprehensive or definite description of a culture? Where to begin?" What we offer in the remainder of this chapter are six *cultural starting points* to reduce the confusion and complexity that cultural differences bring to relationships:

- High Context – Low Context
- Individualism – Communitarianism

- Universalism – Particularism
- Specificity – Diffuseness
- Sequential Time – Synchronous Time
- Low Power Distance – High Power Distance

These starting points are sometimes called *dimensions of culture* (Hall 1976; Hofstede 1984). We prefer to refer to them as *starting points* (Hampden-Turner and Trompenaars 2000) to avoid the impression of dichotomized, fixed-point descriptions of particular cultural traits.

These starting points offer one way of beginning to decode cultural ways of making meaning. All may be relevant to members of one cultural group, or a combination may be applicable, or some variation may occur as conditions change. In some cases, few of these starting points may be salient. Ultimately our message is that there are *no* fixed answers to understanding the dynamics of culture, but there are guiding lights to draw upon along the way.

The stories that follow illustrate the range of differences associated with these cultural starting points. Be aware of the fluidity of culture: the location of a particular cultural preference on the continuum is different depending on the situation, the issue, and the meaning-making processes of those involved. Notice the meaning and relative comfort of each of the starting points for you as you explore and question the stories with a spirit of curiosity and reflection. Do not shy away from ambiguity and those cultural events that are not amenable to easy analysis.

High-Context – Low-Context Cultures

Cultures differ by communication styles—that is, how people relate to and with others. In the cultural groups to which we belong, we all fall somewhere on the continuum between high-context and low-context communication, starting points suggested by anthropologist Edward T. Hall (1976). In high-context cultures, nonverbal communication is emphasized. Meaning is conveyed by context and behavior more than actual words. High-context communication is best understood by the expression, "Read between the lines." People rely on shared understandings to give communication meaning. High-context communication is therefore more indirect than low-context communication.

For example, in cultures where children have internalized respect for, and deference to, elders, the entrance of an elder into a room of seated people will be marked by the younger persons offering their seats to the elder. No verbal communication takes place, but the value and meaning attached to age communicates a message to everybody present. Those offering up their seats are acknowledging the status and leadership of the elder, as well as communicating their respect for her.

High-context communication happens in many settings, not just the national cultures that Hall and others identified as having a preference for it. In families, organizations, and communities, we rely heavily on context to communicate messages. Even if you've never been in a mosque, church, or temple, the behavior of others cues you to observe silence or use a low voice at particular times. In the realm of politics, high-context communication is the norm. For example, Leonie Sandercock writes about the predominantly white Capetown Council in South Africa publicizing their plan for combating urban disorder while promoting integration as a way of masking its negative view of "the arrival and presence of non-whites in the inner city . . . particularly [those] considered to be marginal, the street vendors, the parking attendants (referred to as 'parking terrorists') and the homeless" (2003, 119). Local residents in Capetown understand these layers of meaning because they live in the context where the transition from apartheid is not the color-blind panacea those outside the country may imagine.

On the other end of the continuum, low-context communication is more verbal and direct with a minimal focus on contextual meaning. Words rather than context are relied upon to give communication meaning, and there is less allowance for implied meanings. Low-context communicators expect their words to be interpreted specifically and literally. Generally, Western cultures tend toward a low-context orientation.

Walk into a fast-food business in the United States, and you will likely encounter low-context communication. An order is given, and within a few seconds, that order is filled. The customer walks away with her food, never thinking of the cultural or racial identity of the server. If the server and customer were interviewed even a few minutes later, they may remember little about the appearance or cultural behaviors of the other because they were simply not salient. What mattered to them was accurate and specific communication, not the context surrounding it.

The differences between high- and low-context communication are most easily seen when two or more people communicate from different starting points. These differences surface even when people think they can easily bridge the cultural gap. Journalist Robert Whiting tells the story of Willie Davis, a practicing Buddhist who went to Japan in 1977 to play for a baseball team called the Dragons. Davis believed that he would find the transition to Japan relatively easy, since Japan was the birthplace of the Soko Gakkai Buddhist tradition he followed.

The religion's sacred chant was an important part of Davis' life. He chanted morning, noon, and night in his room, even on the team bus. He chanted in the locker room before games, expecting that his direct and specific prayers for the team's success would be appreciated by his teammates. But it "gave the others the feeling they were at a Buddhist funeral," according to his coach (1989, 86). While Davis expected a literal interpretation of his prayer for team success, the team's high-context association with the prayers led them to feel upset. Likely, their high-context signals were missed or misinterpreted by Davis, and relations between him and the team degenerated steadily. That season, the team failed to achieve good results on the field, even with some very talented players, including Davis.

When miscommunication occurs across cultural boundaries, checking for low- and high-context starting points is a good bet. Because the low-context communicator values directness, it may not occur to him to notice unspoken signals or silence as a sign that something is amiss. Because the high-context communicator values indirectness, it may not occur to her, or it may feel uncomfortable, to state things directly.

Table 3.1 summarizes the general communication characteristics of low-context and high-context cultures. No cultural group relies on only one communication starting point. Generally members integrate some combination of high- and low-context communication as they rely on both contextual and literal meanings in their interactions.

It is less important to classify communication as high or low context than it is to understand the balance of importance of nonverbal or verbal cues in any communication. Without this understanding, those who utlize

Table 3.1
**General Communication Orientations of High-
and Low-Context Cultures**

High Context	Low Context
Nonverbal communication emphasized	Verbal communication emphasized
Contextual, implied meaning	Specific, literal meaning
Indirect, covert	Direct, overt
Implicit message	Explicit message
Reactions reserved	Reactions on the surface

high-context starting points may be looking for shades of meaning that are not present, and those who prefer low-context communication may miss important nuances of meaning (LeBaron 2003).

Individualism – Communitarianism

Consider these two conceptions of self and identity.

> I am a tall tree reaching up toward the sky in all my mighty magnificence. I began as a weak sapling but have now grown tall as the land I stand on is fertile and healthy. It allows me to reach my full potential. I know I can reach for the stars and one day I believe my branches will touch them. I have been cared for by the finest gardeners and have been transplanted in a beautiful forest. I am all that I have, all that I do, and all that I have achieved. I continue to aspire to be the finest and strongest tree in the forest—and I dream of the day when star-dust will sparkle on my leaves.

✳✳✳

> I am a bright, shiny thread in a rainbow blanket. As I weave in and out with other equally bright threads, I stand out for I am a unique color and composition. At the same time I am also subsumed into this vivid, loud display of color in this magnificent creation that blankets all. My complementary relationship with the other unique threads allows me to be noticed and to be cloaked all at once. We come together in a beautiful, knitted rhythm of patterns and yet this very joining is what makes our unique lines and individual patterned routes more visible. I am because we are—in this beautiful rainbow blanket.

Both of these metaphorical pieces were composed during a writing exercise on self-awareness and identity. The first metaphor is my American friend Will's description of himself in North American society. The second rainbow blanket metaphor depicts my South African identity.

Will's description of himself as a tree growing tall on fertile land represents the potential he has, and continues to have, in the land of opportunity, the United States. His identity is bound up in a culture of achievement, growth, and personal fulfillment. It is a culture that encourages endless possibilities based on hard work, commitment, and drive. Will defines himself by all that he has been able to achieve in life and what he aspires to achieve. Even though he is a part of a forest, his primary focus is on his individuality and independence.

My identity and self-awareness arises from collective South African society. Interdependence characterizes relationships there and individual members have a responsibility to preserve and uplift our larger family and community. My individuality is enhanced because of the community of which I am a part. As mentioned in chapter one, *ubuntu*, a Pan-African concept that means "humanness or personhood," represents the community orientation of most African cultures. Translated, *ubuntu* refers to "A person being a person through other persons."

The distinct differences in these two conceptions of identity are what researchers Hampden-Turner and Trompenaars label individualism-communitarianism starting points (2000). While no cultural group can be identified with only one end of this value continuum, Will's cultural orientation tends toward the individualism starting point, while communitarianism is more salient as a starting point for me.

As with high- and low-context starting points, individualism and communitarianism are best understood with an example of conflict. Universities in the United States have experienced conflicts relating to individualism and communitarianism in their application of policies relating to academic conduct, especially plagiarism. While scholarly opinions diverge about how much of the problem can be attributed to cultural misunderstanding, there is considerable evidence that plagiarism is often not well understood by foreign students from diverse parts of the world. Students from more collectivist countries may not attach the same importance to individual work as their more individualist American counterparts. They may come from places where the very idea of personal property is nonexistent, such as the Baltic states under Soviet rule (Russikov, Fucaloro and Salkauskiene 2003). In writing projects involving collaboration, peer review, and group contributions, appropriate attribution of authorship may become even more problematic, and these problems are exacerbated by the assumptions associated with individualist and communitarian starting points.

Table 3.2 summarizes the general values that are likely to be privileged by individualist and communitarian cultures.

In addition to understanding and identifying the values underlying communitarian and individualist cultures, a useful way to explore these starting points is to be aware of accepted forms of greeting and introduction (Novinger 2001). In individualist cultures, people will introduce themselves directly and

Table 3.2
General Orientations Privileged by
Individualism – Communitarianism

Individualism	*Communitarianism*
Relationships of separate co-existence	Relationships of living together
Competition	Cooperation
Independence	Filial piety (deference toward elders)
Individual achievement	Shared aspirations and progress
Personal growth and fulfillment	Reputation of the group
Self-reliance	Interdependence
Autonomy	Group harmony and cohesion
Individual responsibility for choices	Group responsibility for choices
Guilt (particularized blame internalized by an individual)	Shame (global sense of unworthiness projected by a group)

independently—for example, "I am John Smith." In some communitarian cultures, people make reference to their kinship ties by using the name of the father, mother, or grandparents—for example, "I am the daughter of Igor Galichina." The woman may not even mention her own name, or she may do so to convey her familial ties.

Universalism–Particularism

The universalism–particularism continuum is described by Hampden-Turner and Trompenaars (2000) and other scholars. Universalism refers to the broad application of rules, laws, and generalizations to most, if not all, people. As such, there is an emphasis on standardization and mass production of the same standard. If universal rules and generalizations exist, then judgments about a behavior, action, or way of life are based on this idea.

At the other end of the continuum, particularism refers to exceptions to the rules and generalizations. Narrower, circumstance-specific meanings are explored. From a particularist starting point, there is an emphasis on uniqueness, innovation, and creativity, and on creating custom-fit behaviors and living.

A simple example that illustrates the universalism – particularism starting point is the area of human rights. Universal standards such as the United Nations Declaration of Human Rights provide prescriptions for what should be included in basic human rights. The definition and application of these standards continues to be contested across national and cultural lines, between south and north, and east and west.

Specifically, female genital mutilation practiced in certain African cultures is considered a gross human rights violation by international standards, and even by some local African standards. Some of the cultural groups, however, have argued from a particularistic starting point that their unique cultural practices, traditions, beliefs, and heritage cannot be subject to international and universal standards; rather, these practices must be evaluated in context, with attention paid to the social and cultural purposes they serve. Universalist starting points prescribe a general code of conduct that trumps this particularist contention. Ultimately this issue is best addressed through respectful dialogue taking into account both sets of starting points.

Another example of these starting points comes from Whiting's book on the experience of Americans playing professional baseball in Japan. Willie Davis, the player described earlier whose chanting was not appreciated by his Japanese teammates, exhibited a more universalist starting point than his Japanese counterparts. While the Japanese were very sensitive to appropriate attire in particular situations, Davis assumed that clothing he liked could be worn nearly everywhere. Because Davis liked his training suit for the baseball team, the Dragons, he had several copies made in different colors. When he wore them in public, Davis assumed that the popularity of his team and baseball in general in Japan would mean that his choice would be appreciated. In fact, Dragon club executives were very upset by his behavior, worrying that Davis was tarnishing the team's dignified image. The Dragons' particularist starting point led them to see the training suit as appropriate only in particular contexts, not in general public settings (1989).

The general values associated with universalist and particularist starting points are summarized in Table 3.3.

Table 3.3
General Orientations Privileged by Universalism – Particularism

Universalism	Particularism
Generalizations	Exceptions
Standardization	Uniqueness
Broad orientation	Narrow orientation
Sameness and similarity	Difference and distinction
Open, static systems	Innovative, dynamic systems
Mass production	Customization
Comparison is possible	Comparison is insignificant
Equality	Special privileges

Cultures draw on both orientations depending on issues, contexts, and players. Remember the rainbow metaphor introduced in Chapter One to describe South African relationships and interactions? The rainbow's distinct and bright colors come together to create a harmonious vision which spans the entire nation and encompasses all, yet each color's particularities are not lost. The metaphor suggests one way to balance universal, harmonizing trends and particular orientations that emphasize diversity and difference. The rainbow metaphor illustrates that the two starting points often exist within a single cultural context.

Specificity – Diffuseness

Not so long ago I attended a meeting for South Africans living in the United States, and interested others, to establish a nongovernmental organization linked to South Africa. The agenda of this first meeting included establishing a board and adopting guiding principles for the organization. Michael, a North American friend who is deeply interested in South Africa accompanied me to the meeting.

Ninety percent of the people who turned up were South African. Three hours were set aside to cover all the agenda items. The meeting proceeded as I expected it would. Much time was taken in discussing the guiding principles for the meeting itself. For each point and new idea that was brought up, many people talked and voiced their opinions, and before any decision was taken, many challenges were posed and support was determined. Discussions were charged and animated; people were passionate and enthusiastic.

At the end of the meeting, Michael and I walked to the parking lot with a group of other South Africans. We were all in high spirits, congratulating each other on a most successful first meeting. When we were finally alone in his car, Michael burst out, "That was the most frustrating experience—how can you call what just happened successful? We sat there for three hours and achieved nothing—there is barely a board, everybody just talked in circles, and there was such tension and suspicion surrounding everything that was said. We didn't even get through much of the agenda and yet everybody thinks this was a success!"

Michael's frustration with the South Africans at the meeting becomes clearer as we examine the continuum of specificity and diffuseness (Hampden-Turner and Trompenaars 2000). These starting points emphasize the degree of attention to the specific versus a more patterned, ambiguous focus. The specific orientation values attention to efficiency, performance, task, and outcome, while the diffuse orientation values attention to process, relationships, and the big picture.

These starting points also help explain conflict in dialogues where people come together to try to build understanding across differences. In a monthly dialogue group of pro-life and pro-choice advocates, tensions arose between those who were happy to get together month after month to share personal stories and explore various images of family and community, and those who wanted the group to take action on specific projects. Interestingly, these differences did not fall neatly on either side of the pro-life, pro-choice division. Some people from each side were content to continue exploring ideas and stories, while some from each side wanted to develop and implement action plans. These differences actually helped the group become closer, because they could see that there were things they shared with those from "the other side," and this changed their image of their counterparts as "someone very different from me" (LeBaron and Carstarphen 1999).

Table 3.4 details the general orientations arising from the starting points of specificity and diffuseness.

In the case of the South African meeting, the South Africans present and my North American friend operated and evaluated what happened from different starting points. Michael's specific focus oriented him toward valuing a definite, measurable outcome in the form of a well-defined board and the completion of all items on the agenda. He valued efficiency and exactness and became frustrated with the circular talking and perceived tensions around everything. North American culture and specifically his legal background directed his attention to

Table 3.4
General Orientations Privileged by Specificity – Diffuseness

Specificity	Diffuseness
Specific focus	Nebulous or fuzzy focus
Efficiency and performance	Relationships and teamwork
Outcome and solutions	Process
Detail orientation	Holistic orientation
Exactness and precision	Ambiguity and ambivalence
Success as measurable and tangible	Success as felt and experienced
Factual and analytical	Relative
Simplification	Complexity
Analysis	Synthesis

getting things done, making good use of time and achieving measurable results. He believed that the South Africans at the meeting achieved nothing. Why then were the South Africans so self-congratulatory?

The South Africans operated from a more diffuse orientation, and from this starting point the meeting was experienced as a complete success. Unlike Michael, whose priority was outcome and results, they gave themselves to the process. The context of the meeting process was defined by South African political culture, which favors and prioritizes democratic participation, public debate, equal voice, and transparency. Within the context of a political history that denied the majority of South Africans voice, outcome was secondary to equal involvement and the development of strong working relationships.

This same political culture determined the type of communication that occurred: the debate and constant questioning around each point that was raised did not represent tension and anger to the South Africans present, but the establishment of a solid communication base and relationships. With such a foundation created in the meeting, whatever came next would have very little chance of failure. The meeting was thus experienced as successful by the South Africans.

The very meaning attached to *specific* and *diffuse* may be different or similar, and in any particular cultural group both may have relevance depending on the meaning attached to these starting points. For the South Africans attending the meeting there was not necessarily a separation between diffuseness and specificity, since operating in a diffuse way brought the specific into focus. For those involved, the process undertaken was itself an outcome—an ideal, concrete result. As such it was efficient and detail-oriented in terms of ensuring adequate preparation for the establishment of the board and the larger organization.

It is possible for people to meander among various starting points drawing on each as appropriate—or to see them not as linear, but circular. A diffuse starting point may lead to specific outcomes. A specific beginning may yield diffuse fruits. In the abortion dialogue example, it was probably necessary to start in a diffuse way, because there was little or no relational foundation for them to trust. Once they had spent some time with abstract and big-picture experiences, those who preferred specific starting points began to get uncomfortable. The resulting tension led them to devise a process that would take diffuse and specific preferences into account.

No one way of proceeding is superior, but a failure to understand the existence and legitimacy of different starting points can fuel miscommunication and escalate conflict. Even framing cultural starting points as a continuum is to advance implicit cultural understandings. This is why we must cultivate comfort with ambiguity and a spirit of inquiry above all. We see this imperative also as it relates to different ways of understanding time.

Sequential – Synchronous Time

All cultures organize themselves around time, but these conceptions of time can be very different. Some cultures organize time sequentially, while others begin from a synchronous starting point (Hampden-Turner and Trompenaars 2000).

Sequential time is what we are familiar with as clock time, where the seconds, minutes, hours, days, weeks, months, and years are ordered and proceed in a linear fashion. It is also referred to as *monochronic* time, as only one thing is focused on at any one point. Time is rigid and exact. Many Western societies offer examples of the sequential time starting point.

Expressions like "Time is money," "Time waits for no man," and "Never put off till tomorrow what you can do today" epitomize a sequential starting point related to time. Seizing time, as in "seizing the moment" or *carpe diem,* is important as time can easily be lost and can never be recovered. In the previous story, Michael was operating from a sequential time starting point. His frustration with the lack of tangible results and his reflection that the meeting was "just a waste of time" reflects his experience of time as an expendable commodity.

In monochronic cultures there is usually a separation of the past, present, and future into distinct life periods, with the major focus being on the present and short-term future. Since time can be lost, this fast-paced lifestyle favors youth, energy, and vitality.

Synchronous time tends to be cyclical, episodic, and circular. It is a more chaotic, spiraling, overlapping conception of time. Also referred to as *polychronic* time, this starting point involves the simultaneous occurrences of many things and the involvement of many people. This approach to time is soft and elastic as it stretches into unlimited and overlapping continuity.

Many Eastern societies embrace a synchronous conception of time which highlights cycles of growth and decay, birth and death, and regeneration. Time is therefore never lost; it recurs in cycles such as the cycle of the seasons or rebirth through reincarnation. Time stretches far beyond the human ego or lifetime. In such societies there is an invisible thread that joins the present to the past while at the same time marking the way into the future. The past, present, and future are therefore connected and intertwined. From many Eastern and African cultural perspectives, fate, destiny and Spirit live in these intertwined spaces and the unfolding of time is only the unfolding of stories already written, waiting to be told and retold. Ancestors who have died are present at any given moment and are to be honored through rituals and invocations.

Table 3.5 summarizes the general orientations of sequential-synchronous time starting points.

Many people have embarrassing stories about different orientations to time—the kind of stories that only become humorous in retrospect. An Indian couple once told about inviting some German friends to their reception. Operating from a sequential time orientation, the German couple arrived ten minutes before the reception was due to start (according to the invitation), to take their seats and get settled in. Upon arriving at the venue they discovered that they were the only ones present. To their horror, the other guests only started drifting in about thirty minutes later and the formalities did not begin until forty minutes after the scheduled start-time. Unfortunately nobody had warned the German couple that "Indian time" tends to be synchronous in nature, and arriving late is an unwritten code for behavior.

Table 3.5
General Orientations Privileged by Sequential-Synchronous Time

Sequential Time	Synchronous Time
Monochronic	Polychronic
Clock time	Recurrent, episodic time
Linear	Cyclical, circular and overlapping
Ordered conception	Ambiguous and chaotic conception
Time as rigid and exact	Time as soft and elastic
Time as finite	Time as repetitive through events
Faster-paced	Slower-paced
Past, present, future separation	Past, present, future integration
Early life (youth) valued	Late life (elderly) valued
Rigid scheduling	Flexible scheduling
Sequenced talking, turn-taking	Overlap talk
Focused, concentration on task	Subject to distractions, interruptions
Punctuality as important	Lateness accepted as normal
Individual determines life	Fate, destiny operates

The German couple later expressed that, in their culture, punctuality is most important and such behavior would be considered very rude and disrespectful. The Indian families on the other hand had a more flexible, ambiguous orientation to time. Even though there was a scheduled time for the formal wedding reception, the celebrations had begun informally two weeks before and would continue into the days to come. The reception was therefore just one event in a long, ongoing period of celebration and the guests who arrived late were hardly being rude or disrespectful. Their celebration of the marriage was continuous and not limited to specific, scheduled time frames, despite what the formal invitation indicated.

As with the other continua, this one becomes most striking when conflict results. In a recent mediation workshop given by my colleague Janne, she noticed a participant knitting during the presentation components. Janne felt concerned about whether the participant was absorbing the material being presented. Later, each participant would have to pass a written and practical evaluation, and Janne was unsure if this participant would be prepared. Also, Janne worried that her lectures were boring, and wondered whether she should take steps to make them more interesting so that participants would pay full attention.

Janne spoke with the student at the break, inquiring about her knitting and whether it took away from her concentration. "Oh no!" the surprised student exclaimed. "It keeps me focused because it occupies my hands with something constructive that I don't have to think about, while they would otherwise be involved in doodling or nailbiting. With my hands in motion knitting, my mind is stimulated but not distracted, and I am able to completely take in what you are saying." The student, comfortable with polychromic time, demonstrated through excellent test results that her instructor's monochromic orientation was not the only route to success.

Power Distance

Imagine this picture: a young social worker graduates from a well-regarded U.S. university and begins her first professional position in a family and community services organization. A trained mediator, she looks forward with excitement to helping families come together across differences. But she runs into challenges in her first days on the job. At one home, she meets with the grandparents and widowed mother of an at-risk youth recently caught in the vicinity of a crime scene. The social worker assessed that the teenager was "acting out" and seeking attention from his mother and grandparents. Family members were emotionally disconnected from each other and there was poor communication between them.

In this home, the grandparents' words and rules prevailed, as they were the elders and heads of the household. The youth was worlds away in his ideas and values from his grandparents, who had come from "the old country." The social worker believed that there was room for compromise and that the mother could play a mediating role between the seemingly distant worlds of her son and his grandparents. It seemed there was potential for the teenager to relate more openly to his mother, who worked outside the home. But the social worker discovered that this solution was almost impossible to execute as the mother was silent, obedient to her parents' demands and rules. The mother never contradicted the elders' views that the youth should just "shape up and accept his responsibility to step into his father's shoes." The social worker soon discovered that understanding the culture of the immigrant adults, as well as the adopted U.S. culture of the teenager, would offer a more revealing problem assessment.

The graduate's U.S.-American mediation training taught her that she should act neutrally, helping weaker parties (the mother and son) attain equality with others (the grandparents). But in this ethnically diverse, largely immigrant urban community in the United States, she found that equality was less a concern than filial piety. How was neutrality possible in this family intervention? What equality could she offer the teen who was not able to express views and ideas that differed from those of his elders?

The graduate quickly discovered that the people with whom she was working had their own distinct understandings of status and hierarchy. These understandings governed their relations with each other and their perceptions of her. Respect for hierarchy led to unwritten rules about authority, leading to the mother's unopposed acceptance of her parents' rule in the home. The graduate's idea of equality—whether within families, or between families and communities—were well-intentioned but in vain. The concept of power distance helps us understand why.

Organizational anthropologist Geert Hofstede's idea of power distance describes the degree of deference and acceptance of unequal power between people (1984). In some cultures, such as the immigrant community that the social worker encountered, a *high-power distance* indicates that some people are considered superior to others because of their social status, gender, race, age, education, birth, personal achievements, family lineage, or other factors. Status within such societies is usually ascribed instead of earned. A general rule is that the more unequally wealth is distributed in a given society the more likely the society uses a high-power distance starting point. High-power distance cultures tend toward hierarchical societal structures, with defined status cleavages and clear authority figures. A high-power starting point was operating in the home of the at-risk youth in the previous example.

In high-power distance cultural settings, deference to those in authority is expected and normalized. Suppose a supervisor calls an employee just before his lunch date with a coworker, asking for something urgent to be done during the lunch period. In a high-power distance setting, that employee is more likely to accede to the supervisor's request, and his friend is likely to understand. However, if his friend has just arrived from a low-power distance culture, that friend may not understand, and may feel slighted and frustrated that the employee did not tell his supervisor he had a prior commitment. Thus, high-power distance starting points shape more formal relations, while low-power distance starting points invite more open conflict and discussion between those at different levels within an organization.

North American culture advocates equality and democracy as starting points and tends to feature *low-power distance*. People hold status and authority because of what they have achieved and accomplished, at least theoretically. Founded on principles of equality and democracy, North America projects the image of the land of opportunity for all. Low-power distance cultures tend toward democratic decision-making, elected leaders, and shared authority. Of course, U.S. American culture also has status and identity cleavages, just as individual initiative may sometimes enhance status in high-power distance settings. No national or regional culture uses high- or low-power distance starting points exclusively.

Table 3.6 depicts the general orientations privileged by high-power and low-power distance cultures.

As she thought about power distance, the social work graduate came to understand that mediation processes based on Western principles of equality and symmetrical power were unfamiliar to, and did not work for, many in the new immigrant community she served. She creatively tailored her mediation practice and role to accommodate the community's high-power distance orientation. Over time, she found ways to involve elders and community leaders in community and family decisions with positive results. She stopped trying to facilitate symmetrical power relations, and started working to bridge the high-power distance worlds of many of the first generation immigrants with the lower-power distance worlds their children and grandchildren encountered

Table 3.6
General Orientations Privileged by High Power Distance – Low Power Distance Cultures

High Power Distance	Low Power Distance
Hierarchical structures	Structures based on equality
Defined status cleavages	Opportunities for all
"Acceptance of one's lot in life"	"Rags to riches"
Ascribed status	Achieved status
Special privilege	Earned accomplishment
Autocratic decisionmaking, leadership	Democratic decision-making, leadership
Clear authority figures	Shared authority
The right to use power	Use of power is limited
"Old money"	"The new rich"

outside their homes. This task was not easy, since she had been taught to help create symmetry in families, and teach them participatory processes for decision-making, but she understood that their values were just as relevant and meaningful to them as her principles were to her.

The social worker's future work was also affected. After her initial cross-cultural experience, she took time to reflect on her cultural assumptions and starting points. She continued this self-introspection every time she interacted with somebody. By continuously being aware of her own cultural starting points, she ensured a readiness and openness to receive and understand others' cultural frames. By recognizing overlapping starting points, the social worker was on her way to cultural fluency in her work with diverse peoples.

Constructing Cultural Flowers: When Starting Points Overlap

Because they are part of human communication and relationships, starting points do not exist in isolation. No one communication strategy or relationship can be understood by reference to only one of the continua outlined in the previous section. There is likely to be high correlation among some of them in certain contexts, though even this correlation will not always hold true. For example, high-context communication starting points often correspond with communitarian starting points, just as low-context communication often occurs where individualist starting points prevail. People who favor group cohesiveness and harmony are more likely to use indirect communication that allows for multiple meanings, saves face, and displays interdependence. Where individualist starting points operate, low-context communication may be preferable because it is direct, expresses individual desires, and displays independence.

Also, as noted earlier, the starting points of any one continuum are not mutually exclusive. For example, it is almost impossible to define an individual without specifying the group or social context of which he is a part. Similarly, any collective group is composed of individuals.

There are no absolute answers and so there cannot be prescriptive patterns for understanding cultures. Starting points are initial clues to the continuous development of cultural understanding. Imagining these starting points as petals, let's consider how we can construct *cultural flowers of understanding* when we encounter others. The flowers will be unique, depending on how we choose to overlap the cultural starting points. Each constructed flower paints a different picture of culture. The flowers may be relevant to completely different cultural groups or the same cultural group in different contexts and changing time periods. These flowers show that cultural starting points overlap in different and continuous patterns to inform our understanding of particular cultures. Depending on the context and relational dynamics, you may have to remove a petal or add more in. Be creative in your flower construction and you will ultimately understand something of the nuances of cultural starting points. Figure 3.1 depicts what some of these cultural flowers can look like.

Let's take an example of Sylvie, the social work graduate, and see how her cultural flower might unfold. Sylvie begins to practice and is quickly confronted with ways her assumptions are not shared by her clients. She recognizes that she needs to explore her own cultural starting points before she can understand her clients and their ways of behaving and meaning-making. Reflecting on her education, Sylvie notices that the mediation and counseling processes she was taught arose from individualist starting points. They tended to see people as individuals who need empowerment or resources, but who can make decisions independently and act on their own initiatives. Of course, her training recognized that these people live in families and communities and that they need to relate constructively to both groups, but the starting point for decision-making and intervention stressed individual choice and consequences. Sylvie draws an individualist petal on her flower.

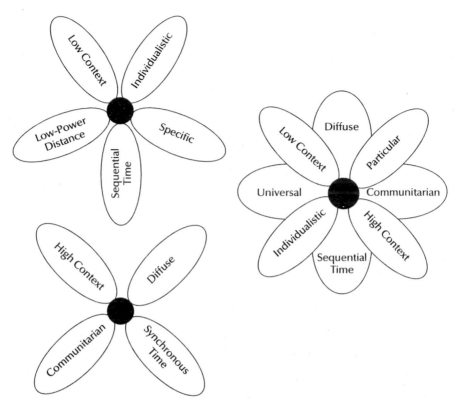

Figure 3.1 Sample Cultural Flower

Reflecting further, Sylvie realizes that she came from a family where communitarian starting points were stressed. Her graduate education had been delayed by a year during which she worked to support her brother as he finished university. He had helped her pay for her social work education. The family was close, and made decisions together about jobs, education, even marriage partners for the children. As Sylvie adds a communitarian petal to her flower, she overlaps it with the individualist petal, realizing that she lives simultaneously in both worlds, shifting back and forth as the context shifts.

Finally, Sylvie adds a sequential time petal to her flower, again overlapping it with the other two petals. This petal represents the pressure she feels at work to manage a large caseload and demonstrate a linear progression of measurable results, even as she struggles with unpredictability and difficult dynamics within the families with whom she works.

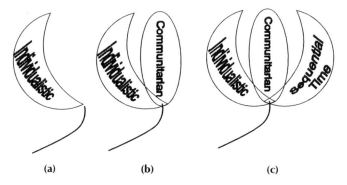

(a)   (b)   (c)

Figure 3.2 Sylvie's Cultural Flower

Sylvie could add other petals, but her flower feels complete for now. It helps her realize why she has experienced such conflict in some of the family situations where she has worked. It is almost as though she has two sets of starting points within herself—individualist and communitarian—both tugging at her while also overlapping with accountability for results in a sequential-time world. Sylvie's academic training made autonomy and independence seem like natural starting points. Her family assumed communal starting points, and she has generally acceded to these, though she has found that foundation limiting at times. In the crush of pressure to achieve results with her client families, Sylvie does not always realize the effects of this inner tug-of-war.

Sylvie can use this process for inner exploration, and for understanding her clients. Put yourself in her place as she considers the mystery of the client she has never met face-to-face an angry, depressed teenager who never emerges from her bedroom. Sylvie finds herself talking to the teen, through a closed door, for more than an hour while the teen's mother sits dejected on a kitchen chair. Let's call the teen Renissa. Renissa is fifteen. She has threatened and attempted suicide several times, and has frequent screaming matches with her mother. Her father is in the military and is away on extended duty. Two other siblings live at home, one older and one younger. Renissa spends many hours and sometimes days locked in her bedroom, unwilling to come out for meals or school. She was in a foster family last year, and was returned to her home after her mother took a parenting course and Renissa agreed to weekly meetings with her mother and a social worker. When Sylvie arrives for her first weekly meeting, replacing a social worker who has been assigned to another case, Renissa refuses to emerge from the bedroom.

Drawing a cultural flower of someone you've never met face-to-face is not easy. Let's consider what Sylvie knows from her long conversation through the door, the case notes of the previous social worker, and Renissa's mother. Renissa's mother relates that her daughter's favorite class in school is art. Renissa has won county awards for her abstract painting, in which she uses broad brush strokes to blend colors. When Sylvie asked if she could see Renissa's art, Renissa described herself as a failed artist, and said there was no point. As they continued to talk through the door, Sylvie notices that Renissa tends to talk holistically, resisting simplification of her situation. Renissa says that the whole system in which she lives is not fair, though Sylvie has not been able to get Renissa to describe her idea of a fair system in detail.

In response to Sylvie's requests to come out and visit for a while, Renissa shoots back that whole lifetimes are elapsing in any given moment, and that this lifetime is not one in which she wishes to come out. These lifetimes are hers, no one else's, and she will be in them how and when she chooses. She adds that her mother is out of her mind half the time, and has unreal expectations. "Obedience is for the old country," Renissa replies in response to a question about her willingness to listen to her mother.

After several attempts at threading question-and-response into a longer conversation, Sylvie sits at the door in silence for a few minutes. Then she knocks. She can hear Renissa inside, talking on the phone to a friend, her typing on her computer keyboard punctuated with frequent beeps from Instant Messenger while she bounces a ball against something that echoes. "Go away!" she shouts in the midst of these activities, "I don't need any of you. I am more mature than all of you."

Renissa at fifteen may be labeled resistant, rebellious, and angry, and these labels may have some validity. But let's look beneath them to five petals that might help us understand some of Renissa's starting points. How does she tend to communicate—with more specificity, or diffuseness? Label the first petal accordingly. How does she see herself—in more individualist or communitarian terms? Label the second petal with your answer. Is the world around her—the child welfare system—presenting her with universalist or particular starting points? Label the third petal accordingly. What can you tell about her orientation to time—does it tend to be synchronous or sequential? Label the fourth petal with your choice. Finally, is she choosing a high- or low-context starting point for communication?

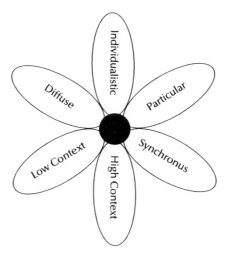

Figure 3.3 Renissa's Cultural Flower

Enter your choice on the fifth petal. Now consider the answer key that follows to see how different or similar your flower looks to the one we've constructed.

Answer key

How does Renissa tend to communicate, with more specificity or diffuseness?
Diffuseness. Renissa speaks holistically, in big-picture terms. She is focused on fair processes, but does not address the details of the process. She feels like a failure, measuring her success internally even though she has won awards. She insists on the complexity of her situation, resisting simplification.

How does she see herself—in more individualist or communitarian terms?
Individualist. Renissa says she can be self-sufficient and doesn't need anyone. She wants to coexist without relating to those in her family. She wants autonomy and independence.

Is the world around her—the child welfare system—presenting her with universalist or particular starting points?
Renissa experiences the world around her as presenting her with ill-fitting universalist prescriptions that get in the way of her self-determination. This

particularist starting point overlaps with her individualist preferences, pulling her in a different direction by virtue of the power of the state to enforce decisions affecting her.

What can you tell about her orientation to time—does it tend to be synchronous or sequential?
Renissa tells Sylvie that whole lifetimes are elapsing in any given moment. This gives us a clue that she is taking a synchronous approach to time.

Is she choosing a high- or low-context starting point for communication?
Renissa is using a mixture of high- and low-context communication. At times, she is very direct and literal, as when she tells Sylvie to go away. At other times, her communication relies not on verbal messages but the context. Refusing to speak or come out of her room conveys a high-context message about her unwillingness to engage. Sylvie is left to try ways of making a connection with Renissa through the door. We can put both high- and low-context petals on the flower for Renissa.

Congratulations on your work with the flower! As you will have seen, there are not always clear answers to the question of starting points. Sometimes, we move back and forth along continua. It is less important to capture a series of starting points accurately than to engage in trying, for it is the effort to understand from the inside out that helps us relate more effectively with others. We must remember, as well, that cultures change and flowers die, so we must replenish our vases of cultural understanding with new flowers that allow for personal and group change over time.

Using Our Multicultural Selves

No person is culture free; as these cultural flowers depict, people are ultimately multicultural beings. We all belong to and are influenced by various cultural groups with different and similar starting points. We embody and express many cultural starting points in our daily lives. As the products of interweaving cultures, our identities and meaning-making capacities extend beyond the reach of any *one* culture. We undergo continual change and our identities, informed by a multitude of cultural starting points, are always *becoming*.

As we have seen, the starting points introduced in this chapter are neither reliable guides to every member of a particular group nor are they fixed in nature. They simply shine the light on possibilities within a culture and invite us to imagine flowers of cultural understanding. Using the starting points provides somewhere to begin our quest for cross-cultural understanding. In this quest, we have the first capacity to achieve cultural understanding of the many influences that shape our identities and meanings. Since we embody multiple cultures, draw meaning from many cultural influences, and relate to a variety of contexts, we are ourselves the links between cultures.

Perhaps this is a good time to stop and consider what *your* cultural flower might look like. Remember, as a multicultural being, you are likely to have diverse cultural flowers that embody different starting points depending on the context. You may want to begin your personal cultural flower construction by thinking of a particular situation, context, problem, or interaction and then assess it in terms of the starting points. As you draw your petals and your flower takes shape, you will surely discover more cultural insights into your situation, but more importantly, about yourself and your ways of being and doing.

Cultural understanding therefore begins with each of us commiting to a process of increasing self-awareness, curious observation, ongoing reflection, and dialogue with others. Equipped with the cultural starting points introduced in this chapter, we are now ready to explore capacities to navigate through culture. Achieving cultural fluency through self-awareness is the subject of Chapter Four.

A Journey Toward Cultural Fluency

Tatsushi (Tats) Arai

Utter silence. My heart pounding. My legs shaking. A sea of people watching me. Somewhere in my mind, a voice was calling, "Tats, come on. You can do it. You have prepared so hard for this. It's just a three-minute speech." I gradually recovered from extreme nervousness and looked around. Standing in front of a microphone, I saw some two hundred junior high school students facing me, along with several teachers on the far right corner of the crowd. Trying to dispel my anxiety, I mustered all the courage that had been hidden somewhere in my body. Slowly I began to read the prepared speech and welcomed the Singaporean guests visiting our school in Tokyo.

It was the first speech I made in English. I was fourteen years old. Nearly twenty years have passed since then. Yet I still remember nearly all the details of that moment: the clear blue sky of the day, echoes of my voice resonating in the schoolyard, and signs of slight confusion on the part of the Singaporean visitors who seemed to be grappling with my heavy Japanese-infused English accent. I remember correcting many grammatical mistakes and awkward sentences with the help of my English teacher when I drafted this speech. I also remember practicing the almost impossible pronunciation of the "r" and "th" sounds numerous times to get ready for the speech. I dreamed that some day, I would become fluent in this mysteriously foreign, yet intriguingly interesting, language. Looking back, I started my journey toward cultural fluency at that moment.

Cultural Fluency

Cultural fluency is our readiness to anticipate, internalize, express, and help shape the process of meaning-making. This process dynamically grows in a social context of interdependence between self and others, enhancing our capacities to

- *anticipate* a range of possible scenarios about how our future relationships will evolve in unfamiliar cultural contexts;
- remain conscious of unfamiliar cultural influences that come to be *embedded* in our meaning-making processes;
- *express* what is deep down in our cultural assumptions, in a way that is understandable to others unfamiliar with our meaning-making patterns; and
- *navigate* the turbulence of cross-cultural dynamics in order to co-create a constructive future together with cultural others.

Cultural fluency evolves from developing these four capacities through experiences with diverse others that stretch our own ideas of normalcy. The first capacity is *anticipatory capacity.* The moment we hear somebody saying, "I can *not only* read," we can anticipate something like, "*but also* write," to follow. Why? Because we know the idiom "not only . . . but also." We can never predict exactly what will follow the "not only" part, but we can roughly anticipate the likely patterns of speech acts that will follow because we are fluent in English. Likewise, anticipatory capacity for cultural fluency is our readiness to expect a range of possible scenarios about how our future relationships might evolve, often with uncertainties and surprises unfolding moment by moment.

The second capacity is *embeddedness.* We anticipate "but also . . ." right after "not only . . ." because we intuitively sense the pattern of English grammatical usage. We do not have to think. The pattern of speech becomes embedded in our meaning making process over time, changing from conscious to unconscious. I remember memorizing these patterns before English tests in junior high. Back then I had to logically think about its meaning and usage repeatedly until I memorized it. Having lived in an English-speaking environment for years, the idiom has become part of me. I now sense it.

The way we acquire fluency in a nonnative language is somewhat similar to our journey toward cultural fluency. Our cultural understanding first anchors in the realm of conscious learning. For example, I vividly remember the first time I observed somebody taking an oath in an American courtroom. I was struck by the mysterious contrast between the profound religious message contained in the oath "I will tell the truth, the whole truth, and nothing but the truth. So help me, God" and the rather disinterested manner in which the court clerk led the witness to recite these serious words for administrative routine. I wondered if the clerk and the witness were truly aware of the serious meaning of the words they were reciting. I also wondered if I was the only person in the courtroom thinking *consciously* about what those words really meant.

Unfamiliar cultural habits of being and doing learned consciously are gradually submerged into our subconscious. This is the process where part of what used to be our conscious reasoning becomes so routinized and internalized in our mind, body, and spirit that we are no longer making conscious efforts to follow the learned habits. While the court clerk seemed to be able to recite the oath without making any conscious effort, I was certain that he had once made a conscious effort to memorize these words. Likewise I now use the English idiom "not only . . . but also . . ." as easily as I ride a bicycle.

From time to time, part of our subconscious gradually slips into our unconscious, where we can no longer recognize the initial shape, color, and flavor of perceptions and behaviors we have internalized. Our unconscious is much deeper than our subconscious, holding a vast reservoir of intuition and imagination outside the reach of conscious reasoning. If our conscious awareness is the tip of the huge iceberg above the surface of the ocean, our subconscious is right beneath the surface, sometimes breaking the surface as tides and temperatures change. Our unconscious, on the other hand, is the vast portion of what is deep down where light does not penetrate.

In our daily life, unconscious patterns of thinking and feeling may surface in dreams, a slip of the tongue, or habitual ways of being and doing. These patterns harbor assumptions that are constantly reshaped and transmitted from one generation to another, carried by the warmth of mothers' milk, grandmas' bedtime stories, and elementary school textbooks that we no longer remember consciously. Cultural assumptions internalized in our unconscious are like unknowingly wearing a pair of yellow glasses, turning everything blue into green, and red into orange. We disagree with cultural others wearing eyeglasses of different colors, without ever understanding the different glasses. Instead we wonder why these cultural outsiders can never accept even the simplest fact that green is green and orange is orange!

The court clerk I saw in the American courtroom may or may not have been a dedicated Christian. But I imagine that he would feel taken aback if the witness concluded the oath by saying, "So help me, Allah," stepping out of the clerk's "common sense" embedded in his unconscious. In short, embeddedness reminds us of unconscious cultural patterns. The process of cultural fluency involves gradually merging new information about ourselves and others into these embedded patterns.

The third capacity is *expressiveness.* "He can not only read but also *writes*" doesn't sound right. We don't need to think about why it's incorrect. We just feel it's incorrect. Yet suppose somebody learning English asks, "This sentence makes perfect sense. Why do you think it's incorrect?" To help out this cultural stranger, we need to activate our database of grammatical rules and patiently explain how the second verb *write* must take the same form as the first verb, *read.* In the meaning-making process shared by English speakers, the mistake is obvious. But when people who don't share the same cultural starting points ask why, we draw on our expressive capacity for explaining those unwritten rules that make up "common sense." This involves probing deep into why we do what we do. It requires surfacing what is beneath the tip of the huge iceberg. It entails becoming a cultural interpreter for dialogue between self and others, describing what colors of eyeglasses we wear and what effects they have on our vision, and cultivating curiosity about outsiders' glasses.

The fourth and final stream is *navigational capacity,* which is our ability to situate ourselves by constructively connecting with others in order to chart a constructive future. It is analogous to reaching an advanced stage of second-language acquisition, where we feel comfortable composing poems and improvising our own unique sense of humor in a new language. It is a process of becoming an active participant in forming and transforming the universe of meaning-making processes that language opens up. We will explore what a navigational process looks like shortly and elaborate on this idea in Chapter Seven. Navigational capacity is necessary for turning our cultural fluency into concrete action for transforming cultural conflicts.

Central to developing cultural fluency is the ongoing cultivation of self-awareness. My moment of extreme nervousness, with my legs shaking and heart pounding—these and many other vicissitudes in my journey toward cultural fluency have been part of my evolving self-awareness, formed and transformed in an endless succession of euphonies and cacophonies. Self-awareness means cultivating our inner observer, so that we are not only making choices about behaviors and interpretations of those behaviors, but are monitoring those choices and behaviors in parallel. As we hone our abilities to self-observe, we see patterns and habitual ways of responding, and also notice choice points where we might wish to respond differently.

Many great philosophers have written about the importance of cultivating self-awareness. J. Krishnamurti (1998) maintains that cultivating a particular quality of attention enhances both self and other-awareness. This quality of attention is different from the way we concentrate on an engrossing book and different from the attention of resistance that comes when we fight distractions. In both of these instances, paying attention means narrowing down our focus. Krishnamurti suggests cultivating awareness that is an "opening out," listening both to the sounds and the silence between the sounds. It is to be exquisitely present to many facets of experience and the silence around experiences. Krishnamurti suggests that if we "know how to listen to what [our] teacher is telling [us] about some historical fact, if [we] can listen without any resistance because our mind has space and silence and is therefore not distracted, [we] will be aware not only of the historical facts but also of the prejudice with which he may be translating it, and of [our] own inward experience." (1998, 138)

Self-awareness in this example is a state of being rather than a set of actions. It is to pay exquisite attention to what is stated and not stated, what is obvious and hidden, and to listen inwardly for understanding of self and other. As we pay exquisite attention to our inner experiences—feelings, thoughts, imaginings, triumphs, and disappointments—and to maintaining spaciousness around these experiences, we become paradoxically more "at home" with ourselves and more able to perceive and make novel choices. As we make novel choices and innovate with others, we deepen our capacities for cultural fluency.

✳✳✳

Of course, the route toward cultural fluency is never a straight line. The stories in this chapter illustrate twists and turns in my journey. They have all contributed to my evolving self-awareness that is the foundation of my work and relationships across cultures.

Having looked at the key dimensions of cultural fluency (*anticipation, embeddedness, expression, and navigation*), and situated self-awareness at the center, we are tempted to ask: What does cultural fluency look like in its entirety? Figure 4.1 presents one way to visualize the image of cultural fluency.

It is difficult to illustrate the flow of a three-dimensional image in this two dimensional space. It is even harder to demonstrate the fourth dimension,

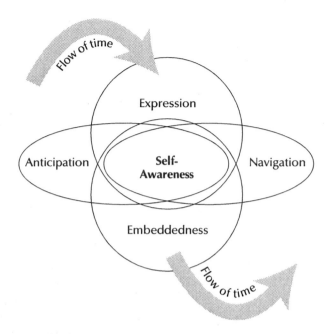

Figure 4.1 Image of Cultural Fluency

time, that sets the tone of evolving fluency. It is clearly impossible to capture the important fifth dimension, sound, corresponding to human voices involved in every moment of dynamic cultural flow. The different shapes in Figure 4.1, representing the four facets of cultural fluency, are catalyzed by self-awareness, which functions as an anchor for meaning-making.

The image presented here is an oversimplification of a complex reality. Throughout my journey toward cultural fluency, I have always felt the need for a simple image of cultural complexity. Otherwise, my legs can be easily swept out from under me by the powerful flow of the current and it would be hard to get my bearings. Perhaps the best question is not whether the image simplifies this reality; it obviously does. A more meaningful question is whether this simplification is useful for navigating the sometimes turbulent dynamics of cross-cultural conflicts. So far, the image has been useful.

✻✻✻

With this in mind, let our journey begin. Our first destination is the southern Rwandan town of Butare, where I worked as the first Japanese lecturer at the country's national university in 1997 and 1998. The story illustrates how I came to appreciate the meaning of formality in Rwandan life, as well as how I reflected on my anticipatory capacity to understand social manifestations of formality in Rwanda. We will then fly to Bosnia, where I dialogued with diverse opinion leaders on post-war reconciliation processes in the summer of 2002. I will contemplate on how I came to rediscover part of my embedded cultural awareness through close interaction with a Bosnian youth. Our journey will then take us to Taiwan, where I married my Taiwanese wife in late 1998. As with any cross-cultural wedding, ours was a rather eventful one, where I was able to learn how important it is to understand and express deep-seated assumptions on the meaning of family life across cultural boundaries. Finally we will journey back to Rwanda and listen to a story about Rwandan twin sisters who had recently lost their dearest brother in battle. I was inspired by the twins to appreciate the significant human potential for coping with a tragic culture of war and for navigating the turbulence of cultural dynamics in conflict.

Anticipatory Capacity: Expecting Uncertainties in Cross-cultural Turbulence

A green military helicopter roared down to the athletic field of the National University of Rwanda. Dust swirled over hundreds of students and lecturers seated on the field and the benches of the football stadium. Rwandan vice president Paul Kagame disembarked, escorted by security guards, including one American. Mr. Kagame walked across the playground and headed straight to the special armchair located at the center of the VIP bench, several yards away from where I was seated with other lecturers. Black limousines pulled up to the VIP section one after another. A round of applause emerged from the students every time a minister got out of a limousine. With the vice president seated deep in his armchair, legs crossed, the national solidarity meeting began. This meeting and the following training sessions at the university were meant to be part of the ongoing nationwide mobilization efforts for unity and reconciliation three years after the war and genocide of 1994.

The event was filled with vitality and passion, expressed by students' songs, poems, dances, and plays evoking fervent patriotism. I observed with great curiosity that all the student performers were facing the vice president and other dignitaries as if they were demonstrating their loyalty specifically to these governmental leaders. After the students' performances and a few other agenda items, the vice president was invited to the microphone for a speech. He picked a small piece of paper out of an inner pocket of his suit, glanced at it, and began to address the audience quite casually and spontaneously. It was a rather long speech for a public function of this sort, lasting nearly one hour. I attentively watched how the students and the rest of the audience listened to him. I was intrigued by the formality and the air of authority demonstrated in the meeting. My curiosity was also drawn to the kind of uniformity and submissiveness expressed by the students' performances. While sensing an unfamiliar tone of formality, I began reflecting back on several previous occasions where I had felt similar kinds of authoritative atmosphere in Rwandan society.

The first time I had felt this tone of formality was when about a dozen of my students invited me and a few other new lecturers to a restaurant near the university. I was invited into the restaurant with my African colleagues. It seemed that seating arrangements emerged spontaneously; yet it was clear that the lecturers were expected to sit on one side and the students on the other in recognition of status. Drinks and brochettes were served. The meeting started with some introductory remarks made by a student representative. There was hardly any two-way communication between the lecturers and the students. Although this gathering was not meant to be a class, the lecturers kept speaking to one student after another while the students listened quietly as if they were not supposed to speak. I was sitting on the lecturers' side, but I hardly spoke because I was busy observing the communication process. It was interesting to note that while the students had organized the event, the lecturers ordered beers continuously and preached authoritatively and passionately to the obedient students.

As I watched this formal student event, I also thought about the meetings that my students often held to select class representatives, share their academic concerns, and discuss administrative issues related to their campus life. In some of these meetings, the class representative maintained a statesman-like tone throughout her opening speech, followed by other students' rebuttals as well as comments of support, all performed with meticulous eloquence and the use of formal language. Sitting there with the other lecturers, I remembered a wedding ceremony held at Butare's city hall. The bride and groom, who were both university administrators, sat on the main stage alongside city officials and invited "dignitaries." Other guests with social status, typically in Western attire, were seated in two rows facing each other at the foot of the stage, with a wide space between the rows for musical performances and dances. The rest of the people, most of whom were bare-footed "ordinary"

Rwandans in non-Western attire, were seated in the section of the general audience looking up at those on the main stage.

I came to suspect that there must be something cultural about the striking consistency with which patterns of formality and authoritativeness were demonstrated repeatedly across different social settings in Rwanda. Later, I understood more about Rwandan cultural formality when I was invited to a student's birthday party. At this party, I saw that his fellow students were seated in a carefully prearranged order and some of them were invited to give prepared speeches as if they were following the protocol of the national assembly.

It would be a mistake to make a sweeping generalization that Rwandan social life is filled with formality, based merely on my observations. But it would not be totally unreasonable to believe that under certain circumstances the Rwandan people I encountered exhibited shared patterns of meaning-making where some kind of formality, authoritative ordering, and status recognition were considered essential for stabilizing their social relationships. For example, as introduced in Chapter Three, it is possible that elements of high-power distance orientations influenced the formality of Rwandan culture. As I formed this working proposition in an attempt to make sense of related experiences in Rwanda, I came to feel that Rwandan society was not as foreign as I had initially thought. This realization helped reduce part of my anxiety about being the "different" person in this community, my workplace, and Rwandan society at large. This proposition later came to serve as a touchstone for my meaning-making process regarding the perceived formality and authoritativeness in Rwandan society. As later events happened, I referred back to this learning as it informed my *anticipatory capacity*.

Having this template for understanding social relations did not necessarily enable me to predict exactly what seating arrangement would be made in a wedding ceremony. Nor would it allow me to tell precisely how the meeting agenda would be set for national solidarity camps in a particular community. Uncertainties and surprises continued to unfold every time I was part of public gatherings. Yet my readiness for uncertainties and surprises was certainly enhanced as I refined my understanding of the parameters within which they were likely to unfold. Most importantly, I no longer sensed authoritative formality as strange and exotic. Repeated observations of social patterns and continuous dialogue with people involved in the social process enabled me to enhance my *anticipatory capacity*, leading to a higher level of cultural fluency in Rwanda.

However, further reflections on my journey toward *anticipatory capacity* building made me realize that there was a crucial missing piece in this reasoning process: What about my cultural lenses through which I was *perceiving* the image of Rwandan formality and authoritativeness? How were my Japanese cultural assumptions interacting with Rwandan meaning-making patterns related to formality and authoritativeness? These questions can never be answered without reflecting on my own "cultural common sense." The next story illustrates part of my ongoing endeavor to become more self-aware.

Embeddedness: Rediscovering Myself in the Mirror of Cultural Others

Bosnia was burning hot in the summer of 2002. "This is global warming," my Bosnian interpreter uttered in a half-joking tone. I was visiting to study Bosnia's reconciliation process. Tarik, as I call him in this story, was an extremely mature college student in his early twenties, majoring in art and design. His command of English was impeccable. Describing himself as a Bosnian Muslim, he shared with me many stories of the war he survived as a teenager.

As we strolled the busy streets of downtown Sarajevo, a distinctly modern and well-fenced building caught my attention. The building was several stories tall and equipped with a super-sized satellite dish and a high-tech security entrance. A large American flag was hung inside the fence. "That's a CIA building," said Tarik. "Really?" I exclaimed in astonishment. I simply couldn't believe that such a high-tech building had been constructed by a foreign government in the middle of this devastated city. I approached the building and took a closer look, hoping that I could find a sign indicating "CIA." Realizing I was not going to be successful in this endeavor, I turned to Tarik and asked, "How do you know this is a CIA building? There is no sign showing that this is the CIA." Perhaps I was demonstrating a bad habit of a social science major: always ask why when you are not sure. I could sense a sign of slight discomfort on Tarik's face. "This *is* a CIA building. Everybody says so," he emphasized, looking me straight in the eyes.

The next day, when we walked by this building again, it suddenly began to rain hard. We hailed a taxi to continue on our way. After conversing with the taxi driver for a moment in Bosnian, Tarik turned to me and said, "See. The taxi driver also says that this is a CIA building." I was unprepared to start our CIA building conversation again. Frankly, I was a little surprised that Tarik not only remembered the conversation from the day before, but he was still trying tenaciously to "prove" his point to me. I inferred that perhaps Tarik had remained frustrated by my disbelief of his comments about the CIA building from the previous day.

Tarik and I visited and interviewed a cross-section of opinion leaders in Sarajevo and elsewhere. Our interviewees were very impressive people, including a head of an interfaith dialogue organization, a Jewish community leader, renowned scholars at the University of Sarajevo, Orthodox and Catholic priests, accomplished journalists, and a representative of a Muslim youth league. Tarik interpreted each interview for me with impressive sophistication and professionalism.

As we moved from one interviewee's place to another, we casually chatted about the findings from the interview we had just completed, especially those things that surprised me. As much as I was interested in what the interviewees said, I took greater interest in what Tarik had to say about them. In addition to sharing with me comments like, "Well, that was a great man. He is a real Bosnian!" Tarik also evaluated whether the interviewee was telling me truths or lies about the war and Bosnian society. Once, after we finished an interview, he told me, "Sorry, Tats. That guy just told you a big lie. Well, this is life." Tarik's comments seemed natural to me. After all, he is among millions of Bosnians whose lives were shattered by the recent war. It is only human to react to others' war-related stories by taking sides. It is also natural to try to convince outsiders like me about the truthfulness of others' stories based on his definition of truth. I neither accepted nor rejected Tarik's claims relating to the truthfulness of the interviewees' remarks. I simply listened and acknowledged what he had to say.

In these interviews, I sought to gather a range of perceptions expressed by different people claiming different versions of truth about why the war occurred and how Bosnian society can find a way forward. From many Bosnian points of view, my exploration was yet another attempt by a curious outsider who could afford to hear "multiple truths"—though nearly every Bosnian was convinced that there was only one acceptable truth. Academic literature on "research methodology" engaging multiple truths must have appeared irrelevant to Tarik, who, like nearly every Bosnian I encountered, was very emotional about the war.

I decided to explain my research method to Tarik, believing that doing so would satisfy his curiosity about why I kept asking exactly the same set of questions to one interviewee after another, and listening to not only the same true stories, but also the ones that were intolerably untrue to him. Tarik patiently interpreted both types of stories for me again and again. After each new "true" story came out, Tarik impressed on me the veracity of that particular account by saying, "You see. That's what I told you. She told you the truth I had already told you." Through him I began to see a universe of truth and untruth resonating with numerous other Bosnian lives that had been acted out in the misery of war.

One day in the middle of our intensive interview schedule, Tarik had to take a morning off to attend a funeral of his academic mentor, who had unexpectedly passed away. The professor had been sick for a while but nobody expected his sudden passing. After the funeral, Tarik and I chatted at the coffee shop we usually frequented. I could see his face filled with the emotion he carried over from the funeral. He told me that he was asked to give an impromptu speech in the ceremony. He narrated part of his speech for me, capturing the rather unorthodox but humorous views that the professor held about different peoples in the world.

Although our conversation shifted freely from one subject to another, an expression of seriousness and tension remained on Tarik's face, perhaps because he mourned the death of someone so close to him. Tarik was disillusioned with hypocritical and materialistic tendencies in human nature, demonstrated so vividly by his friends and neighbors during the war. He mentioned how his hair began to turn white from fear and stress because of the war and because of a personal crisis. He expressed hopelessness about the human potential for positive change. He shared with me his wish that the Final Day of Judgment would come soon and this hypocritical world of materialism would cease to exist. Then we somehow wandered back to our earlier discussion on the authenticity of multiple truth claims.

This time, I felt a little emotional and sorry for this Bosnian youth who, despite being so young, was determinedly hopeless about the future. I could not suppress my impulse to instill some kind of realistic optimism in his mind. So I became insistent. I shared my personal reflections on how people can change if they strive to make a difference. I used some examples of positive change in different parts of the world that I had witnessed. As I shared these examples, I probably became a little pedantic. I systematically explained social scientific approaches of rationalism that advocate single universal truths, and relativism that counsels accepting multiple truths as authentic in their own terms. My intent was to awaken him to the value of listening to multiple truth claims from multiple perspectives, so that we could explore how to reconcile different positions.

Back in my apartment that night, I felt uneasy. Many thoughts came to my mind about my discussion with Tarik at the café. I also thought about the CIA building and Tarik's evaluation of the truthfulness of some interviewees' perceptions of the war. My instinct was that a common thread somehow connected all these experiences. It occurred to me that at least part of Tarik's belief in one undisputed truth came from his commitment to taking sides in polarized Bosnian society, as well as from his trust in Allah's unequivocal judgment of what is right and what is wrong. In addition, I suspected that his belief in a single truth also came from his family background, education, particular experiences he had during the war, and numerous other factors of which I was not even aware.

In Tarik's social universe, there was little value in hearing true and untrue stories again and again for "methodological triangulation" because the truth, once told, holds its universal value without being retold. His Japanese visitor should have believed in the CIA building in Sarajevo once Tarik swore the truthfulness of his judgment, supported by others like the taxi driver. More important, as I interviewed more people to investigate the truthfulness of what Tarik had already told me, I probably appeared to him to distrust the truthfulness of his words. Such behavior on my part might signal distrust not only in Tarik's words but also in his character. Perhaps some of Tarik's assumptions about life surfaced in our conversation that afternoon as he was reminded of the fragility of human life by his professor's unexpected death. My explanations may not have been exactly right. But I am certain that they were not entirely baseless. Something was missing in my reasoning. What about the perceptual lenses through which I was observing Tarik's meaning-making process? What about myself? I mean, my *self.*

As I reflected, I came to regret the way I had spoken to him. I regretted it because I could see that this kind of intellectualism rarely captures the heart of someone who has been emotionally affected by indescribable tragedies. Why didn't I listen to him more patiently and carefully in order to understand how he came to feel so hopeless? Why wasn't I big enough to appreciate his sense of truth at a much deeper level? Why was I driven to "correct" him so impulsively? Why was my self and other-awareness so limited?

In retrospect, I have come to realize that part of my uncertainties about Tarik's meaning-making had to do with my own ways of making meaning as informed by my background. I was born and brought up in a small rural town in the north central part of Japan's main island. My hometown is a land of myths rooted in centuries of Japanese agrarian tradition. As a child, I was thrilled by school sumo-wrestling tournaments, community gatherings for good harvests, rituals for good health attended by barefooted children running across fires made in rice fields, and numerous other events sponsored by local Shinto shrines and temples. I also remember visiting a small pond up in the mountains, where a white eel was believed to be living as a god and protector for local people. Near the pond was a small house where an old lady lived. She and my family were very close friends. Every time my father and I visited there, she came out and greeted us warmly. She believed in the white eel. Perhaps my father didn't, and I was not sure about it. But I didn't mind having a mysterious white eel swimming somewhere in that pond. Interestingly, now, many years later, I feel as if I had seen the beautiful white eel in the clean quiet pond. I can clearly picture it in my mind as I close my eyes. The white eel became a truth in the small universe of my childhood.

It has been several years since I began my training as a social science major in an American university. It has also been a long time since I was introduced to ideas that initially felt strange, including academic thoughts on rationalism and relativism. Rationalists claim that there is a single standard of truthful knowledge, just as there is only one sun and one moon. As discussed in Chapter Three, rationalists begin with a universalist starting point. According to rationalism, the universally valid standard for truth exists irrespective of human perception to recognize the standard.

Relativists believe that multiple truths can coexist side by side in society and nature. They begin from a particularist starting point. According to relativism, our reality is never independent of human perception, and there are as many "truths" as can be perceived. Initially, I felt this dichotomy to be quite unfamiliar. My sense of unfamiliarity came from my Asian roots in Buddhist thought, where oneness of human perception and metaphysical reality is a fundamental premise for our understanding of society and nature.

After years of training in Western social science, I have come to feel more comfortable with the dichotomy between rationalism and relativism. Now the dichotomy is not only familiar to me, but it is deeply embedded in my meaning-making process. When I designed the methodology for the interviews in Bosnia, I took it for granted that there were multiple truths in Bosnian society, consistent with relativism. When Tarik attempted to demonstrate the truthfulness of his and others' views, his behavior did not instantaneously appeal to me as consistent with my own meaning-making process. I reflected that Tarik's claim about the CIA building was not categorically different from the white eel in my universe of social reality, except that the CIA building claim was much more plausible than the omnipotence of the white eel.

I do not think the Western discourse on rationalism and relativism is useless. Nor do I think that Tarik's belief in the universally defined truth is as baseless as my belief in the white eel. It is important to retain and enhance appreciation of different meaning-making processes through which truth is defined. I learned from my interaction with Tarik and numerous other friends in Bosnia that what used to be an unfamiliar Western academic discourse has been embedded deeply in my meaning-making process. Once a pattern of thinking and feeling gets embedded in the realm of the subconscious and unconscious, it is extremely difficult to reflect on how a meaning-making process has been formed and transformed. I have found that it is even harder, and often nearly impossible, to sort out how my meaning-making process is interacting with those of culturally different others.

I was also reminded by this experience that culturally constructed perceptions are always relative in nature. Tarik's claim of truth appeared different from mine because my understanding of truth was different from his. Self and others exist in a dynamically evolving relationship reflected in the mirror of self-awareness. Realizing this made me appreciate the value of being humble and self-reflective when interacting with others in cross-cultural settings.

Another important lesson I learned was that cultural influences are multilayered. Tarik's meaning-making structures have been shaped by Bosnian tradition and modernity, the unique urban life in Sarajevo, Islam and other religious and philosophical discourses, youth culture, the culture of war, and a variety of other factors intertwined with one another. My cultural lenses have evolved from my immersion in Japanese society and education; the agrarian communal life that affected my childhood; the American social science community in which I received rigorous academic training; and countless other factors that shape my meaning-making structures. These cultural influences constantly interact with one another in forming and transforming my self-awareness. At the same time, they interact with the cultural influences of others in the social universe of interdependence.

Developing cultural fluency is a sustained process where our cultural understanding first anchors in the realm of consciousness and gradually merges into our subconscious and unconscious. Because cultural fluency depends so much on self-awareness, it requires effort to continuously reflect on our conscious, subconscious, and unconscious realms of meaning-making when faced with the need to reexamine our own cultural assumptions. Expressing such assumptions to culturally unfamiliar others requires even more strenuous efforts. In the next story on expressive capacity, we will get a sense of what the difficulty is like. Our journey continues to Taiwan in late 1997.

Expressive Capacity: Describing Indescribable Feelings

Spontaneous conversations sprouted and continued here and there across dinner tables. Laughter burst out, spread, disappeared, and reappeared across the room at the wedding ceremony. Sitting at the bridegroom's seat next to my Taiwanese wife Yu Chun, I could hardly see anybody paying attention to the invited parliamentarian delivering a long political speech. Before the ceremony, I received a detailed lecture on the culture of Taiwanese weddings from my wife. I had been informed that Yu Chun's parents invited the parliamentarian to our wedding, just as other Taiwanese families would do for their weddings. But I could not help sensing a slight cultural shock as I witnessed the almost complete absence of attention paid by some two hundred invitees to the ceremony's program unfolding on the main stage. While I enjoyed watching this spectacle, I reflected on how I came to throw myself into the succession of these unfamiliar events for the wedding, which Yu Chun's family had prepared so earnestly for us.

Yu Chun and I were engaged one year before this wedding ceremony held in the southern Taiwanese city of Kaoshung, where she was born and raised until she came to Japan at the age of nineteen. The year-long process of preparing for our wedding was turbulent, revealing a number of different, and often conflicting, assumptions held by my family in Japan and hers in Taiwan. Several months before the wedding, I proposed to my Taiwanese in-laws that Yu Chun and I organize a simple, inexpensive gathering for our marriage, inviting a handful of close friends, family members, and relatives from both sides. We did not plan on wearing special outfits, accepting gifts of money, or returning equally expensive goods to gift givers, as many Japanese do for their weddings. The venue would be a small but homey Japanese barbecue restaurant that my cousin ran in my hometown.

Several months later, we found ourselves en route to a totally different destination. Back then Yu Chun and my family lived in different parts of Japan, her family lived in Taiwan, and I was working in Rwanda. After exchanging numerous communications via fax and telephone between

Japan, Taiwan, and Rwanda, the agreement was reached that we would hold a grand ceremony in Yu Chun's hometown in Taiwan and another smaller but formal wedding in my hometown in Japan, with each side flying to the other side at least once. On my way from Rwanda to Taiwan to attend the first wedding in Yu Chun's hometown, I couldn't help feeling slightly uneasy about this final decision. What created this huge gap between Yu Chun's and my initial suggestion and the outcome of our cross-cultural negotiation?

When our initial plan for a simple, inexpensive wedding was communicated to her Taiwanese parents, we were preoccupied with our financial reality. As a lecturer paid in local terms by a Rwandan public university, I could barely afford an air ticket to visit Taiwan. The thought of imposing an extra financial burden on both our Japanese and Taiwanese parents pained me. Besides, Yu Chun and I shared a vision of living a life of financial parsimony. With this in mind, we felt that celebrating with a simple, inexpensive wedding would carry a symbolic meaning consistent with our long-term vision. Most fundamentally, the essence of marriage is a union between two individuals, so the wedding should be designed in whatever way that satisfies the couple's needs, so long as they do not fundamentally contradict the needs of important others. Yu Chun and I agreed that, for weddings, the families, relatives, and friends of the couple should support the selected format, seeing the individuals' happiness as a building block for group harmony.

Though they are not necessarily "progressive" by today's standard in Japanese society, my parents felt comfortable with accepting the elements of modern individualism in our initial wedding plan. On the other hand, they advised us to consider what my wife's Taiwanese family had to say about our suggestion. "Parents of a daughter would want to see her wearing a beautiful wedding dress in a beautiful wedding ceremony. Perhaps a bride is different from a bridegroom from the parents' point of view. So you need to listen to Yu Chun's parents carefully," my mother said to me.

And she was right. The most important consideration of Yu Chun's parents was to make sure that she, as their beloved daughter, would be able to have a grand ceremony of departure. For them, Yu Chun was about to leave their custody, and the wedding signified the final duty and responsibility that they as parents had to fulfill before their daughter began a life of her own. At this turning point of their and Yu Chun's lives, they wanted to decide how to celebrate the wedding. Their views were important, not ours, because in their culture it was essential to include circles of close friends, neighbors, and family members in our union.

Consistent with Taiwanese traditions, Yu Chun's parents felt the need to create a public occasion with a large wedding ceremony. I learned from Yu Chun that particularly in her family tradition, there was a strong aspiration to invite as many relatives and friends as financially possible, in order to openly demonstrate their fairness, sociability, and accountability in the eyes of the public. A large wedding proves the legitimacy of the couple's union, as well as the family's sociability.

Inviting many neighbors and acquaintances is considered a way to bring about good fortune for the couple and the families involved. *Engi*, translated as "codependent origination," is a traditional concept shared widely by Asian societies under varying degrees of Buddhist influence. It evokes a worldview where a variety of causes and effects are constantly co-arising and merging into one another simultaneously, with no single phenomenon in nature and society evolving in isolation. In the social context of public celebrations such as wedding ceremonies in Taiwan, *engi* means inviting a wide range of people whose good wishes will bless the couple. While relatives and close friends are invited to publicly demonstrate the families' sociability, less close acquaintances are welcomed because they symbolize *engi*, bringing together as many influences as possible to create good fortune. In our wedding, for example, Yu Chun's mother invited a street vendor in her neighborhood whose name she did not even know. By today's Japanese standard, such a casual invitation would make no sense. But from our Taiwanese family's point of view, this and many other similar invitations extended to "familiar strangers" were important to bring about good fortune for the departure of their dearest daughter.

Looking back, I have a number of reservations about my views on Japanese and Taiwanese cultures related to our wedding. I am sure that some of the value differences described here relate to the characters of the particular individuals involved, like myself, rather than widely shared cultural assumptions on both sides. It is also possible that cultural and other types of social influence are transient from one generation to another, and vary from one locality to another in both Taiwan and Japan. Nevertheless, I still feel that part of the difficulty in our effort to bridge the two families was undeniably cultural in nature because different meaning-making patterns complicated our attempts to reconcile the different positions expressed.

Five years after the wedding ceremony, our two families enjoy a friendly relationship and mutual respect, despite our inability to communicate with each other without Yu Chun's interpretation in Taiwanese and Japanese.

Every time I look at my wedding photos, many thoughts come to my mind, both happy and slightly puzzling ones. I now realize that this experience provides an opportunity for me to expand my expressive capacity for cultural fluency.

Reflecting on my meaning-making process, my initial position was undoubtedly justifiable, given the need for making a financially conscious decision and the modern value of individual independence widely shared in my generation. At a much deeper level, my feelings were based on the assumption that our families should consider Yu Chun's and my happiness, and the collective welfare of our families would naturally follow. My Japanese family shared more or less similar feelings. Reflecting on my wife's Taiwanese parents' views, Yu Chun and I now understand how they viewed a wedding ceremony primarily as *their* social opportunity for demonstrating the Taiwanese family's respectful position in public and for accumulating good fortune. At a deeper level, their belief seemed to be based on the firm conviction that constructing the family's network of social relationships through the wedding was an essential foundation for their daughter's happiness and their own, with the couple's individual happiness naturally following from the larger context of social harmony.

If I had had more anticipatory capacity to understand the cultural assumptions embedded in the mindsets of our Taiwanese and Japanese families, I could have helped articulate some of the roots of Yu Chun's and my difficulties with her family's interpretations. It may have been possible to acknowledge the underlying values of different wedding plans suggested, including the need for social relationship building and the respect for individual self-actualization. Articulating these and other fundamental values and cultural assumptions, if done considerately and respectfully, could have contributed to mutual understanding and sustained closeness. Once these ideas were articulated and shared, it could have been possible to interrupt the momentum of position-taking over the wedding plan, and to jointly explore a variety of creative and affordable ways to meet each other's cultural expectations.

Expressive capacity evolves from sustained efforts to develop self-awareness. It involves describing almost indescribable feelings and beliefs embedded in our meaning-making processes. Some of these cognitive and emotive processes are shared within and across cultural contexts, while others are not. Building an expressive capacity bridges the gap between different meaning-making processes. Throughout my ongoing journey toward cultural fluency, I have experienced and witnessed more failures than successes in creating cultural bridges. But this personal reflection does not stop me from believing in the human capacity to appreciate and further cross-cultural understanding with a view to cultivating fertile common ground for constructive, shared meaning-making. The next story illustrates this point. We journey back to Rwanda, where I witnessed not only indescribable tragedies of genocide but also significant human ingenuity in navigating turbulence in the aftermath of war.

Navigational Capacity: Sailing across Turbulent Waters

It was a quiet morning in 1998. I was working as a lecturer at the National University of Rwanda. That morning, I hurried to the classroom where about a dozen students were waiting for me. Most of my students came to Rwanda after the genocide of 1994 from Uganda, Tanzania, Kenya, and other countries where they had been born and raised as second-generation refugees.

As soon as I entered the classroom, I immediately felt some serious tension in the atmosphere. What caught my attention the next moment were the twin sisters, whom I will call Aidah and Flora, crying hard. Their classmates remained helplessly silent. One of them approached me and discreetly informed me, "They just learned from the university staff that their brother was killed." I learned that the twins' brother had been a soldier stationed in a village in the northern part of Rwanda, which was just ambushed by an overwhelming number of former genociders who had been hiding and reorganizing in the mountains nearby. Having heard many stories of this kind in Rwanda, I couldn't help thinking about the dreadful possibility that their brother's death was one of indescribable brutality. The twins must have been more painfully aware of this possibility than I was. No words of condolence came to my mind. Whatever I could say to them would have been helplessly superficial. The only thing I managed to tell them was, "Please go home. Go to your family. They need you as much as you need them. Don't worry about today's class and the mid-term exam we will have soon. Take some days off and let us know when you are ready to join us again." With this, they left the classroom.

That evening's radio news confirmed that my fear was not baseless. The outnumbered government soldiers hopelessly defended themselves and the villagers until they were relentlessly massacred. The twins' brother was among them. I imagined the scene of the massacre. The disheartening image of the twins crying haunted me. I could no longer distance myself from this incident. The story became part of me. I could not sleep that night.

A few days later, there was a knock on the door of my apartment. My students often came to my apartment, so it was part of my daily routine to receive young visitors. But this time, I was totally surprised. Aidah and Flora were standing at the door, with intelligent smiles beaming from behind their glasses. "Good morning, Sir," they greeted me with their usual politeness. "Wow," I couldn't help exclaiming. "Are you two okay now?" I asked. "Yes, we are. Thank you for asking," they replied reassuringly. I invited them in. We sat on the bamboo chairs in my small living room and talked.

As I looked at Aidah and Flora, I could not see the slightest sign of sadness on their faces. "Sir, I think we are ready for the mid-term exam we just missed," they said. I simply could not believe what I had just heard. I asked them repeatedly, "Are you sure? Don't you need a little more time before you come back to school?" The twins were determined to resume their studies immediately. Reflecting on their brother's passing, Aidah added in a quiet strong tone, "This is part of our life. We are okay now. We have to move on." In talking with them, I learned how they perceived their brother's death and how they made an effort to turn this tragedy into an opportunity to renew their commitment to the future. I had read somewhere that this kind of personal transformation would be possible in theory, but I never expected that I would witness one. In my mind, the image of their brother's tragic death was still fresh. I was puzzled by the gap between the image of their brother's death and the reality unfolding before me. I was overwhelmed by the twins' strength and self-mastery. A few days later, they sat for their make-up exams and passed with outstanding results.

I have mulled over this incident many times since then, trying to understand the seemingly unfathomable depth of the twins' capacity to accept the hardest challenge in life and their readiness to envision a future beyond their brother's death. I have no doubt that they remained saddened by the tragedy even while they demonstrated extraordinary self-mastery. Still a question remained in my mind: Where was their self-mastery coming from? As I observed them over time, I suspected part of it might have come from their own personalities, encouragement from important others, their philosophical orientations, and perhaps countless other factors, many of which I was not even aware. Yet, was that all?

Having observed many tragic experiences of a similar nature in post-genocide Rwanda, I have come to believe that their coping mechanism had something to do with the reality of living with the tragic experiences of war.

At the core of this coping process was a "culture of war," in which human life is perceived as helplessly transient while at the same time remaining precious precisely because of its transience and fragility.

Born and raised as Rwandan refugees in neighboring Uganda, Aidah and Flora were repatriated after the 1994 genocide. Their life in Rwanda was a process of cultural adaptation to a homeland in which they had never lived. This process of cultural adaptation was not only transnational in nature; it was also demanded that they accept the pervasive culture of war, of which their brother, as a soldier for the refugees' repatriation movement, had been a constant reminder and symbolic representation.

Even after the genocide, sporadic fighting continued between former genociders and the new government forces in the country's northwestern region. Soldiers and civilians died on both sides every day. The news of battle-related casualties was broadcast on a routine basis. Death was routinized and expected as part of Rwandan social life. Despite this general social trend, when Aidah and Flora first heard the news of their brother's death, they were traumatically saddened. The pervasive culture of war never attenuated the preciousness of a particular human life. Life was so precious because it *meant* something painfully personal to them, with its human voice, human face, and countless moments of closeness the twins had shared with their deceased brother.

Aidah and Flora came to reconcile their personal sorrow with the culture of war after only a few days of self-reflection and encouragement. They were well aware of their sadness. They were also aware of the social expectations about human death set by the tragic reality of war-torn Rwandan society. With conscious effort, they refused to be overwhelmed by their personal sadness. At the same time, they refused to accept the banality of human death routinized in the culture of war. They took the third path: get back to normal life as soon as possible and aspire to live a life of self-actualization on behalf of the deceased brother. Am I reading between the lines too imaginatively? I don't believe so, as I observed the twins' unwavering enthusiasm for their studies, their future dreams to become capable journalists, and their respect for human life after the death of their brother.

Navigating across turbulent cross-cultural dynamics requires strenuous efforts to reflect on self, others, and the cultural context in which they are situated. I learned from the twins that it is possible to not only grasp the dynamism of cultural turbulence, but also to create our own way of situating ourselves in cultural contexts where we are foreign. As we do this, cultural adaptation gives way to the development of navigational capacity. We are transformed in a process where our self-awareness leads us to see shades of meanings and where self becomes an indispensable part of the drama of intercultural dynamics. In short, navigational capacity is our readiness for co-creating a constructive future, based on our awareness of both the challenges and opportunities presented by a given social context.

The Way Forward

My journey continues. It has been an eventful one thus far, but I expect more learning experiences are still to come. The four dimensions of cultural fluency have been helpful in my journey. Reflecting on the insights gained from the stories presented in this chapter, we can now summarize concrete steps to develop cultural fluency as follows:

To build *anticipatory capacity:*

- observe patterns of being and doing demonstrated by cultural others, taking into consideration how they characterize who they are and what they care about;
- articulate what their patterns of meaning-making are, while always treating our template of cultural interpretation as tentative and subject to continuous revision;
- reflect on how our own meaning-making patterns have been shaped, by reflecting carefully on how we have come to perceive who we are and what we care about;
- consider how the meaning-making patterns of cultural others interact with our own, acknowledging that cultural understanding is always co-created by constant interaction between self and others;
- remain willing to reshape our interpretive lenses by incorporating new insights gained from self-reflection, as well as from observation of cultural others.

To understand *embeddedness:*

- acknowledge that there are deep-seated assumptions affecting our habitual way of being and doing at the subconscious and unconscious levels of meaning-making;
- ask ourselves why we feel unfamiliar with cultural outsiders when a difference is felt, keeping in mind that our own cultural assumptions have helped shape the perceived difference;

- explore what cultural assumptions we have adopted to form our meaning-making process, by way of sustained self-reflection and dialogue with cultural others;
- reflect on how our experiences in childhood as well as at later stages of our life have shaped and reshaped who we are and what we care about;
- also reflect on how cultural others have come to develop their assumptions, by applying the same way of thinking in our dialogue with them.

To develop *expressive capacity:*

- articulate why we care about what we care about, by unpacking the meanings embedded in our ways of being and doing;
- encourage cultural others to articulate their meaning-making processes the same way;
- suspend value judgments and probe each other's assumptions as deeply and broadly as possible, exploring the kind of empathic language that will allow us to bridge our meaning-making patterns with theirs.

To expand *navigational capacity:*

- recognize what cultural expectations affect us in a given social context, as well as what meaning-making patterns we have brought with us into the context;
- decide how we want to co-create a future together with the cultural others in the context of interdependence, building on both differences and commonalities between our meaning-making patterns and theirs;
- take the first step forward with courage, and flexibly adjust our actions to the unfolding reality.

As illustrated by the stories in this chapter, these four dimensions are intertwined with one another. Yet they are cumulative in a sense: navigational capacity presupposes expressive capacity, which requires awareness of embeddedness and anticipatory capacity. At the same time, there is always a mutual feedback effect. For example, our attempts to express cultural assumptions often reveal fundamental misunderstandings that have been created in the anticipatory process.

A failed endeavor of cross-cultural navigation may be appreciated in retrospect as a great contribution to social harmony, if the tension created by the perceived failure turns into a renewed opportunity for expressing hidden assumptions and indescribable feelings. Despite these and numerous other complexities of our journey, there is at least one constant reality where these four dimensions converge and diverge—that is, the continuity of *self,* reinforcing again the centrality of self-awareness. The manifestations of cross-cultural turbulence unfolding before our eyes are perceptual images reflected in the mirror of self-awareness, which is being shaped and reshaped in the social context of interdependence.

Now it is your turn to embark on your journey. *You,* who have just traveled with me to Rwandan ceremonies, the "CIA building" in Bosnia, my Taiwanese wedding, and the scene of the twin sisters crying. What would you say to a Bosnian youth holding a totally different assumption of truth from yours? What if you were faced with the challenge of cross-cultural communication where you and your in-laws had contradictory ideas of how to celebrate an important occasion? What would you do if an important family member were just massacred in your homeland, to which you had been dreaming of returning after years of hardship in exile? These are all hypothetical questions. The "what if?" rhetoric implies that you are not in the stories. And because you are not, I am doubtful that the reflections and lessons I have drawn from my journey are applicable without substantial modifications. One of the most convincing reasons for my doubt is that your meaning-making process is not likely to be the same as mine and that of other characters who have appeared in the stories on my journey. This is precisely the reason why everyone needs to design and embark on his or her own journey toward cultural fluency. Welcome to your journey.

✳✳✳

My journey started with the first public speech I made in English when I was a junior high school student. Since then, I have felt the same kind of extreme nervousness every time I had to jump into an unfamiliar cultural context. As I hear my heart pounding and feel my legs shaking in the face of uncertainties unfolding in cultural turbulence, I quietly repeat exactly what I told myself twenty years ago: "Tats, come on. You can do it." I feel like I have not grown much, but recently I have come to realize that this is a healthy unending process.

Our journey toward cultural fluency is a sustained process, where the frontier of the present merges into future uncertainties evolving moment by moment. Our understanding of the four capacities anchored in our self-awareness certainly helps us fix our eyes on the frontier of the dynamic present. But our cultural fluency doesn't come with assurances about exactly what the future holds. Perhaps I sensed this image of temporal continuity standing before the two hundred students and several Singaporean visitors in Japan all those years ago. I am glad that I mustered the courage to jump into the uncertainties and gained a little confidence. I am also grateful for the nervousness and anxiety that revisit me every now and then, reminding me that the conscious effort to humbly reflect on my inner dynamics is essential to appreciate the bounty of cross-cultural understanding.

When the Waters of Culture
and Conflict Meet

Tatsushi (Tats) Arai*

Sunset
When the burning sky gently touches the horizon
Sand dunes whisper to travelers on horseback
"Hurry to the oasis before it gets dark"

Four parties from different directions
North, south, east, and west
Meet at the crossroads of civilizations

Utterly exhausted and thirsty
Men, women, children
Young and old
Delighted to find a place to rest at last
Thousands of miles away from home

Alas!
The water in the oasis is very low
Barely enough to quench the thirst of one party
The travelers sit in a circle
Staring at the dwindling water

---

*With acknowledgement of Karenjot Bhangoo's contributions to early versions of this chapter

The chief of the party from the north raises his voice,
"This water belongs to us. You all go away"
Looking at the other parties in defiance

A traveler from the south responds,
"No, let's share it equally among all parties"

A traveler from the west suggests,
"Let's talk and figure out exactly what each party wants—
Water to drink, grass around the water to feed horses, or its comforting atmosphere—
We can then decide who takes what and how much"

A traveler from the east reflects,
"The beauty of this oasis has quenched the thirst in our hearts
Giving us the strength of spirit to carry on our way
And that's more than enough for us"

At the Crossroads of Civilizations

At first glance, the northerners in this poem appear individualistic and competitive, claiming monopoly over the water. The southerners are more communitarian and cooperative, attempting to share the scarce water with the other parties. The westerners are rationalistic and analytical, trying to sort out the parties' respective interests and maximize ways to satisfy everyone's needs. The easterners seem to be contemplative, self-reflective, and inward-looking, valuing what the water symbolizes in their hearts. Given the range of perspectives the four parties bring, what do the water and oasis *mean* to them? Why do they respond to the situation the ways they do? By exploring these and other questions, we will discover how culture and conflict interact with one another.

As we have seen in Chapter Two, conflict is a difference within a person or between two or more people that touches them where they make meanings or experience their identities. Even though people may feel threatened in their approaches to making meaning or their identities, few people articulate conflict this way. Conflicts play out through struggles or competitions related to roles, relationships, or resources. They involve power and psychological needs for recognition and respect. People in conflict are often focused on "the other" as the source of the problem, and they tend not to look beneath the surface to the deeper roots of their differences.

As we also explored in Chapters Two and Three, culture refers to underground rivers that connect us to others in the groups we belong to. How are these two sets of ideas related to each other? To answer this question, we will examine three aspects of the interaction of culture and conflict:

- Culture assigns meanings to conflict, telling us what the conflict is about;
- Conflict, in turn, stimulates cultural changes and continuity by shaping the cultural lenses through which we interpret what the conflict is about;
- Culture and conflict are intertwined, constantly shaping and reshaping each other in an evolving interactive process.

The interactive relationship between culture and conflict is depicted in Figure 5.1.

At the oasis, the travelers interact in various ways, revealing their cultural assumptions. Throughout this chapter, we will continuously revisit the oasis, delve into the travelers' minds and hearts, and explore the variety of social and historical contexts from which they have come. Before exploring the ways culture and conflict are intertwined, we will look more closely at how conflict evolves. We will examine conflict dynamics. We will pay close attention to how cross-cultural differences influence conflict and how conflict appears as a tangible reality. We will also consider how conflict polarizes and dehumanizes relationships, as well as how it expands in scope by engaging more issues and parties. After observing how conflict dynamics evolve, we will explore how culture shapes and reshapes conflict. We will see that culture frames the universe of our conflict behavior, tells us what action appears preferable, separates "us" from "them" in identity orientation, connects past

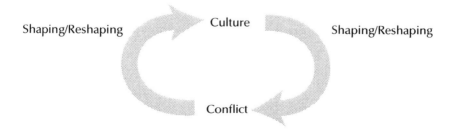

Figure 5.1 Interactive Dynamics of Conflict and Culture

traumas to future glories, and spreads conflict across social contexts by means of shared symbols.

Our next question is how conflict shapes and reshapes culture. We will highlight the process by which cultural messages are transmitted by cultural carriers. Cultural carriers refer to both abstract ideas and concrete objects that carry symbolic meanings within and across social contexts of conflict. We will consider how significant social events, such as intensive violence, people's movements, mergers of cultural groups, and social system changes reshape culture by changing cultural carriers.

Culture and conflict are intertwined in three arenas of social life: time, social relationship, and identity. We will explore their dynamics through two alternative scenarios of how the travelers' interactions might evolve. Ready? Let our journey begin.

Conflict Dynamics

Conflict can be envisioned in multiple ways. It may seem static, like a complex knot, mysterious and impossible to undo. As with a tangled knot, the origins of conflicts are often elusive. People involved may be so enmeshed in the conflict that its beginnings are lost to the fuzzy boundary between fact and fable. A more dynamic metaphor for conflict is a storm moving over the mountains, born of the interaction of elements, unnoticed until the gathering clouds are about to lose their watery cargo. Once conflict begins, it can lie dormant or it may gather force and momentum like a storm accelerating as it squeezes through a narrow valley. Conflict is not a linear event—it may rage fiercely for a time, and then become silent in a lull between episodes.

Conflict lives in stories told to children that communicate who is, and is not, one of "us." It breathes purpose into lifetimes and offers a frame in which the pictures of large- and small-scale events make sense. Just as storms and knots may be useful—storms for bringing needed rain, and knots for securing things—conflicts may answer needs of people involved. They offer a sense of belonging, a way of enacting a quest for justice, and the promise of constructive social change. But conflicts are also potentially destructive: storms of conflict may violently wash away acres of food crops, swallowing humans and animals in large numbers and smashing bridges that are lifelines between towns and villages. Conflicts are neither wholly constructive nor destructive; they are dynamic processes that often gather strength as they develop, capturing increasing numbers of people and issues, wielding substantial power and generating lasting impacts in the lives of those involved.

Like storms, conflicts take on their own lives, with their own unique courses of development and effects. Just as no two storms are identical, no two conflicts are the same. And just as storms eventually dissipate, yielding to the calm of a sunny day, so conflict dynamics sometimes change and may even transform enemies into friends. People involved can find new resources and ways forward, and live into new relationships. Just as the elements of the storm do not merely disappear, but change form, so the conflict continues to affect the lives of those involved, continuing to influence lives if only in stories and souvenirs.

Both storms and conflicts are dynamic, systemic processes. They may come full circle, with the tumult and disruption they brought relegated to memory. Like the molecules of rain never disappearing in the ecosystem, conflict potential is ubiquitous in our social universe, manifesting in different forms, shapes, and sizes. The travelers' conflict over scarce water at the oasis is but a small manifestation of vast storms and potential storms gathering continuously in the ecosystem of human relationships.

Conflicts may form unnoticed as people gradually become aware of differences. Differences can turn into conflict when there are scarce resources, or when one or another of those involved feels threatened by the other. Conflicts tend to be more intense when the people involved are interdependent, like the people at the oasis, because they may not see a way for everyone to get what they need and want. As people came into relationship with each other at the oasis, their perceptions of overlapping needs created tension, tension that was thickened by their different ways of trying to meet their needs and their overall sense of scarcity and threat.

Of course, differences alone do not necessarily lead to conflict. Many differences between individuals and groups exist in social life, but they do not necessarily threaten how people make meaning or experience their identities. The people at the oasis may have quite different ideas about the meaning of life, for example, including different ways of valuing and making sense of difficult experiences. But these differences will not generate conflict unless they play out in the physical world over resources or in the felt and sensed world where, for example, needs for recognition and security can fuel claims of ownership and control.

In cross-cultural contexts, human differences in language, religion, age, gender, skin color, and the place of origin are visible markers of cultural variations. At deeper and less visible levels, patterns of meaning-making also characterize differences between people. Meaning-making relates to habits of *attention*. Do we tend to notice danger, possibility, connection, or what's missing in a situation? These varying ways of paying attention lead to different perceptions, and perceptual diversity is often part of the tangle of conflict dynamics. Meaning-making also relates to values—how we order and hold what is dear to us, and how these values relate to our understandings of overarching questions like the purpose of life and the meaning of family, time, and work. When interdependent people make meaning differently, valuing and perceiving the same situation with different eyes, conflict can arise. When the situation or resources appear limited, it is easy to slip into seeing the other as a competitor or an adversary.

Let's go back to the travelers approaching the oasis. They were utterly exhausted, hot, and thirsty, hoping to find water. The growing urgency to quench their thirsts created the foundation for a potential conflict at the oasis. As the travelers encountered each other, they realized the interdependence of their needs and desires and the different ways they were approaching the scarcity of water. As they encountered each other, their emerging awareness of interdependence and competition transformed the potential conflict into a "real" conflict.

Conflict is most intense when people are interdependent and when resources—physical like water or less tangible like status—are scarce or perceived to be scarce. If these ingredients are not present, people can walk away and solve their problems independently. Think of a grocery store in the United States: Someone beside me takes the apple I have my eye on, but a conflict is unlikely to arise because I have no ongoing relationship or interdependence with the other shopper. Not only that, but there is another apple right beside it that is quite acceptable to me. Given the scarce water at the oasis, walking away was not an option.

Interdependence in conflict may be welcome or unwelcome, subtle or salient, cooperative or competitive, constructive or destructive—or both of each of these pairs at the same time, depending on people's interpretive lenses. Conflict hurts people most when their interdependence is so essential that they cannot do away with it despite the difficulties of remaining interdependent, such as for friends or lovers. When such a dilemma is felt, it is often hard to be silent. Emotional turbulence surfaces in actions and interpretations. Satisfying desires becomes stressful and may appear impossible in the face of others seeking to achieve their aspirations. All of these dynamics affected travelers at the oasis. We look in on them again to see how they address their unfolding conflict.

✳✳✳

Gradually, the travelers became aware of the increasing urgency of their needs and desires for the scarce water. They began to talk with each other in several simultaneous conversations within and between their groups. Some of the young people in the group from the north spoke in hushed tones about whether they could divert the water away from the watchful eyes of the other groups. A few older members of the western group wondered together whether their early arrival shouldn't give them priority. Someone suggested drawing straws to see who would drink first. There was growing sense of tension in the air.

Conflict often escalates, polarizing human relationships, as opposing groups form. People in conflict often converge into camps split between perceived good and evil, right and wrong, just and unjust. Once the split begins, mistrust may grow, deepening the rift between "our side" and "their side." A sense of "we-ness" and "they-ness" emerges. Those within the same group look for more reasons to distrust the other side and trust their own. As the parties' attitudes become rigid, they feel more confident in predicting that the other side will grow increasingly evil, uncompromising, and offensive, while their side will remain good, generous, and defensive. Taken to an extreme, the other side is perceived as *less* than human.

The interactions between the travelers from the north, south, and west gradually evolve into heated debates over who is right and who is wrong, while the concerned travelers from the east observe the three other groups attentively. Both the egalitarian southerners and rational, analytic westerners feel that the competitive northerners are egoistic and unreasonable. The southerners and westerners form a cautious alliance in the face of the common opponents from the north. The northerners feel threatened when they see that the westerners and southerners are working together to outnumber and outmaneuver them. Consequently, the northerners sense the need to strengthen unity amongst themselves, confident that their strength will help them prevail in the emerging competition. Two camps come into being. The cleavage deepens as insults are exchanged. At that point, the southerners and the westerners both feel the water is too important and limited to be shared with the others, especially with others who do not play fairly.

People in destructive conflict begin to dehumanize their adversaries when the conflict polarizes relationships. The sense of "we-ness" and "they-ness" escalates, where "they" appear less worthy than "we" are. People tend to see themselves as patient, generous, and open, while perceiving others as closed, unreasonable, and selfish. Because the adversaries are so evil, questions arise about whether they should be treated with respect. Their lives and welfare may gradually be seen as less worthy than those of reasonable people because of their evil and malevolent natures. Coercive action appears necessary in extreme cases because the adversaries are so committed to their frames of mind that further attempts to talk with those on the other side appear to be a waste of precious time. These relational spirals feed on themselves, generating corroborative evidence like multiple self-fulfilled prophecies, and the reciprocal dehumanization of the "other side" continues to feed the conflict.

At the oasis, the rift continues to grow between the alliance of the southerners and westerners, on the one hand, and the northerners, on the other. One of the northerners shouts, "You cowards, leave immediately!" The southerners and westerners grow more impatient with the northerners. A young man from the westerners' party stands up angrily and responds to the northerners, "You selfish people can't even hear what we are saying. If you can't talk with us about how to divide the water, you don't deserve your share. It is *you* people who need to go away right now!" A man from the north shouts back even louder, "Shut up, coward. If you are thirsty, eat grass and satisfy yourselves just like small critters in the desert do!" Emotion runs higher as more insults are exchanged. Gradually each party comes to see the others as stubborn enemies unworthy of respectful human treatment.

As the relationships between people in conflict deteriorate, they begin to focus not only on the initial issues that have provoked the conflict, but increasingly on the *character* of the adversaries. People and problems become so inseparable that everything the adversaries do appears evil. Indeed, the adversaries themselves seem evil at the core. The more intensively distrusting individuals and groups become in their interactions, the more reasons for distrust they find in the behavior of each other. Conflict deepens and escalates like gathering storm clouds grow heavier passing over the sea.

Tension continues to grow at the oasis. The northerners stare at the westerners and say pejoratively, "Hey, cowards. You all have strange beards and mustaches. Your horses are as fat as pigs. Where on earth are you from?"

The westerners are now openly defiant, responding to the northerners angrily, "We are talking about the water, not about our appearances or our horses. But let me tell you something. You people all stink. When did you last bathe? Or do you ever bathe?" Laughter arises among the westerners and southerners, fueling the northerners' resentment further. With these bitter insults exchanged, water is no longer the only, nor even the most important issue in the conflict. Beards, mustaches, horses, odors, and winning begins to matter. Their relationships—interdependent and entangled—matter. They are too involved to walk away now. Not only do they need and want the water, but they now have a stronger interest in the others not acquiring it. The conflict is multilayered, deeper than it was when originally triggered by the issue of how to distribute the water.

Conflict spreads as more people become involved. As people in conflict are increasingly convinced that they are right and their adversaries are wrong, they look for others to join their camp and discourage them from joining their adversaries' camps. Newcomers on their side are good. Those joining their adversaries' sides are evil. As more people get involved in the conflict, its scope expands, making the conflict even more complex and harder to resolve.

A small group of merchants arrive at the oasis while the travelers' arguments continue. They wonder why the travelers are shouting at one another around the small spring. A young merchant approaches the crowd. In spite of the tense atmosphere, he begins in a friendly tone, "Hello. What is going on here?" A westerner replies deploringly, "Oh, young man, you have come at a perfect time! These thugs from the north are threatening us. We just want to talk about how to share the water here. Please help us deal with their stubbornness." A northerner hastens to raise his voice in rebuttal, calling "Hey, young man, don't listen to those cowards! They have just insulted us with nasty words. They said we stink! How dare they say that? You've got to help us here!" While the merchants stand still, not knowing what to do, each camp tries to recruit the newcomers for support. The conflict is about to spread in scope, as more people are invited to join. Utterly confused, the young merchant sighs and says, "Well, it doesn't look like there is anything we can do about this. You are adults. Why don't you talk together and work out your problem yourselves? We'd better go now." With this, the merchants leave the oasis discretely, hurrying to their next destination before darkness falls.

These interactions between the travelers show that the shape of conflict can shift, changing its character dynamically. Had the merchants become involved, the conflict would have shifted, escalating or de-escalating depending on their behavior. But the merchants were not drawn in by the traveler's invitations. The merchants found the accusations and insults confusing and threatening, and chose to leave rather than involving themselves further in the fray.

The merchants' response is not unusual. Many people avoid conflict when they can. Often, people try to avoid conflict even when they are involved in it as someone who has control over a scarce resource or who is in a relationship with someone who is unhappy with the terms of the relationship. In these cases, avoidance may act like an inflated ball kept under the water—when it is released, it has a lot of force and momentum that can no longer be ignored. For this reason, avoidance is not a durable strategy for interdependent people—conflict does not disappear if ignored. But it takes wisdom and understanding to effectively engage conflict, especially across cultural and worldview differences.

How Culture Shapes and Reshapes Conflict

Cultural differences make conflict harder to resolve because they expand the potential for misunderstandings and misperceptions. Because of this, some people have questioned whether cultural differences themselves cause conflict. Scholars have looked at global society, sometimes arguing that different civilizations inevitably clash in conflicts. At the global level, Samuel P. Huntington's book *The Clash of Civilizations and the Remaking of World Order* (1997) supports this assumption. At the grassroots level, too, talks of intractable cultural differences abound, particularly in times of crisis. For example, in interviews I conducted with different American faith communities immediately after the attacks on September 11, 2001, a widely shared perception emerged that different faith and cultural traditions exacerbate destructive conflicts.

The relationship between culture and conflict is actually more complicated. The perception that cultural differences cause or escalate conflict obscures the ways that cultural differences can contribute to constructive relationship-building. Whether cultural differences turn into destructive conflicts depends on how we appreciate and work with the differences. It is important to be crystal clear that cultural differences do *not* inevitably lead to destructive conflicts. The following chapters of this book will show some ways differences can be synergistic, even across cultural boundaries.

If cultural differences do not necessarily cause conflict, then why do we see so many conflicts between different cultural groups in our workplaces, schools, local communities, countries, and global society? One answer is that we may not be interested in stepping outside our own frames of reference. It takes energy and a spirit of inquiry to stretch into someone else's way of seeing a situation. The more certain we are that we are "right" about something, the less curious we will likely be about alternative ways of seeing it.

Another way of explaining the plethora of conflicts is that we are often not aware of creative and workable ways to turn cross-cultural differences into opportunities for constructive relationship building. In many cross-cultural encounters, like the travelers' interactions at the oasis, others' ways of meaning-making may seem so opaque and improbable that we fail to tap deep into our emotional and intellectual capacities to appreciate them. Rather than inquire into the differences, we feel overwhelmed with complexities and retreat to comfortable understandings and habits. Only if we choose to be curious about how others make meaning do we begin to appreciate cultural differences as starting points for constructive relationship building.

How does culture shape and reshape conflict? There are several reasons why cultural differences *appear* to cause conflict. Culture frames the outer boundaries of our mind's vision, so that the cultural outsiders' terrain that lies beyond our horizon is difficult to recognize. Culture tells us subtly why we do what we do, rendering us unfamiliar with the lives of cultural outsiders. We tend to equate this unfamiliarity with strangeness, polarizing relationships between "us" and "them." Culture also carries shared memories and expectations across historical periods and geographic areas by means of symbols that touch our hearts and minds. When these symbols are manipulated to exacerbate conflict, cultural differences and similarities emerge as factors to either divide or unite people. Let's look at each of these issues more closely.

Culture frames the universe of our conflict behavior. It presents the parameters within which "all possible options" are considered in coping with the conflict at hand. It sets outer boundaries of the terrain that we consider traveling. It also gives us a 360-degree panorama of the horizon in our mind's eye, while remaining silent about what lies beyond that horizon. These feelings are so powerful that we either dismiss universes that lie outside our cultural boundaries as less significant, or even "forget" that other universes exist at all!

Let's return to the oasis for a moment and see how culture frames conflict behavior. The travelers' conflict is escalating. Shouting intensifies as night falls. As the discussion gets heated, the southerners call the northerners egoists who care about nothing but their own survival and well-being. The northerners dismiss the southerners as idealistic and naïve, arguing that the southerners are hiding their lack of courage to confront their competitors under their professed wish to cooperate. Each camp feels that the other side's claims and cultural assumptions are unimaginable nonsense by its own standards. Any compromise suggested by one side would be a gesture of generosity from its own viewpoint. A rejection of such a compromise by the other side would only reconfirm the suspected irrationality and intransigence of the other side. Relationships among the travelers become more uncomfortable. Yet they are now bound by their inescapable interdependence, as well as by their dilemma over how to share the limited water.

Culture sets the boundaries of all possible options available for the travelers to work through their conflict. Still, there is a way to step outside these boundaries: to inquire about how others' cultural ideas make sense. The northerners, westerners, and southerners could talk, for example, with people like the easterners, who believe that the beauty of the water, of the oasis itself, is in unlimited supply. Does the appreciation of the beauty quench the travelers' thirst? No, at least not in a physiological sense. Yet such appreciation would certainly help the other three parties realize that there is an unknown cultural terrain outside their boundaries. Does this imply that the easterners are culturally superior to the other travelers? No, because each pattern of meaning-making makes sense in its own terms within its own context. This does not mean that each of them is perfect, only that they each make sense when viewed from the inside out. Only once the attempt is made to view cultural ways of meaning making from the inside out is there any basis for assessing which cultural way of seeing things may be most adaptive or useful in any given context. In other words, *dialogue with genuine curiosity* is a precondition for constructively addressing cultural conflict.

But the people at the oasis do not feel genuine curiosity, and they do not engage in constructive communication. When confronted by the northern individualists, the egalitarian southerners claim that the northerners have broken God's rule of equality for generous giving and sharing. The southerners contend that sharing is an essential value in their family and community life. They believe that generous deeds following God's will in times of need have implications not only for the present lifetime but also for their afterlife. For the southerners, sharing is a virtue embedded in their meaning-making process. While not all southerners are committed to the egalitarian aspiration in the same way, there is at least a shared tacit assumption that sharing *is* a virtue. Deviants from this standard may be tolerated, but they are certainly not welcomed as heroes within the groups' cultural universe. These characteristics of the southerners' meaning-making patterns help explain their insistence and strong feelings; for them sharing is as natural as breathing.

Culture makes certain goals and behaviors in conflict appear more natural, preferable, and legitimate. It helps us understand why we do what we do in conflict. It guides us to choose certain courses of action or inaction over other options. To the southerners, sharing is intuitive and normal. Remembering the "big picture" and God's place in all things is a given. But these "givens" are not shared by those in other groups, at least not in the same way.

To make matters more complicated, actors within cultural groups have varying motives. When people want power or influence, they sometimes use cultural differences to manipulate and polarize relationships, shaping and reshaping their sense of who "we" are and who "they" are in conflict. Stereotypes may be reinforced. Awareness of cultural differences in these circumstances furthers polarization, deepening the cleavage between "us" and "them." It also sets expectations about what is good and evil, just and unjust, moral and immoral. As a result, the existence and manipulation of cultural differences facilitates the psychological process where people come to believe that "we are good" and "they are bad."

Examples of this abound in our multicultural cities and in the fault lines between and among communities. The police, accused of racial profiling, may very publicly make changes in procedures, but react internally with defensiveness, feeling less able to do their jobs as they remain confident about their stereotypes of specific identity groups. Environmentalists, convinced of the myriad harms that will arise from a development, cannot conceive of the developer as anything but greedy and Machiavellian, and so may miss opportunities to find meaningful ways to engage with the development company. Developers, in turn, are reinforced in their views that environmentalists are obstructionist, unconstructive and unrealistic. Both sides may amplify these images with their own constituents to justify unwillingness to engage with the "other." And so the conflicts continue and escalate, just as they do at the oasis.

In the polarized relationships among the travelers, the southerners and westerners both feel that the northerners are egocentric and selfish. The northerners believe that establishing their right to water is an act of bravery and courage. For them, the southerners and westerners' attempt to divide the limited resource reveals their naiveté and cowardice, demonstrating their inability to confront opposition and show strong leadership. Because of the different cultural lenses they wear, the travelers interpret each other's positions as unfamiliar, unacceptable, and unworthy of respect.

Take a step further and look at how culture links the past, present, and future as conflicts evolve historically. Myths, heroes, and traumas emerge and slip into grandmothers' bedtime stories, folklores, street and building names, monuments standing at street corners, exhibits at art museums, school textbooks, and songs played at festivals. Collective memories of historical conflicts, such as the Nazi holocaust, the nuclear explosion in Hiroshima, and South African apartheid, continuously evolve for generations. They tell us what and who to hate and what and who to glorify at present and in the future.

Cultural memories also transform conflict potential in society, shaping and reshaping human relationships continuously. Thousands of miles away from home, the reflection on the water at the oasis reminds the travelers from the east of a funeral scene, in which ashes of their revered ancestor were sprinkled over the surface of a sacred river running through their village. They nod to each other as the sun glints on the water, thinning to a wavy line on the surface of the oasis before disappearing. Their shared memory urges them to muster inner strength to continue their way forward. For the easterners, it is unimaginable to fight over water.

Historical continuity of cultural memories often surprises us. Cultures have conflict potential deep within them because they always exist in relationship to other cultures, and never in a vacuum. Manifesting in different characters, magnitudes, and intensities, deep cultures of conflict evolve over generations. "This is our *crusade*," said President George W. Bush, expressing his resolve to confront the security threat to the United States in the aftermath of the September 11 attacks in 2001. Intended or unintended, the speech implies that the war between Christians and Muslims over eight hundred years ago still carries a symbolic message today, reappearing in a reference that—intentionally or unintentionally—evokes a deep-rooted enemy image.

Finally, culture spreads conflict across families, communities, countries, and other social contexts through shared symbols and experiences. Like winds carrying pollen from one cactus to another, cultural messages travel beyond the immediate context of the conflict at hand. The messages are delivered by cultural carriers, such as ethnic symbols shared by diasporas of the same cultural roots, religious aspirations held by believers across countries, and memories of social oppression and liberation experienced by peoples around the world. A televised image of a burning national flag carries cultural messages, provoking hatred, revenge, glory, apathy, and a number of other sentiments, depending on the viewers' cultural lenses. A burning flag is not merely an object; it is also a symbolic carrier of emotional experiences that remain fresh in people's hearts.

In the easterners' camp, a little girl clings to her grandfather's sleeves. She watches the travelers' interactions intently. "Grandpa, I am scared. Are they going to fight?" she asks. The old man looks into her eyes. He then looks up at the sunset sky, deep in thought. "Oh, dear. Nobody knows. Anger makes people blind," he says with concern. "Look, grandpa! Look at the necklaces and pendants the big men from the north wear. I have seen the bad people in our hometown wearing the same necklaces and pendants. Grandpa, I think those horrible people from the north believe in the same religion as those bad people in our hometown." The little girl has no hesitation about expressing what's on her mind. This time, the old man replies firmly, "Oh, my dear! Don't call them horrible. We haven't even spoken to them. We don't even know them."

But the old man is fully aware that the girl has a point. Considering the unique religious icons they carry, the northerners appear to share the same faith with his neighbors who have a reputation for being cruel and unsociable in his hometown. Suppressing this association, the old man tells the girl gently, "My dear, it's no good to say that their faith is bad. It's *what they do* that makes them good or bad."

The girl is still adamant. "No, no, grandpa. They are *all* bad people. Those bad neighbors were mean to us, do you remember? I don't like them. I will tell my friends about these bad people when we return home." In the girl's mind, the images of the northern "bullies" at the oasis and the "bad neighbors" back home overlap, with the northerners' religious icons connecting her negative experiences, past and present. Cultural experiences and expectations give the little girl cues about how to view this conflict.

Culture, as in this example and many others, shapes conflict in many ways. It frames the universe of our conflict behavior, tells us what action to take and why, defines who we are and who they are, links past tragedies with future glories, and expands the geographic scope of conflict. We now reverse our way of thinking and ask: how does conflict shape and reshape culture?

How Conflict Shapes and Reshapes Culture

Conflict facilitates both cultural changes and continuity. Events related to social conflict form new cultural carriers and transform existing ones. Cultural carriers are concrete objects as well as abstract ideas that convey symbolic messages within and across social contexts. Where can we find cultural carriers? Everywhere. Think for a moment about favorite folklore and fairy tales, morals, and proverbs that teachers taught us at elementary school, cartoons and pictures animating history textbooks, the national anthems we sing, rituals and religious ceremonies we attend, and national heroes that public buildings, universities, airports, and streets are named after. We remember our favorite childhood stories—the colors and textures of illustrations as well as the story-lines—because they are associated through our senses with a time and place when we discovered our place in the world.

In Washington, DC, people supported or opposed the name change of the airport there to Ronald Reagan Washington National Airport because they understood the power of symbols. These symbols surround us as subtly and naturally as air, without telling us how they shape and reshape the way we make meanings. Conflict affects culture most deeply when it transforms the kind of cultural carriers that penetrate our identity. These carriers touch our minds and hearts where we sense who we are—our identities—and what we care about—our meanings and values.

We can see this phenomenon clearly in tracking symbols that enter our collective consciousness. What did the World Trade Center towers conjure for people before September 11, 2001? They may have variously evoked awe, pride, envy, admiration, or frustration. Many Americans saw them as a source of awe and wonder—evidence of the marvels of modern engineering and the strength and vision of the country. Few Americans associated the towers with negative images of American identity. This changed forever on the morning of September 11, 2001 as Americans awoke to the meaning of the towers to those who planned the attacks. The attacks brought with them the eventual and unwelcome realization that some people from other parts of the world saw the towers as symbols of the financial empire of the United States and its policies of market capitalism and military strength.

Everyone has personal experiences of symbols that have entered their consciousness, acting as anchors for identity, relationships, or values. A little girl loses her stuffed rabbit. While her mother tells her another can be bought, she is inconsolable. Inquiring further, we learn that the rabbit was given to her by her father before he moved overseas after her parents' divorce. When he gave it to her, he told her the story of the Velveteen Rabbit who becomes more real as he is loved. This became her favorite story and the stuffed rabbit was her connection to the story, to the idea of "holding onto love," and her father. For her, a new rabbit cannot conjure up the same memories nor can it substitute as a carrier of this story or the accompanying feelings of love, safety and connection. She is devastated again by the loss, both the loss of her rabbit and the loss of daily contact with her father that the rabbit symbolized.

What changes the meanings associated with cultural carriers most significantly in social and interpersonal conflict? A simple answer is: large events, on a worldwide scale or a personal level. Whether the symbol is the Trade Towers or a stuffed rabbit, the impact of the symbol is larger than life. These events are so large in scope that our minds can hardly capture them adequately unless we release our imagination freely, going beyond the small oasis and the desert that have set the stage for our journey thus far. Four types of conflict-related phenomena are particularly salient, considering their important impact on culture:

- intensive protracted violence;
- forced movements of people;
- mergers of different cultural groups; and
- introduction of new systems of thinking.

Let's explore these phenomena by considering relevant cultural carriers at both the interpersonal and societal levels.

✳✳✳

Widespread intensive violence, such as international war, genocide, nuclear explosions, and large-scale terrorist attacks, shape and reshape culture with a broad range of social ramifications. War, for example, creates heroes and epics, often remembered for centuries. The heroes and epics are told and retold in children's picture books, museum tours, historical documentaries and movies, religious rituals, and even gossip over afternoon tea. They slowly permeate our cultural terrain just as raindrops quietly dissolve into rivers. They sometimes re-emerge in our collective awareness, particularly when we are faced with crises. They call for unity when our "old enemies" are felt in the atmosphere of fervent patriotism as well as long-awaited reconciliation.

On a large scale, the dropping of the atomic bomb at Hiroshima and Nagasaki was a history-altering event. Sadako, a young Japanese girl living not far from the explosion, was less than a year old. Miraculously, she escaped injury though many around her died. When she was 12, she began experiencing dizziness and fatigue and was diagnosed with leukemia. Sadako began folding paper cranes after learning from her best friend about a legend that promised the restoration of health to one who folded a thousand cranes. Before she died, she finished 644 paper cranes. After her death, a monument was built to her memory called the Children's Peace Monument. Since then, millions of cranes have been folded by children the world over in honor of Sadako's dream and the spirit of Hiroshima, symbolizing solidarity in the campaign to abolish nuclear weapons and realize lasting peace.

Sadako's personal struggle came to symbolize the devastation experienced by countless Japanese victims and a dream of peace shared around the world. Sometimes, an interpersonal conflict spawns internal scars that are less visible, but no less real. A little girl sexually abused by her father suffers wounds in her heart and in the deep culture of her family as a whole. At times she may feel fearful of masculinity or sexuality, moving away from things that symbolize the nightmares of her childhood. An old dress she comes upon makes her feel sick, though she can't remember why. In the microcosm of her life, the traumatic memory shapes and reshapes her meaning-making patterns that resonate with the interpretive lenses of her family and loved ones around her.

Culture is also shaped and reshaped by social conflicts forcing a large number of people out of their motherland. Relocated to makeshift camps and unfamiliar dwellings, refugees in exile tend to idealize the image of their native country over time. They often create myths and stories to be shared with children and grandchildren that give meaning to their experiences and anchor the old ways for the young. Forced relocation places them in unfamiliar social contexts where their cultural carriers are made and remade in evolving patterns of meaning-making.

Hmong people came by the thousands to the United States in the 1970s and 1980s following the war in Laos. They had been promised aid by the Americans in exchange for their assistance in the war effort, but many experienced a sense of broken promises, languishing in refugee camps and settling in the United States after long waits. Once in America, the struggles continued, as employment and housing were hard to obtain, and intergenerational conflicts were common. A Hmong public health administrator, Bruce Thowpaou Bliatout, explains that what Euro Americans call mental illness were regarded as liver problems for the Hmong. "Difficult liver," as it is translated, arises from soul loss because of grief for lost family, status, home or country (Fadiman 1997, 203). The symptoms are excessive worrying, crying, confusion, disjointed speech, loss of sleep and appetite, and delusions. Hmong refugees were often incapacitated by this loss of home, and the image of a sick liver became a cultural carrier for this ache.

At the interpersonal level, an example of involuntary relocation is found in an adopted orphan, carrying her deceased mother's photo. The visual image conveys the unforgettable touch of tenderness that will be remembered forever in her heart. The picture and the meanings that it carries shape and reshape her self-awareness that interacts with the patterns of relationship building in her new family.

Unlike forced relocation, a merger of different cultural groups is a more mutual and voluntary process. Although it is not necessarily a consequence of destructive conflict, such a merger helps form potential roots of conflict, as well as carrying the potential for social harmony. At the societal level, national groups merging to form a single state come to share an anthem, national flag, passport, and currency. These and other cultural carriers help shape a new sense of nationhood. Sometimes the carriers may function to marginalize those who fail to catch up with the new momentum of nation building. Either way, mergers of different social groups shape and reshape culture, both transforming and exacerbating conflict potential in society.

For decades, Yugoslavia was such a nation. United under Josip Broz Tito at the end of World War II, the republics of Bosnia-Herzegovina, Macedonia, Montenegro, Croatia, Serbia, and Slovenia adopted one flag, one anthem, and one socialist identity. When Tito died in 1980, Yugoslavs looked around for a uniting leader. They had been prepared for his demise by the slogan, "After Tito—Tito," but there was no new Tito. The country split into old identities, as nationalist flames were fanned by Slobodan Milošević. Dissent kept growing. Serbs complained that ethnic Albanians in Kosovo were persecuting them. Croats and Slovenes resented the fact that tourism money earned from their republics went to subsidize Kosovo and other poorer parts of the republic. Albanians in Kosovo demonstrated for their own republic or union with Albania. Conflict continues in the region and the Yugoslav identity is no more.

At the interpersonal level, an intercultural marriage creates a confluence of two national cultures. It shapes new patterns of meaning-making and reshapes existing ones carried by the spouses of different cultural roots. As we have seen in Chapter Four on cultural fluency, the intercultural marriage between my Taiwanese wife, Yu Chun, and myself reveals different cultural assumptions and unexpected conflicts between the Japanese and Taiwanese families. From these and many similar experiences, we can see that the more conflicts a couple experiences, the more unfamiliar cultural assumptions are revealed to educate the two partners.

Consider the relatively simple questions that the two families ask whenever they meet: what food should be served for dinner and what kind of seasoning should be used for cooking? Yu Chun's family is vegetarian, following a philosophical and religious tradition. My family runs a traditional Japanese restaurant, taking pride in fish cuisines. My Japanese father feels that vegetarian food is "tasteless" and "palatable only for grasshoppers." Yu Chun's Taiwanese parents are unwilling to take a sip of Japanese soup prepared by my family, if there is fish-based seasoning in it. From the Taiwanese family's point of view, eating fish and meat means "inflicting violence on sentient beings," and those eating them will "go to hell." One can never underestimate the tension and anxiety felt when our two families jointly plan a menu for dinner. The conflict is deeply felt.

Yet, as soon as the two families begin dialogue about *why* and *how* they have come to develop their dietary habits, a wealth of opportunities emerge, where both sides can empathize with each other while listening to personal stories and value statements embedded in their respective dietary habits. The families don't convert each other, but they do learn more about each other's meaning-making patterns. They prepare a colorful mixture of dishes for the dinner table, where vegetarian dishes are juxtaposed with palatable non-vegetarian dishes that do not look "aesthetically grotesque" from the vegetarians' point of view. Both family members extend their chopsticks to whatever they can eat. The shared dinner table symbolizes an emerging shared identity, catalyzed by food as a cultural carrier.

Finally, large-scale conflicts introduce new ideologies, political tenets, and other systems of thinking that shape and reshape culture. Revolutions, colonization, and politically motivated consecration of a nation drastically change patterns of meaning-making and relationship-building. Revolutions make heroes, colonialism brings about new elitist positions for socio-economic exploitation, and religious conversion replaces existing deities with new ones. These changes penetrate undercurrents of culture, facilitated by new cultural carriers.

The transition to democratic elections in South Africa is an example of a positive outcome of a large-scale conflict. Music played a huge carrier role in that transition, as South Africans from diverse cultural traditions came together in communities and across lines that had divided them for decades to harmonize and dance together. The film *Amandla: Revolution in Four-Part Harmony* chronicles the central role of music in this transition, tracing the power of song to communicate, motivate, console, unite and catalyze change. Named for the Xhosa word for power, *Amandla* celebrates the way music not only sustained struggle and guided change, but carried the soul of people re-inventing themselves and their country (Hirsh 2002).

At the interpersonal level, a little child raised by an unfamiliar step-mother, still suffering from his parents' divorce, is thrown into a new mode of communicative gestures, such as touching and kissing—or lack thereof. The gestures carry new patterns of meaning-making for the child. His parents' divorce changes the family context in which he lives, and has ripples into the social context as he is now perceived differently and treated differently by people he encounters.

Intensive violence, forced and voluntary movements of people, and the introduction of new systems of relationship-building shape and reshape culture at a deep level. These events are so significant that affected people not only remember them forever, but also remind their children and grandchildren not to forget them. In this sense, the impact created by these conflict-related phenomena is *irreversible*, leaving inerasable marks in our minds and spirits, and sometimes even on parts of our bodies. Such sustained impact reshapes the cultural lenses through which we interpret future conflicts. Considering the succession of these changes, we realize that culture influences conflict and conflict in turn affects culture. In short, culture and conflict are inextricably intertwined, not only at the oasis but in multiple aspects of inter-personal and social dynamics.

Exploring Alternative Scenarios for the Journey Ahead

Having journeyed through the travelers' interactions at the oasis, their recollections of personal histories, and numerous other contexts of cross-cultural dramas, we have learned how conflict dynamics evolve, how culture influences conflict, how conflict affects culture, and finally, how these two things, culture and conflict, are intertwined. Following is a brief summary of what we have learned so far about conflict dynamics:

- The potential for conflict may exist but remain unnoticed when differences between people do not hurt or trigger them in places where they make meanings and sense their evolving identities;

- Conflict emerges when people realize that their differences matter in the context of interdependence;
- Conflict polarizes relationships, sharpening a sense of "we-ness" and "they-ness;"
- Conflict de-humanizes adversaries, making them seem unworthy of human treatment;
- Conflict deepens when there are more issues involved;
- Conflict spreads in scope when more parties are involved;

Culture shapes and reshapes conflict in the following and other ways:

- Culture frames the possibilities for conflict behaviors;
- Culture tells us what kind of behaviors are preferable in a given conflict, and why;
- Culture tells us who "we" are and who "they" are in conflict;
- Culture connects the past, present, and future of conflict dynamics;
- Culture helps spread conflict across social contexts, catalyzed by shared symbols;

Conflict shapes and reshapes culture in the following and other ways:

- Conflict changes cultural carriers that deliver meanings;
- Widespread violence reshapes culture by generating traumas and glories;
- Forced relocation of people often leads to envisioning an idealized image of home;
- Mergers of cultural groups inspire the creation of cultural confluence symbols;
- Social institutions and ideologies create and perpetuate cultural symbols and continuity;

Culture and conflict are inextricably intertwined in the following and other ways:

- Culture shapes our sense of time, and conflict facilitates its transformation;
- Culture frames preferred patterns of relationship, and conflict reshapes them;
- Culture makes us feel who we are, and conflict reshapes our identities;

Remember the image of conflict-culture interaction captured in Figure 5.1, and presented earlier in this chapter? Let's revisit it briefly, as it provides a useful template for visually summarizing the main ideas explored in this chapter.

Now that we have journeyed through the dramas at the oasis and elsewhere, we have learned enough lessons to redesign this diagram and make it more comprehensive. Figure 5.2 captures a small portion of the vast arena where culture and conflict interact and evolve.

Do we need to memorize all the details in Figure 5.2? Absolutely not. Its details are not as important as its basic image, which provides a way to think and feel our way through cross-cultural conflict. In your journey, keep in mind the simpler Figure 5.1, which illustrates an interactive process of culture and conflict shaping and reshaping each other. As you experience your own cross-cultural dramas involving family, coworkers, unfamiliar visitors, neighbors, rival companies, recreational circles, and even nations, come back to this simple image frequently. Modify its shape and image in your own way. Add necessary details to its basic image if they help you to guide your journey through conflict. Each of our lives is unique. So is your journey toward understanding culture and conflict in the universe of your life. I hope that the footsteps left by the travelers, illustrated in Figure 5.2, give you at least one insightful example of a cross-cultural journey. With this image in mind, we return once more to the oasis. Sadly, the conflict is escalating. Something has to be done to stop the travelers from fighting.

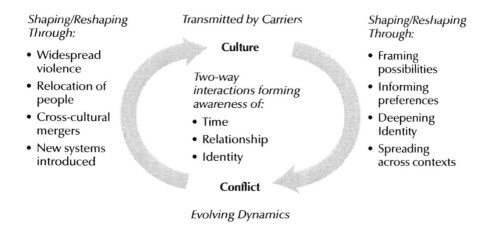

Figure 5.2 Interactive Dynamics of Conflict and Culture: An Example of Applications

At the oasis, everybody remains tense. Exhausted children lie asleep on the sand. Sunlight slowly breaks the darkness. The sun begins to rise again. As they awake, the travelers return to exchanging bitter insults, and people in the northerners' camp prepare to fight. United, the westerners and southerners have also taken up arms, determined to defend themselves from the northern "barbarians." The easterners have finally come out, attempting, in vain, to mediate among the angry parties. The story continues.

Angry travelers stand up
Swords of vengeance in hand
Roars of anger echoing in the sky
Shaking the sand dunes awake in surprise

"Charge!"
One man shouts
Spearheading into the enemy camp

Whizzing over the men charging
An arrow flies like a flash of lightning

Thud!
The arrow lands with a dull sound
Then comes a mother's cry from the southerners' camp
Galvanizing the whole universe

Alas!
The arrow finds its way right into the beating heart of her little boy
With his eyes wide open to the sky
His blood flows like a little river

His life struggles to take one last breath
Mustering all his energy to utter the very last word
"Mama . . ."
The little boy closes his eyes
Firmly embraced in his mother's arms
His little soul merges into the universe
Never to return to the warmth of his mother

Time stops
The travelers drop their swords in awe
All watch the scene intently

The mother looks up resolutely
With tears of anger overflowing in her eyes
She picks a sword of vengeance in hand
Staring at all travelers around, the allies and enemies alike
Speaking out with firm conviction
"Who killed my son?"

That moment
A little girl points to the spring and shouts
"Look, water is coming out!"
Like a geyser gushing up to the ground
Water begins to overflow ceaselessly
The small spring grows larger and deeper

The travelers watch this abundance in awe
Some delighted and overjoyed
Yet the young mother remains impassive and resolute
"Water doesn't matter anymore. This is about my son and about who
I am."
The sword of anger remains firmly in her hand

What is this conflict about? Is this about water? Is this about face-saving, given the bitter insults exchanged? Or is this about the mother avenging her child's death? Having explored conflict and culture, you may have your answers. I have my own. The men, women, and children at the oasis would each have their own opinion, too. There is no right or wrong answer. However, every view is *authentic* in terms of the particular cultural lenses of those in conflict at the oasis. To understand how the interactions between culture and conflict play out, let us share one possible way to look at this conflict, from the perspective of the mother who has just lost her son.

Conflict dynamics evolve, shaped by painful events. When the angry travelers began shouting, the mother wanted to distance herself from the escalating conflict. She believed that the conflict was about how to divide the water as equitably as possible, embracing the southerners' egalitarian and communitarian orientation. Even after the continuous exchange of insults polarized the relationships and dehumanized people to each other, her only concern was to protect her son from harm. But the moment he was killed, the conflict was reshaped drastically in her eyes. It was now about how to sustain her identity as a mother and how to get revenge and justice given the evil she, and her son, encountered.

The conflict is deepened, the issues expanded. For this mother, the lines between good and evil, right and wrong, were redrawn when her son was killed.

Culture shapes conflict. At the outset of the conflict, the mother preferred to settle their differences by dividing the available water as fairly as possible. For her, sharing was the *only* way the differences could be reconciled, consistent with the common theme of the numerous bedtime stories that she told her son. Conflict shapes culture. When her only child was killed, she was no longer a mother but a bereaved parent. Her identity was transformed, with an irreversible impact. She felt as if she had nothing to lose anymore, not even her own life. The passionate urge to distinguish good from evil, long dormant in the depths of her heart, has emerged as a driving force in her life. Culture and conflict interacted with one another in shaping this mother's behavior and reshaping the conflict.

Let's further expand our imagination and consider another possible way for the desert scenario to unfold. Wind the clock back to the moment the travelers were about to fight.

Angry travelers stand up
Swords of vengeance in hand
All of a sudden
A voice cries out from somewhere in the distance
"Oh, my goodness. Help!"
A pregnant woman in the northerners' camp lying on the ground
Struggles with excruciating pain
As her labor has just begun

A man spearheading the northerners turns back
"Oh, my dear! Why now? Not now for heaven's sake!"
The man drops his sword
Rushing to his wife

Time freezes
Everyone watches the scene unfolding

The man holds his wife in his arms
"Oh, God! What am I supposed to do?"
Then a voice, out of nowhere
"I know what to do"
An old man approaches the man and his wife from the westerners' camp
"I am a doctor"

Offering his help in a quiet tone
The northerner swallows the bitterness still boiling in his heart
"Come help my wife . . . please"
Uttered in a helplessly timid voice
The oasis suddenly becomes a hospital
Southerners fetch a bucket of water from the spring that is now a source
of healing
Easterners offer all the blankets they have, preparing a makeshift bed
for delivery
Men, woman, and children hold their breath
All watch the scene intently

Sunrise
When fresh beacons of light spark into the sky
A newborn baby cries out with all her might
Resonating within the depths of the travelers' hearts

The doctor turns to the anxious man
Reassuring him with a gentle smile
"Everything is OK now, father"
The man looks into the westerner's eyes and says
"Thank you"
With tears of relief in his eyes

Has the conflict disappeared? No. The travelers are still thirsty. Many still remember the bitter insults exchanged. Their desire for water and revenge has not disappeared altogether. Then why aren't they fighting any longer? Again, there is no right or wrong answer. It may be that this new life, at least temporarily, rehumanized their relationships. The newborn baby *meant* something so important that their urge for vengeance subsided—or at least the bitter feelings became less important than their anticipation of a new life, despite their different cultural lenses. The travelers' latest experience suggests that in conflicts colored by various cultural lenses, and marked by deep polarization, options for rehumanizing people and realizing our interdependence do exist.

This chapter has helped us observe some of the ways cross-cultural conflict can evolve. In the ocean of human relationships in daily life, knowable aspects of culture and conflict are limited. Sensing the vast arena of unknowable dynamics, we continue our journey ahead with both humility and anticipation of exciting discoveries. Despite the uncertainties that remain, by now we have some understanding of how conflict and culture evolve and change. But we have yet to explore how to create constructive social changes *purposefully*. Metaphorically, the present chapter and the previous ones have shed some light on how tides in the ocean shape and reshape, yet they have informed us little about how to navigate the tides as skillful sailors. We now take up this challenge, asking questions like: How can we find ways to bridge cultural differences in conflict? How do we know what changes open up opportunities to reshape cross-cultural conflict constructively? Through an exploration of capacities and skills for intercultural conflict resolution and an advisory map to guide our journey, we will endeavor to answer these questions in Chapters Six and Seven.

CHAPTER SIX

Capacities and Skills for Intercultural Conflict Resolution

Karenjot Bhangoo and Venashri Pillay

The previous chapters have provided us with detailed explorations of culture, cultural fluency, conflict, and the way culture and conflict are intertwined. Through the interactions of the traveling groups around the oasis in Chapter Five, we have explored how culture and conflict continuously shape and reshape each other. Chapter Seven addresses intercultural conflict resolution in greater depth and presents an advisory map as a navigational instrument for bridging conflicts across cultures. Before we are introduced to the advisory map, this chapter offers capacities and skills to facilitate and deepen intercultural conflict resolution.

Do you remember your last road trip to a new place? You may have experienced excitement at the prospect of visiting a new place, but some anxiety and trepidation about the long journey ahead and the unfamiliar road. Even if you had a map and plotted your route, you were probably aware of the possibility that you might get lost, encounter a detour, or just get very tired from the change and exertion. Do you remember how you prepared for these possibilities? You may have plotted alternative routes, made sure your car was ready, invited a friend to share the driving, recorded your favorite music, or packed a picnic lunch to have along the way. These steps could have increased your positive experience of the trip.

The skills presented in this chapter aim to do the same thing: help prepare you for the challenges of encountering difference and change by providing concrete, specific tools to bridge differences. The skills will help us when we are feeling stuck, when we encounter a boulder in the road, or when we are tired at the thought of continuing.

The capacities presented are the foundation of cultural fluency in conflict—a continuing path of development built over a lifetime. The capacities inform how the skills can be used and magnify the effects of the skills. Capacities are broad, general abilities that may come naturally to us, and can be further developed. For example, a painter's capacity for creative expression is exercised through brush-stroke skills; capacity for love is manifest through parenting skills; and journalists' capacities for inquiry are developed through improving interviewing skills. We all have capacities and skills—some we use automatically without being aware that they are an everyday part of our interactions, while others lie dormant and are activated only occasionally, depending on the context. As we live, we develop new capacities and learn new skills.

Overview of Capacities and Skills for Intercultural Conflict Resolution

A multitude of capacities and skills are available to assist us in intercultural conflict resolution. Many have been mentioned in previous chapters. In this chapter, we focus on three important and necessary capacities, as well as nine specific skills that give these capacities expression. Table 6.1 outlines the capacities and corresponding skills.

Relationships and interdependence are at the center of successfully bridging conflict. Capacities for *flexibility, creative engagement,* and *momentum* help us recognize our interdependence and strengthen our relationships, moving beyond a sense of ourselves as isolated and disconnected from each other. The capacity for *flexibility* asks that we remain open to difference. Through the skills of pattern interruption, sitting with discomfort, and dancing with surprises, we cultivate this capacity. The capacity for *creative engagement* encourages us to be inventive in encountering and interacting with others. The three skills which facilitate creative engagement are metaphor, storytelling, and ritual. As we apply these capacities and skills, we build the third capacity: *momentum* for moving forward. Momentum keeps engagement and interaction alive as we build relationships. Revealing uncertainty, pausing, and intuition are skills that help sustain momentum.

Table 6.1
Overview of Capacities and Skills for Intercultural Conflict Resolution

Capacities	Skills
Flexibility	Interrupting Patterns
	Sitting with Discomfort
	Dancing with Surprises
Creative Engagement	Metaphor
	Storytelling
	Ritual
Momentum	Revealing Uncertainty
	Pausing
	Intuition

Flexibility

What happens when you are confronted with a person or a practice that is completely different from you or what you believe to be acceptable? As we write this, two small communities—Colorado City, Utah, in the United States, and Bountiful, British Columbia, in Canada—are embroiled in a legal and social conflict over their choice of family lifestyle. The people of these secluded communities have maintained polygamous practices for generations, despite U.S. and Canadian law that declare polygamy illegal. They remained "under the radar" of larger society for years, but now officials are intent on investigating and prosecuting polygamists. In both communities, elders and many of the "sister-wives" interviewed insist that they are happy and that the larger U.S. and Canadian societies do not understand their beliefs, religion, and lifestyle. As this conflict unfolds through the news media we are reminded of a similar situation that happened, thousands of miles away, on another continent.

Lebo was a recent university graduate in South Africa, pleased that she would soon be embarking on her journey as a successful, independent career woman. Her first job as a community social worker brought her in contact with a rural community in Kwa-Zulu Natal, South Africa. Lebo grew up and was educated in the city, removed from many traditional African practices observed in rural parts of the country.

One of her first clients was a young boy whose mother was the third wife to his father. Even though the mother was not Lebo's client officially, she felt it her duty as a woman to help this mother get out of what Lebo believed was an oppressive, polygamous marriage. She felt this poor woman definitely needed to be empowered to leave her sexist husband. Armed with strong feminist beliefs, Lebo started to talk to the mother about women's rights, letting her know that no matter how desperate she felt, she did not have to suffer the dominance of any man. She passionately shared her opinions that women are strong and should not be suppressed or oppressed by men. She suggested to this mother that polygamy enables men to continue the oppression of women, and offered to help the mother extricate herself from this situation.

Imagine Lebo's surprise when the mother burst out laughing. Lebo was shocked, angered, and insulted by the mother's strange reaction. At this, the mother ceased laughter, and shook her head in disgust. "Women like *you* keep other women disempowered, not their husbands!" she retorted. Lebo was confused and outraged. She left, and the two never spoke again. But Lebo was unsettled by the experience, and asked herself questions about the opaque situation: What had the woman meant? And should she have handled the situation differently?

Weeks later, Lebo received a letter from the mother who explained that she felt it *her* duty as a woman to let Lebo know what she thought. She explained that she was a strong, proud, empowered woman who celebrated her ability to choose. She *chose* the happy lifestyle she shared with her husband, his two other wives, and all their children. She enjoyed the support she got from the other women and was fine with sharing her caring husband. She ended by suggesting that women like Lebo who remain inflexible, judgmental, and closed to others' lifestyles are the ones doing women a disservice in the end. While the note did not change Lebo's views on polygamy, it did cause her to reflect more on her capacities for flexibility and openness to difference. Lebo continued her work in the community with a resolve to replace judgment with flexibility.

The situation is somewhat different in Bountiful and Colorado City. National legal and social norms do not condone polygamy. At the same time, both countries have guarantees of freedom of religion. Resolving this tension between cultural and religious practices is more than just a legal matter—it requires the flexibility of seeing the world from inside the skin of others if only to understand how their ways of being make sense to them.

Flexibility asks that we remain open to difference as we encounter others. The capacity for flexibility means suspending judgment and perceiving with a spirit of inquiry. Suspending judgment is not to abandon our beliefs or values, but to create a space for curiosity inside ourselves and between us and others. Had Lebo exercised her capacity for flexibility, she would have replaced her judgment that the mother was disempowered with a spirit of curiosity about the mother's life choices.

Who knows what will happen in Colorado City or Bountiful? In a democratic society, laws must be upheld or changed. But enforcement of laws will not change beliefs or stamp out the practice of polygamy for those who believe it to be ordained of God. There are places where the arm of the law cannot reach, and gray areas that cry out for cultural bridging more than legal enforcement. Where law, culture, and custom intersect with local and constitutional values, understanding is at least as important as legal boundaries. At a minimum, Lebo's experience reminds us to suspend judgment about communities like Colorado City and Bountiful and to explore their beliefs in the context of their religion and values. We will not adopt their beliefs and abandon our own, but as we replace judgment with understanding, relationships can be built that may foster ongoing dialogue and more progress in protecting women and children than legal enforcement.

Being flexible means suspending judgment and entertaining ambiguity and complexity. Developing comfort with ambiguity allows us to hold and explore seemingly contradictory and opposite perspectives as we seek to broaden our understanding and gain deeper insights. By engaging ambiguity and complexity, we give ourselves permission to understand nuances, recognizing that no person or group is static or one-dimensional. Context matters—we act differently with members of our "in-groups" than outsiders; we make different choices when we feel threatened or our identity is at stake than if the issue is a matter of preference rather than principle. By deepening our ability to engage ambiguity and complexity, the capacity for flexibility facilitates intercultural conflict resolution. The three skills of interrupting patterns, sitting with discomfort, and dancing with surprise help foster and express our capacity for flexibility.

Interrupting Patterns

Imagine the mind as one large, organized filing cabinet. In our files, we store categories of information that we draw on to make sense of our world—they shape our thoughts, feelings, and actions. People in groups to which we belong have similar files in their filing cabinets that lead them to think, feel, and act in similar particular, patterned ways. When we encounter difference and unfamiliarity, we go to these inner files. Sometimes, our files for people or situations may be inadequate or missing. In these cases, it is easy to substitute a negative judgment for information. The line between noticing a difference and ranking that difference below our "common sense" way of responding is a very thin one. Sometimes, when we interact with others and the experience is positive, we find a way to align it with existing understandings, and create a new file or category for our cabinets. But if the information we hold already, what we believe to be true, moral, and right, feels threatened by the difference, then judgment ensues. We slam our filing cabinet shut and short-circuit inquiry about the different experience, person, or encounter.

Lebo's "filing cabinet" contained a file with her particular views about marriage and relationships arising from cultural norms reflected in law. Her file, easily accessed when she encountered the woman in the polygamous relationship, told her that polygamy was wrong and oppressive for women. Instead of altering her existing files of information or creating new ones about marriage and relationships, she defaulted to negative existing files. These preset files prevented a different perspective: thinking that a woman could actually *choose* polygamy and be happy did not fit with Lebo's beliefs. These ideas had the potential to disrupt the filing cabinet of her mind and spin it into unsettled chaos. We need organized mental filing cabinets and files to keep our lives feeling coherent, ordered, and controlled. The judgments invoked by negative or thin information in our files protect us from chaos and facilitate our ongoing functioning in society. They allow us a sense of safety when confronted with uncertainty. But judgments also create barriers to people who are different from us as they flow from stereotypes and prejudices.

Developing flexibility requires that we continually adjust our mental files and categories in evolving, fluid, and dynamic ways. How do we achieve this? As we struggle to understand an intercultural conflict, we can imagine deliberately allowing disruption in our filing cabinets. Choosing to embrace and hold ambiguity—even for a brief time—furthers our understanding of others. We are likely to experience discomfort initially, but it helps when we remember that we are not trading our beliefs for theirs, only trying to understand their beliefs in context.

We can interrupt patterns by simply asking a set of questions. Before you consider the questions below think of a belief or perspective that you hold strongly—for example, where do you stand on controversial topics like polygamy, abortion, same-sex marriage, or ritual sacrifice?

- **Why do you hold this belief or view? Where does it come from?** On closer reflections, Lebo could have realized that her belief that "polygamy is wrong" was influenced by her religious teachings, social context, familial upbringing, feminist-influenced education, and media messages, all of which reinforced her association of polygamy with abusive and oppressive men.

- **How does this belief influence you and your life?** Lebo's strong negative views on polygamy intercepted a spirit of inquiry and made it difficult for her to form an empathic bond with the mother. She did not see another alternative or perspective, but felt that it was her responsibility to "save" women in such predicaments. She saw her choice of monogamy as superior, and this attitude of superiority impaired the formation of a helping relationship.

- **Now, assume the completely opposite view to the one you hold. What is it? How does it make sense for those who hold this view? What can you imagine might reinforce this view for those who hold it?** Had Lebo thought of polygamy as a worldview rather than interposing a negative judgment, she might have inquired about the social context in which it arises and is sustained. She might have thought about how a communal and rural lifestyle requires sharing and interdependence for survival, remembering that group child-rearing is not an uncommon African practice, and that multiple adult partners and parents may create a more supportive and loving home. She may also have remembered that this choice of lifestyle, like her monogamous beliefs, is also rooted in tradition, custom, and religion.

- **With this alternative belief, what would your world look and feel like now?** Lebo's world would definitely be more ambiguous and complex. It might be more uncertain and maybe even uncomfortable if she retained this understanding of polygamy in context. Her world may also suddenly feel larger, more expansive, and open to multiple perspectives and people living in diverse ways. Lebo would have been more prepared and open to engage the mother with a sense of respect and keenness to learn. She would have started her interaction differently and established a foundation for building a new relationship instead of damaging it the way she did. None of this would have required that she change her views on polygamy, only that she be open to understanding a way of life different from her own.

This kind of exploration is harder than it sounds. It is not easy to understand a worldview that supports a perspective that seems completely wrong or misguided. Our tendency is to evaluate views different from our own using values and assumptions embedded in our personal worldviews. To truly explore differences, it is important to try to work from the inside out: to imagine how the different view makes sense rather than marvel at its strangeness or patent wrongness. We can ask ourselves the question, "How can I imagine this view making sense? How does it serve those who hold it?" stepping away from our inclination to justify or defend our own contrary beliefs and values.

As we ask these questions we practice suspending judgment and finding alternative ways of understanding others. If Lebo had interrupted her thought patterns by posing these questions to herself as soon as she found out her client came from a polygamous family, she would have been less likely to jump to judgments and more likely to engage the mother in constructive dialogue through her openness and flexibility. Then, Lebo might have been able to work with the mother constructively without adopting the mother's beliefs.

Sitting with Discomfort

When Lebo first received the mother's letter, her judgment precluded her from entertaining a positive view on polygamy. Reading the letter, she became even more defensive. Her resistant stance caused her increasing uneasiness—she could not forget the mother's letter, but she could not accept the mother's perspective.

The intensity of Lebo's feelings kept the issue in her awareness. Sitting with the uncomfortable feelings gave Lebo the time and space to reflect on her thoughts and actions. Finally, she decided to look at the issue again with more openness, even though polygamy seemed so foreign to her. Lebo could have stifled her discomfort by reaffirming her view that the mother was oppressed. This would have been the easy way out—it is natural for us to want to remove discomfort and unpleasant feelings from our daily experiences. But, as Lebo's experience shows, using these unpleasant feelings as a cue for reflection allows us the opportunity to move toward flexibility in thought and action.

Let's consider another example, this time of Venashri's experience as a new social worker, working with children and families in an African township in South Africa for a nongovernmental organization. After years of apartheid and separation from other groups, an Indian working in an African community was unusual. Her biggest challenge early on was being accepted. She sensed that the parents and some of her African coworkers were uncomfortable working with her, as she was with them. None of them were accustomed to this situation. The initial tension in the air persisted.

Venashri thought that knowing the local African language was enough to bridge differences and make relationships work, but she continued to face resistance from the community. She followed the textbook instructions of trying to learn the other culture and reaching out to build relationships, yet when she did this, she found people becoming more distant. Strangely, her first breakthrough with a local family came when she stopped trying so hard and openly admitted that she didn't know much about their culture. Without realizing it at that time, she was actually sitting with the resistance and discomfort she was encountering, and this became the first step to reducing tensions.

As Venashri stopped trying to learn or reach out, it actually gave the local people an opportunity to approach her in their own time, space, and way. Doing nothing, letting the space just exist without trying to fill, fix, create, organize, manage, or plan, allowed others to reach her. She let go, and when she did, the local people themselves filled the uncomfortable space by reaching out to her. Sitting with the discomfort allowed new things to blossom in the space between her and the families. Venashri also realized that working in this different setting brought her to increased awareness of her own culture. As she shared more about herself and her culture, others shared too, further increasing her understanding of the local African culture. She discovered that the magic moments of understanding can actually occur through sitting with silences, distance, and resistance.

The act of sitting with discomfort or resistance requires that we develop a way of letting uneasy and difficult experiences just *be* for a while. It does not imply avoiding the conflict situation, but that sitting with difficult feelings can be a way of engaging the conflict. As we do this, we stretch our capacity for flexibility in intercultural conflict.

Dancing with Surprise

Flexibility is also enhanced when we invite surprise into our interactions. When we encounter something unexpected, we are surprised. How do you deal with surprises? Do you cringe at the thought of being unprepared for something? Or are you energized by the unexpected? Surprises in interactions are magic moments for change. When we are surprised, we may be momentarily still as we decide on a way to deal with the unexpected. Welcoming the surprise, dancing with it, letting it influence our thoughts, feelings, and actions will create openness to the other and may transform a tense interaction.

Returning to Lebo's story, she experienced surprise when the mother burst out laughing after Lebo had delivered her "empowerment speech." Lebo was shocked by the mother's strange response; it was not what she expected. But rather than embrace and share the surprise of laughter at what seemed an inappropriate time, she became angry because she perceived that the mother was mocking and insulting her. This in turn triggered an angry response from the mother.

What if Lebo had interrupted her reflexive response by using her experience of surprise as a cue to react in a different way? What if Lebo had shared the mother's laughter, recognizing that the situation was a challenge for both of them? This may have changed the tone and atmosphere of their interaction. If Lebo had shown genuine curiosity in asking what was funny, the mother would not have needed to defend herself against judgment. Even if the mother's laughter meant something other than amusement, Lebo's genuine inquiry would have invited explanation and communication, rather than increased anger and resistance. Lebo would have been using the skill of dancing with surprise, incorporating the surprise into her movement. We dance with it, explore and experience it, and see where it leads.

Recall Al's story introduced in Chapter Three, which took us on a journey to the rural island community south of Mindanao, Philippines, where a death was mourned. Al noted that death in his community is a solemn occasion to be mourned. Remember his surprise when he realized that death was celebrated in the Balut Saranggani community that he was visiting. Mourners were celebrators, participating in festivities with food, dance, and music. Al found himself gasping in surprise at their different way of dealing with death.

There may not have been time to ask many questions about the origins of the customs and traditions in which this community engaged. Confronted with surprise, Al chose to embrace it and experience it. He danced in the celebration, appreciating the difference and not worrying about processing what was happening through his own cultural lenses to make meaning of it. Through his participation in the festivities, Al developed a deeper understanding of the Balut-Saranggani people and the meanings they attach to death and life. When he embraced the new mourning ritual and joined in, he opened himself to the local people and learned about their culture. Unlike Lebo, Al's choice to dance with surprise created the opportunity for openness, flexibility, and building relationships. Al was choosing to engage creatively—another important capacity for cultural fluency.

Creative Engagement

The capacity for creative engagement encourages us to be inventive in encountering and interacting with others. In difficult intercultural interactions, we may feel hesitant to continue engaging for fear that we may generate more conflict. Creative engagement encourages us to find innovative, non-threatening ways to interact with others when conflict arises. This capacity emphasizes the gifts we have for relating to others—we are in essence relational creatures. When we relate to others in ways that acknowledge our interdependence, whether as members of a wider community, a region, or the human family, we smooth out the negative effects of conflicts. While this is less easy in conflictual interactions than harmonious ones, it is even more important. Creative engagement keeps open the possibility of conflict as a generator of positive change, learning, and growth.

Engaging with others is the first step to understanding different perspectives and beliefs. Through creative engagement, aspects of the conflict that were previously unknown or hidden can become clear, allowing for greater meaning-making and understanding across differences. Creative engagement enables discovery and the invention of new ways to be together, important aspects of the advisory map presented later in Chapter Seven.

Metaphor, storytelling, and ritual all facilitate creative relationship building. The skills of using metaphor, story, and ritual are important to helping people understand the cultural logic of others in intercultural conflict situations (LeBaron 2003). We will explore each of these skills in turn as they facilitate creative engagement, beginning with an example of the usefulness of metaphor as a skill for dialogue in an intercultural conflict in Canada.

Metaphor

Among indigenous peoples with long histories in Canada live immigrants from many parts of the world. Transitioning to a new country can be difficult for immigrants. Challenges relating to language, religion, and cultural ways of being arise as families move from their "home" cultures to the Canadian mosaic. Established groups may have difficulty understanding and accepting new people and their differences. Racism and discrimination create even more difficulty for people in transition.

Sikh immigrants from northern India have long been a part of communities on the west coast of British Columbia, Canada. They brought their language, religion, and customs along as they came in waves starting over a hundred years ago to help build the railroad and work with the rich natural resources of the coast. Through the years, they encountered many challenges arising from misunderstandings, racism, and lack of acceptance. These challenges converged into a significant conflict when Sikh people wanted to build a temple in a small coastal town where they could worship and share community.

European-Canadian residents of the town opposed the construction of the temple. They believed that the increase in traffic would disrupt their peaceful neighborhood. They feared the change and worried about what these unknown and different people might do. They boldly voiced their opinions and tried to halt the construction of the temple through a petition to local government.

Facing this resistance was very difficult for the Sikh community. British Columbia was their new home, and they wanted to belong. Erecting a temple was vitally important both for the practice of their religious beliefs and as a symbol of their identity. The Sikhs were shocked by the Euro-Canadians' reactions. They felt even more unwelcome than before, and saw the resistance to the temple as another manifestation of the Euro-Canadians' prejudice and discriminatory behavior toward them.

This intercultural conflict between Sikh and other residents of the town festered. The Sikhs realized that they needed a way to communicate the importance of the temple and its relationship to their community values. They also wanted to step out of the back-and-forth debate that was keeping everyone from moving forward. As they struggled with what to do, they used a Punjabi metaphor that spoke to their difficulty in trying to move ahead in the face of resistance. The Punjabi metaphor literally translates to "flipping the Ganges toward Pahoway."

The Ganges in India is a sacred river that flows from an ice cave in the Himalayas to the Bay of Bengal. Pahoway refers to a place on the upper side of the Ganges River near the Himalayas. The Ganges does not actually flow toward Pahoway, so the metaphor refers to the impossibility of changing something that has been constant for a long time, something part of the accustomed landscape. This metaphor captured the sense of struggle and pain the Sikh community encountered in planning their temple. The resistance they faced not just in terms of building the temple but also with regard to their settling in British Columbia felt no less difficult and impossible than trying to "flip the Ganges toward Pahoway." Members of the Sikh community became energized as they used the metaphor because it helped them express their depth of feeling and mounting discouragement.

After a while, someone suggested that representatives of both the Sikh community and Euro-Canadian residents get together to talk informally. When they did, the Sikh leader used the metaphor to explain how Sikh people had experienced the community's resistance. The metaphor helped the Euro-Canadians realize how the conflict over the temple felt connected to many other struggles, and the intensity of their Sikh neighbors' pain. For the first time since the temple had been proposed, Euro-Canadians got a glimpse of their neighbors' despair and sense of failure. The metaphor had resonance for those who heard it; each of them had experienced challenging times when they felt like they were trying to change something unchangeable. As they empathized with the Sikhs, the Euro-Canadians could no longer perceive them as "other"—depersonalized and disconnected from themselves.

As the Euro-Canadians shifted their perceptions of the Sikhs, there was more openness to dialogue. There was an opening for the Sikhs to inquire and learn more about the thoughts, fears, and concerns of the Euro-Canadians. From this turning point, their interactions changed in constructive directions. A basis for relationship had been created through the metaphor and their willingness to engage in dialogue that saw them through the construction of the Sikh temple and the resolution of other community issues.

The metaphor played a significant role in advancing the dialogue and creative engagement. It was powerful even though it had to be translated from Punjabi into English. The river metaphor was particularly strong because it was a shared symbol that reminded residents of their common natural heritage and interdependence. The image of the Ganges became a stepping stone from technical and logistical conflict about situating the temple to dialogue about the feelings and meanings each side was attaching to the temple.

Metaphors can be powerful mediums for facilitating shared understanding in intercultural conflict because they evoke sensory and emotional resonance, or empathy. They help contextualize and communicate experiences. Metaphors provide creative ways into meaningful conversations because they convey expansive images that facilitate shared understanding across differences. They can also save face and smooth communication by conveying strong or complex feelings that might not be easily expressed directly. The Ganges metaphor did all of this, and it acted as an anchor for those people involved. In subsequent months and years when issues of community hardship, resistance to change, and new conflicts arose, people from both communities again referred to the impossibility of changing the direction of the mighty Ganges, and found solutions that worked for both sides.

Storytelling

Transport yourself to a time when you read or listened to your favorite childhood story. It may have been at the feet of your grandfather seated in his creaky rocking chair or turning the pages of a favorite book on a rainy afternoon. Remember what it felt like to be transported into the story as the words jumped out at you and magically took on life. You were suddenly the knight in shining armor, the magical fairy-princess, the poor little orphan, the wise owl, the little train that could, or the conflicted serpent. No matter what the story, or the character with whom you identified, you inevitably got drawn into the emotions that unfolded. You lived the story for that brief time. This is the wonder of stories and storytelling. They welcome us into new worlds, providing the opportunity to know what others feel like from the inside out.

Storytelling helps us relate easily to others. For a brief time, we replace the storyteller's journey with our own. In the example of the Sikh and Euro-Canadian conflict, storytelling was another tool used by members of both communities to create understanding and bridge the gap.

The Sikh leader sat down with his Euro-Canadian counterpart and shared a story about himself and his people. Moving away from his position about building the temple, he offered something more private: the struggles of his family and their transition to Canada. He spoke about how hard it was to find a job in a foreign place. Once he found a job, he had to endure racist slogans and slurs as part of his daily existence. As he related his personal story of hardship and struggle, the emotions that were part of these experiences were plain.

The Euro-Canadian neighbor felt the emotion of the Sikh leader. As his words were spoken, his pain came into the room, affecting them both. He listened quietly for some time, allowing the Sikh leader to complete his story. He was surprised that he identified so strongly with the feelings expressed. Then, the Euro-Canadian shared his own story. The emotional openness of the Sikh leader implicitly invited him to follow suit. His story also involved hardships. He talked about the difficulties of raising a family and trying to find work in a small town. He recalled the struggles of his ancestors when they first came to Canada.

Although they had different experiences, the shared stories helped the men realize their similarities, including shared hopes and dreams for their families and future lives in Canada. The stories bridged a cultural gap and allowed both men to find common yarns of understanding.

As they developed ease with each other and their conversation, a more relaxed and open atmosphere facilitated conversation about the temple and other community issues. Storytelling helped them focus on what connected them rather than what divided them as they moved from adversaries to shared identities as men, fathers, workers, and community residents. Stories formed the groundwork for other conversations, movement toward shared understanding, and creative engagement.

Ritual

Sometimes, stories are shared through rituals—times when thought is set aside and we focus on feelings, sensations, and relationships. Rituals can be comforting as they remind us of our identities and the meanings of our cultures, and they may be used to mark or smooth transitions. Just as stories helped the Sikh leader and his Euro-Canadian counterparts create understanding, rituals can be important in helping bridge differences and uncomfortable change, as illustrated in the story of Jabu.

Jabu recently relocated to his home country of South Africa after living in the United States for several years. He originally left South Africa in his late teens. Although he grew up in a traditional Zulu home in South Africa, he became very disconnected from his culture and traditions during his time in the United States. He embraced a modern Western lifestyle, dismissing his Zulu traditions and customs.

Upon Jabu's return to South Africa, he experienced many problems. As much as he was thrilled to finally be home with his extended family, he also realized that he no longer identified with people in his family and community. He found that he was often getting into arguments with his dad and other elders about his lifestyle. He liked his independence and found himself impatient with the more communal orientation of his family. For example, he did not understand why it was such a big deal to his parents that he missed a distant relative's prayer ceremony for some important personal errands he had to get done. He felt that his family was being insensitive to his needs and wishes.

As time went on and he was unable to find a good job, his stress mounted. His father and other community elders continuously pointed out that he had not fulfilled certain Zulu customs and traditions, and that was why he was not successful. Jabu responded with anger due to his perception that his family was unsupportive, and the conflict between him and family members festered. Jabu's father felt extremely hurt and insulted by Jabu. He felt that he and his traditions held the solution to all Jabu's problems, but his son was rejecting him and his way of life. A few more months passed. Jabu was more frustrated than ever. He avoided his old neighborhood and was barely on speaking terms with his family. Eventually, only out of desperation and to placate his father, he agreed to participate in a ritual about which his father had been talking for awhile.

The ritual was conducted by his family elders and was held in honor of the ancestors. A goat was sacrificed, *impepho* (an incense plant) was burnt to cleanse Jabu and the family, and the eldest family member called out to the ancestors to welcome Jabu back to the family home and to guide and bless him on his job search and his way in life. The ritual was concluded with a shared meal in a festive atmosphere.

As Jabu participated in the ritual, he started to reflect more about his customs, traditions, and family. Gradually, as he began to participate more willingly and genuinely in the ritual, Jabu noticed the pride on his father's face. For the first time since he had returned to South Africa, he began to feel connected to his father, his family, and his people. No words were being spoken, but Jabu came to realize the meaning attached to family, community, and traditions in the Zulu community as the ritual progressed. He realized that his suffering had always been the suffering of his family too, and they were supporting him in the most powerful way they knew by calling on the powers and blessings of the ancestors. The ritual marked his family's shared hopes, dreams, and well wishes for Jabu.

Jabu's participation in the ritual helped create a shared foundation for ongoing relationships of mutuality and openness. Later, when the ritual was over and he had gained more understanding of the ways in which his family *did* support him, he was able to have an in-depth conversation with his father about Zulu traditions and in turn share with his father some of his experiences in the United States. A new relational foundation between himself and his father emerged. He is still not quite sure whether paying tribute to his ancestors resulted in him getting his dream job a few weeks later, but he did know that he left that ritual feeling more connected to his family and himself.

Through the ritual, Jabu learned about his people and their meaning-making processes without anyone giving explicit explanations. The actions in the ritual spoke more meaningfully to him than any of his father's explanations ever had. Through the ritual he *felt* meaning come alive.

Jabu's story illustrates the power of ritual to catalyze cultural fluency. We all have rituals—times outside the ordinary when we are acting rather than thinking—whether we are observing a family birthday, performing sacred acts in a place of worship, or spending time alone in the mountains. Rituals are vessels that help us observe, mark, and transition changes in identity, meaning or status.

Often, we engage in rituals with people in identity groups to which we belong, whether families, work groups, or communities. In these cases, rituals help reinforce group cohesion. But rituals can also be powerful tools to facilitate engagement across differences, as in Jabu's story. The ritual brought the meaning-making process of his family and the Zulu people alive for Jabu. It had a strong impact because it created a bridge of feeling across limiting assumptions that made a space for a new quality of relating between Jabu and his family.

In intercultural conflict, ritual's gifts of connecting and emphasizing shared meaning become very important. In many cultures of the world, conflict resolution processes begin with cleansing rituals, are accompanied by rituals to appease the ancestors, and conclude with sharing a meal or celebration to symbolize the release of bad spirits and the restoration of relationships. Rituals connect people to the unseen but vital realms of identity and deeply held values.

Rituals may smooth communication between adversaries by replacing hurtful words with experiences of powerful emotions. They transport people from their polarized stances, shifting their attention to positive aspirations and connective thinking.

Rituals are also important for their marking function, as was the case in Jabu's story. So often, we move out of phases of our lives without stopping to observe and mark their meaning. Both negative losses and positive successes deserve to be marked. Sharing them in community brings others into the circle in a way that makes burdens lighter and spreads the joy of successes. Rituals also provide closure, signaling to everyone that a new phase has begun and the old one has been put to rest. They emphasize the preciousness of relationships, present and past, and underline our interdependence with each other. Rituals also save face by bringing us together without requiring that we name every obstacle we faced in arriving.

In conflict resolution, marking even small successes can be very important. Celebrating achievements, both large and small, marks progress and positive change. Otherwise, it is easy to become discouraged and disheartened, especially in protracted conflict situations. Rituals also create bookmarks to which we can come back as we measure our progress over a longer period of time. Thus, they contribute to hope and momentum, the next capacity for intercultural conflict resolution.

Momentum

Our capacity for momentum encourages us to keep at it, whether "it" is learning about ourselves and others or engaging particularly challenging difficulties. Momentum implies continuous motion—and the benefits that accrue to someone already on their way to a goal. In conflict resolution, momentum is not a straight line. Being still at times during the journey can also facilitate momentum in achieving a resolution. In conflict resolution, momentum can even include doubling back to pick up new pieces of understanding to roll into the eventual closure as the conflict is addressed.

Maintaining momentum means paying focused attention and going forward in the face of obstacles. The capacity for momentum keeps us engaged and our relationships vital. It gets us through the stuck parts of the journey, helps us remove boulders in the road, and reminds us to remain courageous in the face of fear and uncertainty. The three skills that help us keep our momentum are revealing uncertainty, pausing, and intuition.

Revealing Uncertainty

Engaging intercultural conflict can be overwhelming, anxiety-provoking, and even frightening, especially if we are not familiar with "the other." We may get frustrated because we don't know where to start or how to proceed, or we may be faced with failure and resistance. It is easy to imagine how momentum can be blocked.

Momentum comes to mind when Venashri recalls her experience as a new social worker in a South African township. She was finding it extremely difficult to bridge the distance between herself and community members. Try as she might, the distance only expanded and she was at a loss as to what to try next. Surprisingly, when Venashri finally acknowledged her frustration at not knowing what to do, a breakthrough occurred. Her training at school had not emphasized acknowledging things she did not know, nor giving voice to the vulnerable, scared thoughts she was having. When she voiced her fears and uncertainty, she finally allowed others to see her as no different from themselves.

She was no longer a remote professional, know-it-all, fixer-of-everything, but also a person with her own feelings, fears, and uncertainty. The local families who lived in uncertain times and led uncertain lives finally saw someone with whom they could identify as she revealed her own uncertainty and fears. They also saw Venashri's humanness—and the bridge of understanding that led her to the local people, and them to her, was finally clear.

Similarly, when the Sikh Canadians conveyed their fears, uncertainty, and struggles to the Euro-Canadians, their conflict over the construction of the temple reached a turning point. Through use of the descriptive metaphor of the Ganges, the Sikhs revealed their feelings and plight. Their Euro-Canadian neighbors could not help but identify with the enormity of the Sikhs' frustration. As the Sikhs revealed their uncertainty and vulnerability about their futures in a new country through metaphor, they were humanized in the eyes of their Euro-Canadian neighbors. They were no longer "those unknown and different people who want to change the neighborhood and disturb the peace." Instead they became "people like us who face the same challenges in life and suffer similar fears and pains." Revealing uncertainty helped the Sikhs and Euro-Canadians find their common humanity despite their many differences and provided a place for them to begin constructive interactions.

When we are in conflict, defensiveness and fear often prevent us from revealing uncertainty. The choice to reveal our flaws and weak points may feel like a loss of power or face, but it can be a humbling experience that reveals interdependence. If we believe that we cannot say anything until we have some answers or a way forward and so we say nothing at all, the distance remains and widens. It is not necessary that we have all the answers or know the way to go. It may be enough to say that we *don't* know or that we are uncertain, afraid, helpless, and alone. Acknowledging we don't know how to proceed invites others to share responsibility for the process and our relationship. Speaking uncertainty is an act of courage that can facilitate movement of people toward each other.

Pausing

I have walked that long road to freedom. . . . But I have discovered the secret that after climbing a great hill, one only finds that there are many more hills to climb. I have taken a moment here to rest, to steal a view of the glorious vista that surrounds me, to look back on the distance I have come. . . . my long walk is not yet ended. (Mandela 1994, 617)

Mandela relates his journey of conflict resolution for himself and the people of South Africa in his autobiography *A Long Walk to Freedom*. He notes that this journey is far from over but that he needs to stop and rest in order to go on. His words of wisdom tell us that that the journey of conflict resolution is dotted with many difficult hills, and while we must persevere, it is important that we also know when to stop and rest so we don't become too tired or weak to reach the next hill.

Working to bridge intercultural conflicts can be draining emotionally, physically, mentally, and spiritually. People are likely to become tired and irritable. In order to maintain momentum, we sometimes need to recharge rather than try more of the same strategies that have not been working. Instead of concentrating harder, exerting more pressure or energy, or returning to the same analysis that reinforces our perspective, it can be helpful to pause. If we don't, we may jeopardize the progress we have already made. To maintain momentum, we sometimes have to stop.

Pausing allows us to rest a little, get a change of scenery, or do something completely different. When we return to our work, we may come with fresh eyes. Stories of inventors and creative geniuses are full of instances where pauses facilitated discoveries and broke impasses. When we are in the grips of conflict, we can sometimes be so focused on holding on to the thin yarns that stand between us and significant loss or disappointment that we are very resistant to pausing. Paradoxically, it may be the best thing we can do.

When Venashri paused in her efforts to build relationships with community members in South Africa and acknowledged her uncertainty, it was not because of great wisdom or discipline. It was because she was frustrated and exhausted. Only weeks later did she realize the value of actually pausing. When she paused, she invited the local people to approach her and in that space, connections happened. When she stopped, the local people could finally begin their attempts to reach her. Sometimes when we are determined to solve an issue, we get so focused on moving forward that others cannot catch up to us even though this is what we seek. Pausing facilitates people reaching us in their own way and time.

Venashri was fortunate that the local people reached out to her when she paused, but what if she had stopped and the distance between herself and the local people remained? Perhaps she would have directed her energies and efforts elsewhere for a time and, when she eventually came back to the task of bridging the gap between herself and the local people, it would have been with renewed energy and refreshed ideas.

Because pausing is difficult to do when much is at stake, it may be helpful to identify a distraction or another concrete task. Physical movement can help—as our bodies move, sometimes the way we have organized our thinking and our perceptions of others shifts, too. When we are trying to help others in conflict, it can be very helpful to assign them a physical task or focus that takes them away from unproductive directions and creates a pause in problem-solving. For example, it may be helpful to ask parties to take a walk or go on a hike, together or separately, to clear their heads, change the setting, and allow fresh thinking to surface.

Pausing should not be used for avoidance in difficult situations or when there is lack of progress. We should, however, monitor ourselves so that we don't continue momentum when the motion is part of a downward spiral. Conflict can spiral up into transformative learning experiences, but it can also spiral down into despair and lasting damage. Pausing may help us discern the direction of our relational spirals.

Intuition

Intuition is *knowing* without necessarily knowing how *the knowing* arrived. How many times have you acted on a hunch, gut feeling, or instinct? Do you recall a time when a nagging feeling, unknown sense, or a knot in the pit of your stomach conveyed something to you? If you are walking in a dark alley alone, you start to walk faster as your heartbeat increases; a gut feeling causes you to call home to check on family; a respected attorney follows his urge to pack up his office and a lucrative job to travel and experience the world. Was there really a reason to walk faster in the alley? Was there a problem at home that needed immediate attention? Was there something deep inside of the lawyer that called him, though he did not know its name?

Intuition is not always accurate in directing us to pay attention, or perhaps we do not always know how to read its signals. It is a bodily experience that can be sudden, unmistakable, and emphatic, or it may be gradual, moving slowly into our consciousness, calling us to act or to stop acting in moments when we would otherwise have continued. Intuition shifts our momentum, giving us a message that asks us to pause and re-evaluate our chosen direction.

In intercultural conflict, intuition provides hunches about ways of progressing. It asks that we pay attention to impulses made tangible in our bodies that guide us in different or new directions. Intuition is typically clear and unambiguous, and thus may be welcome when we feel ourselves in the thicket of unresolved intercultural conflicts.

People report different physical indicators of intuition. Some experience heart palpitations, sweaty palms, feelings of uneasiness, trembling legs, or knots in the pits of their stomachs. For others it is less obvious as it slowly seeps into consciousness as a thought or idea that will not disappear. Everyone's body has its own lexicon that can be learned and increasingly respected and understood. The messages conveyed by our bodies help us through conflict by providing valuable clues and creative new ideas about how to proceed.

In the South African township, Venashri had a flash of intuition that told her to stop her efforts aimed at connecting to the locals. Though she was resistant to this message, listening to it helped her achieve a breakthrough. Intuition prompted the Sikh Canadian leader to share a Punjabi metaphor with his Euro-Canadian counterpart. Again, the result was a positive shift in their interaction. In the following example, intuition helped people step through an opening to change their relationships to each other.

It was the afternoon of the third day of a problem-solving workshop in a diverse not-for-profit organization. Everyone was tired, but they had made halting progress in addressing some of the issues that had blocked productivity and positive relations over the past few years. There were still issues unaddressed, and a sense of foreboding about the issue of leadership. The executive director—we'll call him Ross—was a thoughtful man, deeply committed to fostering awareness and initiative in his staff. He was scrupulously honest, sincerely caring, and visionary.

But there were problems. Ross was so focused on honesty that he sometimes confronted his staff in ways that left legacies of profound pain and embarrassment. He was so committed to excellence in the organization that he sometimes lost track of the forest for the trees, spending endless evening and weekend hours dotting "i's" and crossing "t's," and he expected his staff to support him with their presence and dedication. People were stressed, tense, and just plain tired.

The facilitator of the workshop realized that rational analysis of leadership style and preferences would not create a safe and complex conversation.

People needed to share their experiences, but they were afraid for their jobs and reticent to step over invisible lines of allegiance between various employees. Ross himself claimed he wanted to hear what his employees had to say about leadership, but he was quite thin-skinned, and the facilitator knew the process had to be handled delicately. Given the fatigue and nervous anticipation of the group, she wondered how to proceed.

The facilitator had used many of the techniques and skills in her repertoire with the workshop participants. They showed a preference for experiential activities, balanced with reflection and incremental conversation. She had a plan for the leadership segment of the workshop, but something in her gut told her it wouldn't work. Pausing, she left a silence for the intuition she was feeling to develop. "What will help this diverse group move forward in a respectful, open way?" she asked internally. The germ of an answer emerged as a mental picture came into her mind. She saw the senior managers tied up while everyone else circulated around, trying alternately to untie knots, avoid the confusion, and find points of entry.

After a break, the facilitator asked the participants if they would be willing to explore leadership in an unusual way. They gave guarded approval. Then, she did two things. First, she used a building exercise as an icebreaker. Dividing everyone into five teams, she gave each a brown paper bag with building toys inside it. The instructions were to take the toys out of the bag and build the tallest structure they could in five minutes. An air of play and competition followed, and laughter filled the room as one of the towers collapsed just as the five minutes were ending. Participants used this experience to talk for a few minutes about leadership roles and styles as they had played out in their groups. They then generalized these points to develop a shared list of touchstones for effective leadership that included ways everyone could participate in the leadership of the organization.

This activity got the participants communicating, but it did not address the issue of Ross's leadership directly. This issue would have remained the elephant in the room, had the facilitator not followed this building activity with another one. She gave members of the senior leadership team three differently colored balls of yarn and asked them to use them in creating a picture of leadership in their diverse organization. Ross sprang into action. He began to wind his ball of yarn around himself and the other members of the senior leadership team. They followed suit. Soon, there were multiple layers of yarn binding them together, and no one could see where the colors began or ended.

The leaders sat in the middle of the room, literally bound together. Staff members displayed a variety of responses: Some tried to help the leaders get untangled; Some helped continue winding the yarn in even more intricate patterns around the leaders; Others did nothing. In the midst of the laughter and the experience of constriction, the play stopped when Ross suddenly realized how his drive for perfection and focus on details had contributed to an intricate enmeshment. He asked everyone to stop what they were doing, and began to talk, first slowly and then with more excitement, from his place at the center of the yarn maze. His vulnerability in the center of the tangle gave him voice to talk about his vulnerability with the organization's board, and this acknowledgement led to others on the staff responding empathically. They eventually unwound the yarn, and had a conversation remarkable for its depth and insight about leadership structures, roles, and approaches, and what needed to shift to make things work better in the organization.

The facilitator fell silent as the talk among the staff and leaders continued. She reflected on how her intuitive picture of the leaders tied up had led her to design an activity that precipitated the conversation. And she resolved, like Venashri did in the township and the Sikh Canadian did in British Columbia, to attend to her intuition for its seeds of wisdom in moments of confusion.

Should we always attend to intuition? Surely we should, though we need a process of discernment before acting on it. Given our definition of intuition as knowing without knowing how the knowing has arisen, it is worth asking where it comes from. Is intuitive sense colored by our own fatigue or judgment? Does it serve the needs of others, ourselves, or a combination? Is it based in fear, or does it come from a place of hope and respect for self and others? Does it fit with a pattern of caretaking of others, and, if so, is the caretaking in their best interests? Answering questions like these will help us discern whether and when to act on our intuition. As we make choices, we maintain momentum and avoid the potholes on the road to conflict resolution.

✳✳✳

The capacities and skills identified and presented in this chapter assist us with engaging difference and change through a relational approach to intercultural conflict resolution. Some of these capacities and skills come naturally to us, depending on the situation or context. Other times, we may find that we resist them, or need to practice them because they are outside our zones of experience or comfort. As we approach conflicts with spirits of curiosity and openness to expanding our repertoires, we are better able to address rifts and strengthen intercultural relationships.

We are now equipped with important capacities and skills to bridge differences, but we need a mental map into which to fit them. What do we do, and when, and how do the steps fit together? These questions are answered in Chapter Seven as we explore an advisory map for intercultural conflict resolution that serves as a navigational instrument to help choose a path and steer well in our collective journeys.

A Map Through Rough Terrain:
A Guide for Intercultural
Conflict Resolution

Nike Carstarphen

Intercultural conflicts we face may be as simple as misunderstandings about the appropriate time to arrive at someone's house for dinner, or as complex as dehumanization of "others" as in the cases of genocide in Rwanda, Apartheid in South Africa, and ethnic cleansing in Bosnia-Herzegovina. The previous chapters offer many suggestions for helping us understand how we might deal with intercultural differences and conflicts at the interpersonal, group, and community levels.

Chapter Three provides us with starting points for understanding culture and cultural differences. Chapter Four helps us develop cultural fluency in order to navigate these cultural differences. Chapter Five illustrates how culture and conflict are intertwined, constantly shaping and reshaping each other, and provides helpful hints for resolution of conflicts across cultures. Chapter Six equips us with important capacities and skills for attempting to engage people across differences and establish relationships.

In this chapter, we offer a map to help navigate the rough terrain of intercultural conflicts. We use the term "map" instead of framework or model to reflect the idea that there are many ways to reach a desired destination, and many maps that may be helpful. As Chapter Three reminds us, there are many ways of seeing, being, and doing in the world. Similarly, there are many routes to improving relationships and productively addressing our conflicts. This map provides touchstones for the journey, and possible starting points and paths toward resolving intercultural conflicts. Think of this map as a navigational guide for the conflict-weary traveler—one that does not present a specific route, but offers alternative routes with the choice of path left to the traveler. No two intercultural conflict journeys will be the same, but the map can illuminate a potential path through the darkness of conflict.

As we have said before, there is no definitive way to map conflict or culture, though we may develop cultural fluency to help us better deal with conflicts. An advisory map is preferable to no map at all, as guideposts are better than miles of unmarked landscape to the traveler with finite food or water. The map helps address cultural conflicts as it

- *Combats feelings of being lost or overwhelmed in the midst of intense conflict.* When people reflect on intense conflicts in their lives, they often report significant frustration and disorientation. It is useful to know something about the origins and dynamics of conflict, how it relates to identity and meaning-making, and how to design a route through it. With these tools, conflict is less likely to be disorienting or overwhelming.
- *Makes alternatives and choices visible.* Until we are aware of the shape conflicts often take and the turning points that may present themselves, we are moving about in a dark place where pits and traps abound. As we learn from reflecting on our own conflicts and listening to others' challenges, we develop a wider repertoire of choices and ways to act on our choices that respect differences yet further progress.
- *Turns our attention to ways conflict can improve relationships and be mutually capacity-building for those involved.* Conflict, as much as many people avoid it, can be educational, constructive, and generative. It can clear the air, clarify boundaries and feelings, reveal vulnerabilities and convictions about ourselves and others, and teach us life-skills for relating well to others. It is also an important engine of social change. The map shows how culturally fluent approaches to conflict can help turn the tide from enmity to inquiry to amity.
- *Points those in conflict to hopefulness and creativity as resources.* It is not enough to want things to be better when in conflict. A positive attitude and expectations, and feelings of efficacy are important to successfully addressing it. With hopefulness, creativity is unleashed, and resourcefulness and resilience make the field of possibilities bigger.

Even as we entertain multiple levels, it is not possible to give a comprehensive list of ways through conflict. As Chapter Two reveals, because cultural factors influencing identity and meaning-making are so complex, bridging intercultural conflict is challenging. The map helps by identifying the shapes conflict can take and by helping us design and choose a way toward resolution. It is not prescriptive, since it leaves specific steps in addressing conflicts to be devised by the people involved in the conflict and their allies. Neither is it purely elicitive, since it offers a series of guideposts to inspire and shape ideas about moving forward.

✳✳✳

Before reading about the map, imagine you are involved in the following conflict at work. As you read the story, ask yourself how you would react to what is unfolding, what you would be feeling and thinking, and what you would do to bridge the differences.

The conflict is set in Transworld Corporation, an engineering firm that employs over one hundred people. The organization is experiencing difficulties among its staff that are having a negative impact on productivity and profits. Morale is low and it is clear that something needs to be done to stem negative spirals of interaction in the company. The executive director hires a conflict resolution consultant to help identify and resolve internal problems.

The consultant knows that it is important to understand the issues from everyone's point of view before proposing any action, so she interviews people at all levels of the organization. Many of the same themes emerge: employees, including management, say that they want better communication among units, greater input into decision-making, improved relationships, greater advancement opportunities, and more attention to diversity issues in the organization. In consultation with the executive director, the consultant assembles a diverse task-force of twelve people to help address the problems at Transworld. The job of the task-force is to develop recommendations for how the organization can improve, boosting employee morale, productivity, and—ultimately—the bottom line. The consultant will facilitate the task-force, which is to meet twice a month for six months.

Members of the task-force are from different units and levels in the organization, but they quickly polarize into two groups. One informal group (Alpha) includes two Africans, two African Americans, and two Latin

Americans. The other self-selected group (Omega) has four European Americans, one Japanese American, and one African American. After listening to the conflict between these groups, it becomes clear to the consultant that they are a microcosm of the organization. They seem to be functioning on completely different wavelengths. Each group sees the other as obstructing the progress of the task-force, and both are becoming increasingly frustrated with each other. The consultant attempts to facilitate constructive discussion, but is not successful in helping them bridge these differences. She recognizes that the problems arise from divergent ways of understanding roles, structures, and relationships within the organization.

The Alpha group thinks that the executive director, as leader of the firm, should be on the task-force so that everyone knows he is serious about the work of the task-force. His absence is a source of mistrust. Their insistence is problematic because many members of this group already distrust the executive director's intentions. They believe his participation would help build trust: it would be an important symbolic step toward repairing damaged relationships and restoring harmony in the organization. They also feel the need to build trust and relationships with members of the Omega group in order to accomplish the tasks assigned to them.

Members of the Alpha group see the task-force as an opportunity to develop a shared vision of what the organization should be like, especially addressing roles and relationships among people. They believe that there are serious structural problems that inhibit teamwork within and across departments. This group's approach to problem solving reflects a polychronic, synchronous sense of time, in which events are seen as interlocking and simultaneous; there are co-dependent and multiple origins of phenomena, and a belief in the recurring or cyclical nature of events through time. They believe that the task-force needs to consider the history of the organization and the turning points when employee relations began to grow sour. Only from this deep understanding of the past can current problems be understood, and a vision developed and implemented for the future. The Alphas approach the problems holistically, taking into account the context, history, and the relationships among people. Their emphasis on relationships is common among people from communitarian-oriented, high-context cultures, as described in Chapter Three.

Omega group members see things quite differently. Omegas are relieved that the executive director is not on the task-force because they can talk more openly. The executive director's absence signals his willingness to delegate responsibility, thereby showing trust and confidence in the task-force members' competence. They feel confident that their recommendations will be taken seriously.

The Omegas' approach to problem-solving draws on a sequential sense of time and reflects the analytic, rational, factual-inductive approach common in dominant U.S. North American culture and individualistic-oriented, low-context settings. They are task-oriented and prefer to develop systematic recommendations and action plans for each of the identified problem areas. Omegas compartmentalize the problems according to function, including decision-making processes, communication protocols, and so on. They are confident that through fine-tuning, changes can be made within the existing structure of the organization. The best approach is to analyze each problem area in detail, identify causes of conflicts, develop solutions, and make recommendations for improvement. Members of this group believe that doing this will improve employee relationships, satisfaction, and productivity, and enhance organizational functioning. By solving present problems, they will be ensuring future success.

Table 7.1 summarizes the differences between the Alpha and Omega groups' problem analysis and problem-solving approaches.

What would you do if you were the consultant trying to bridge the differences between these two groups? What would you do if you were on the task-force? With which side might you find resonance? Given your preferences, how would you help address the conflict in a way that takes both sides' perspectives and values into account?

✳✳✳

The following map, Figure 7.2, offers a way of understanding and navigating intercultural conflicts like this one. Of course, there is no easy formula for what to do. Each situation and group of people is too different to offer a recipe. Taken together with the previous chapters, the map guides us through some important elements of intercultural conflict resolution and poses questions to deepen our insights. The map will help us envision different ways through intercultural conflict, whether we are in the midst of it or trying to help others. As we explore the map, we will use Transworld Corporation and other examples to illustrate its applications.

The map is centered in a relational view of conflict. It is no use separating people from problems, because you need the people to get a wise solution. By

Table 7.1
Transworld Organizational Conflict

	Alpha group	Omega group
People	Include director to build trust and relationships; and representatives from all levels and departments	Include representatives from all levels and departments. Top leader not necessary on task-force
	Shared responsibilities. Task-force works with director to develop vision and recommendations	Delegated responsibilities. Task-force works independently to develop recommendations
	Shared decision-making	Director makes decisions with input from subordinates
	Build trust and relationships with the Omega group	Focus on problem areas to indirectly foster better relationships
Purpose	Develop shared vision and recommendations to achieve vision	Identify problems, recommend solutions
	Relationship building in order to be able to work together and achieve tasks	Task-focused, through which relationships will be built by working together
Perceived Problem	Poor leadership, damaged relationships, distrust	Fine-tuning of organizational processes — change within existing structure
	Structural flaws — need to change organizational structure	
Process	Past — present — future are intertwined; synchronous time	Present — future focus; sequential time
	Holistic approach	Analytical approach

creating ways to understand and address personal, cultural, and social norms and expectations, the map shows ways to re-imagine troubled relationships. Depicted as circles to symbolize its continuous, nonlinear nature, the map includes four broad parts: preparation, discovery, creation, and rejuvenation.

Preparation involves understanding the webs of relationships and considering ways of bringing people together across differences. Discovery deepens this inquiry as we come to see how past, present, and future leave their traces on our relationships. Creating involves coming together to strengthen relationships and invent options for constructive problem-solving. Rejuvenation includes nurturing and sustaining relationships through ongoing constructive engagement. At the center of the circle is relationship—brilliant technical or analytic approaches are doomed to fail without the creative engagement of people to discern a way through conflict.

There are multiple entry points into the circles depending on the context and people involved. All stages interact together and form a dynamic, cyclical process. People may go through this process together, face-to-face and directly, or they may be engaged in indirect communication or even separate, linked processes. Even when people are not in the same room, relational considerations remain at the center of the map.

With relationship at the center, we prepare, discover, create, and rejuvenate as we address differences. People prepare by opening their hearts and minds to the journey, if not each other. Is there a thin crack through which those involved might peer to imagine less painful relationships? Often, the process starts with such a crack, and the process of engagement creates more space for the light to enter. As the process continues, discovery enlivens us—we explore

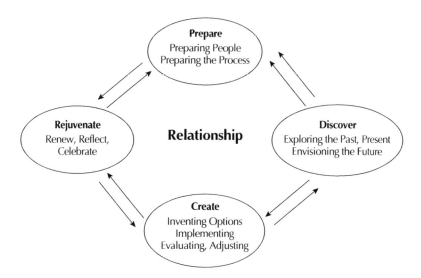

Figure 7.2 Advisory Map for Intercultural Conflict Resolution

our past in ways that don't keep us stuck and our futures in ways that bring hope. We create new relationships and shifts in negative histories as we invent new ways to be together. Evaluating our efforts at change helps us make adjustments as we go along. We build relational bridges in our hearts and minds that transform our behaviors and relationships. We remember to pause, renewing our energy and revisiting our vision, to keep rejuvenated and spirited as we proceed.

Relationship at the Center

When we hold relationship at the center of our map, it reminds us that we are ultimately interdependent. Our relationships are carriers for our identities, passions, and meanings. Whether it is our conflict or we are helping others, we are always part of a relational system. With relationship at the center of the map, we are also reminded us that conflict resolution across cultures is most successful when we watch for connections with others, holding them in our hearts and minds. When we are threatened, it is difficult to think of the "other" as a human relation, as precious and infinite as ourselves, yet it is never more important. When relationships are scarred by oppression, violence, and other injustices, it is very hard to keep connection in our awareness. Yet distance and separation will only lead to more of the same; relational awareness keeps the possibilities for coexistence alive without compromising rights or values.

Intercultural conflict resolution works best when individuals or groups *recognize* their interdependence. As an old professor of mine often said, "The whole world needs the whole world." No matter how much people in conflict may resist this understanding, we are all interdependent to some degree. It is common in conflicts for people from different sides to see themselves as completely separate. They may confuse separateness or distinctness with independence when it is actually their interdependence that keeps them engaged in relationship, whether harmonious or conflictual. The tendency to ignore interdependence is exacerbated when people or groups are from different cultures with little reciprocal understanding. It arises from a belief that we don't need others and don't need to concern ourselves about the lives of those near or far who are not part of our group. This sense of separation is becoming harder to maintain in the face of modernization, globalization, and media exposure. A positive outcome of this change may be that we see ways to reach out across the globe, realizing that when we ignore, denigrate or hurt others, we ultimately hurt ourselves. The shared awareness of our interconnectedness makes social healing and positive change possible.

Having relationship in the center of the circle helps us be mindful of the importance of connection for achieving positive outcomes. This dynamic is clearly illustrated in a series of interviews I conducted with two Jewish-Palestinian dialogue groups in California. The first of these groups, the Jewish-Palestinian Living Room Dialogue Group, has about thirty active members who have met for over ten years. The second group, inspired by the first, has about fifteen active members and has met for over five years. In both groups, the Palestinian and Jewish members have developed deep friendships and engaged in action-oriented projects to improve the daily lives of Israelis and Palestinians and to foster peace and reconciliation between the two groups in the United States and the Middle East. These brave people, who dare to engage in dialogue despite criticism from their peers, have underlined their fundamental belief that "We are in this [Israeli/Palestinian conflict] together and we must find a way out together." When they encounter difficulties or feel frustration and anger, they draw strength from their touchstone of connection and continue to dialogue and support each other rather than retreat into separateness.

People do not always begin resolving conflict with awareness of connection in their hearts. In the Jewish-Palestinian dialogues, many of the participants came to the dialogue with clear "us versus them" perspectives. For these participants, the idea of connection developed through the dialogue; recognizing their interconnected relationship was a turning point for many. As they built relationships, awareness of their cultural and historical commonalities replaced their sense of separation. They also learned more about differences between them through sharing hopes, dreams, and fears. Over time, they began to see each other as complex and precious people, people with whom they could empathize, rather than as enemies. These shifts in hearts and minds helped them embrace their connections as a foundation for solving problems. As their relationships were nurtured and celebrated by the participants and leaders, their connections became anchors to help them stay focused and united.

A sense of connection was initially lacking in the Transworld Corporation. The consultant falsely assumed that the task-force members already had a sense of connection based on their shared history at Transworld and their common desires to improve the organization. Therefore, she paid insufficient attention to developing a sense of relationship among task-force members at the start of the process. There was an immediate push by the consultant supported by Omega group members to focus on problem-solving and developing recommendations. It was easy for the consultant to identify more with the Omegas, whose views were closer to her own. When difficulties emerged in the overall group, there was no vision of connection to help anchor them. Instead, the group degenerated into two rival camps.

Realizing her mistake, the consultant then focused on developing a sense of connection. She did this mainly by having each of the members describe their reasons for participating in the task-force, their general hopes for what they wanted to achieve, and the connections they saw between their departments and individual positions. She then emphasized the commonalities in their reasons and goals, and pointed out the interdependence between people and departments. This discussion helped create the beginning of a relational foundation. The consultant also began watching for the task-force members to show signs of viewing themselves as having overlapping identities, shared concerns, and goals, and then reinforced these commonalities. A sense of connection ultimately arises from within groups, but it can also be nurtured by outsiders as in the case of this consultant and the Alphas and Omegas.

Acknowledging connection may require more strength and courage than might be anticipated. It can be difficult and requires much work, but once the journey is undertaken, realizing connection can be therapeutic. For example, in conflict situations where there are clear victims—such as during Apartheid in South Africa—it might be extremely difficult for victims to conceive of a connection with their oppressors and victimizers, or for those in power to conceive of a connection with those they see as inferior or dangerous. Yet even in South Africa, a sense of connection that included all groups had to be conceived and embraced before reconciliation among all the groups became possible. This sense of connection was fostered by innumerable individuals and groups within South Africa before Apartheid ended and was further embodied in the post-Apartheid Truth and Reconciliation Commission.

The idea of connection is essential to bridging intercultural differences and boosting resilience. Keeping relationship at the center of our hearts and minds will serve as a constant reminder of the purpose of engagement.

Prepare: People and Process

Imagine yourself going to an unfamiliar country. What would you do to prepare for the trip? Whatever preparations you make, your journey will likely be filled with unexpected twists and turns. The map encourages us to prepare for the journey of resolving intercultural conflict in order to better engage the obstacles and opportunities that await us.

There are two important aspects to preparation: the *people* in the conflict and the *process*. Preparing the people includes encouraging open hearts and minds to contribute to a positive atmosphere for engagement. Preparing the process means assessing the situation, identifying who needs to be a part of the journey and their cultural lenses, and developing a range of approaches that will help bridge differences.

Preparation may be formal or informal; it may be incremental or achieved by leaps and bounds. It may include detailed planning and anticipating spontaneous changes. Preparation may be subtle and indirect based on cultural patterns, personal preferences, and previous experiences; or, we might consciously prepare to deal with differences. Preparation may be done by those involved in the conflict, with or without help from someone external to the conflict.

To prepare does not mean we will *be* prepared. Preparation is ongoing throughout our journey. However, as we considered ways to build cultural fluency in Chapter Four, we found we can *anticipate* a range of possible scenarios of how interactions may unfold and where they may take us. We cannot know or control what will actually happen because change and dynamism are constant parts of human interaction. Preparation is about getting as ready as possible for the unexpected, attuning ourselves to a range of cultural lenses, and nurturing a spirit of inquiry.

Prepare the People

If building connection is the route to intercultural conflict resolution, then people are central to this process, as illustrated by relationship situated at the center of our map. When we are *open*, we expand our creative energy. Our relationships offer us unlimited potential to continually invent new ways to acknowledge and value each other as we pursue individual and collective needs and aspirations. What can we do to nurture open minds and hearts in order to create a positive atmosphere for bridging differences? While these efforts are part of an ongoing process, there are several things we can do. The first and easiest place to start is with ourselves.

Open Our Minds and Hearts. Imagine the vast possibilities that emerge when we can free our hearts and minds to develop positive attitudes and expectations about human challenges and people. In order to do that, we need to know ourselves and how we interpret and experience the world. We have to understand what shapes our worldview, and be able to recognize where and how our perspectives can be expanded. Chapter Four emphasized that cultural fluency is centered in self-awareness and Chapter Six reminded us that open-mindedness can be developed through our capacity for flexibility. Flexibility allows us to remain open to difference and suspend judgment as we encounter others. Through Lebo's story related in Chapter Six, we learned that suspending judgment does not entail abandoning our beliefs or values, but creating a space for curiosity within ourselves and in our relationships. The skills of interrupting patterns and sitting with discomfort, described in the previous chapter, assist in opening our hearts and minds to difference.

Multiple perspectives become more visible when we are open-minded and ready to learn with each other. Taking time to reflect on your perspectives and possible views of others expands open-mindedness and flexibility. It is also important to survey your full range of emotions related to the conflict situation. It is easy to push negative or unpleasant emotions aside because they bring discomfort. At the same time, we screen out positive feelings for the "other," because empathy makes a poor friend for enmity. Welcoming feelings is easier once we realize that emotions are nothing more than internal prompts that tell us that everything is okay or something needs to change. We may not be completely aware of the full range of our emotions and what we have screened out, but we can learn more as we do some inner exploration. We accept that others in the conflict also have a full range of emotions and feelings.

Going back to Lebo's story from the previous chapter, if she had been open-minded and in touch with her worldviews and feelings about marriage and relationships, she would have had a more constructive exchange with the mother in the polygamous marriage.

Create a Positive Atmosphere. Have you ever had days where everything seemed to go wrong and you wished you could go back to bed and start all over again, or days where everything seemed to go smoothly? It seemed that whatever happened the moment you awoke set the tone for the rest of the day. The same dynamic can happen when we try to resolve differences. How we approach others will set the tone for the interaction. Creating a positive climate for the process helps relieve some of the inevitable anxiety that accompanies confronting our differences. It expands the positive potential of coming together by encouraging connection, openness, cooperation, creativity, and flexibility that contribute to positive expectations and deepening relationships.

There are many approaches available to set a positive tone that awakens people to the benefits of working together to create positive outcomes. How we engage in these efforts will depend on the situation and the different cultural starting points of those involved. A variety of helpful approaches and skills are outlined in Chapter Six.

We can encourage an atmosphere of constructive engagement through using creative approaches. Creative approaches help people step out of well-worn perceptions to see things from a fresh perspective. Facilitators from the Network for Life and Choice (a pro-life/pro-choice dialogue group formerly with the peace-building organization Search for Common Ground in Washington, D.C.) used the symbol of overlapping circles to open their dialogue process on abortion. This symbol (Figure 7.3) illustrates that all groups in conflict are interconnected and have both different and overlapping concerns, values, beliefs, experiences, and dreams. This symbol of common ground helped put participants into a positive frame of mind. It turned their attention to understanding their real differences while building a relationship based on their commonalities. It grounded their ongoing dialogues in ways that led to joint action projects. Through dialogue, pro-life and pro-choice advocates came together to develop joint initiatives on adoption and prevention of teen pregnancy, among other projects.

Nonverbal forms of communication and the physical setting can also help set a positive tone. The location of meetings is important, as I learned one summer when I mediated between two rival gangs that had been fighting

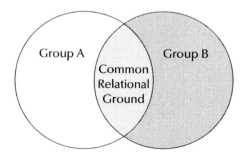

Figure 7.3 Common Ground Symbol

each other for many years. We took five leaders from each side for a weekend retreat in the woods to participate in experiential team-building activities and build relationships through face-to-face dialogue. The retreat center—graced with colorful trees, an inviting lake, and peaceful surroundings—helped encourage constructive and creative interactions. Circles and side-by-side seating reinforced that no one was more important than the other and downplayed an adversarial dynamic. Chairs without tables reduced the sense of a physical separation and emphasized joint vulnerability. Hospitality—food, drinks, and creature comforts—evoked the symbolic "breaking bread" or "sharing from a common bowl," common forms of relationship building in most cultures.

Music, dancing, singing, and other rituals may also open hearts and bring people together. In Chapter Six, we learned of the power of rituals like these through Jabu's experience. Participation in the Zulu family ritual created a shift for Jabu, and bonded him to his family. Similarly, in one of the Jewish-Palestinian dialogue groups mentioned earlier, the group opened their dialogue process with Jewish, Muslim, and Christian prayers for peace and unity. The prayers brought tears to their eyes because they were so pleased to be learning and sharing meaningful rituals with each other. In the gang mediation, I opened the dialogue with a ritual burning of incense to symbolize cleansing negative energies and hostility to help us begin on a positive note. As some of the tension dissolved in the smoke and drifted out the window, the young men became more relaxed and open. They embraced the symbolism of the ritual and volunteered to lead it at subsequent meetings until they successfully resolved their conflict. These rituals all contributed to transforming relationships so that problems could be constructively addressed.

Of course, saying prayers or burning incense is not appropriate in every conflict. It is important to open processes in positive ways that fit specific situations. Sometimes, it is possible to ask people what might be meaningful to them that could be transferred into the new setting. Ideally, all the people involved in the conflict work together to identify ways of opening everyone's hearts and minds, whether informally or more formally. In formal settings, trusted leaders or facilitators can help identify shared symbols or rituals for coming together. For example, during the third meeting at Transworld Corporation, the consultant used the common ground symbol of overlapping circles to emphasize shared goals to the two groups. This symbol helped set a more positive tone that continued throughout the meeting.

Prepare the Process

Preparing the process includes assessing conflict dynamics, identifying who needs to be involved, and developing process options for bridging differences. As was the case at Transworld Corporation, the challenge in intercultural conflicts is that people from different cultures may have very different perspectives on these issues.

Assessing the Situation. Assessing the situation is an ongoing process, but it should begin early to improve understanding of conflict dynamics and allow weighing of options for intervention. We may start with meditation to focus and open ourselves to insight as taught in diverse spiritual traditions. Taking the time to rest, reflect, and renew our energies allows us the time and space to clear our heads and hearts to receive new perspectives.

We can reflect on what we already know about the conflict, asking questions like these of ourselves and, whenever possible, of others: What types of cultural differences may be influencing the people and the situation? How are people experiencing what is happening? What is driving people and what do they want? How are people dealing with differences? What approaches might help now? This reflection will not necessarily yield definitive answers, but it will help with preparation. Ideally, everyone involved in the conflict will have the opportunity to assess the situation and work together on the best approach to address differences.

We can also seek guidance from others—friends, family, colleagues, supervisors, elders, spirits, or ancestors. People familiar with the cultural dynamics or histories of those involved can serve as cultural informants to help explain and interpret the situation and offer advice on how to proceed.

As we know, Transworld Corporation hired a consultant to assist in resolving tensions between employees. What could the consultant have done to assist people in assessing the situation? She could have set aside some meditative time early on in a joint session. Employees could have been given questions like those mentioned earlier and asked to take some quiet time to reflect on them. Later, she could have facilitated a discussion to elicit shared and individual perspectives of the situation and ideas for addressing it.

Identifying Who Is Involved. Identifying who is involved in a conflict seems like such a simple undertaking. However, as the Alphas and Omegas at Transworld Corporation found, answers to this question are influenced by cultural understandings. The Alphas wanted the executive director on the task-force and the Omegas did not. The consultant asked each group to explain their reasons and assumptions, and then asked them to come up with possible solutions. The result was that the task-force asked the executive director to come to the next meeting to show his support for their work. They also asked him to come for the first half hour of several subsequent meetings so they could give him updates, ask him questions and clarify issues, and get his feedback. This new approach satisfied both the Alphas and Omegas.

Another story illustrates different conceptions of who should be included in resolving a conflict. I was asked to mediate a conflict between two teenagers, Joe and Ricky, who had had a fight after school. Joe is Anglo-American and his family has lived in the United States for many generations. Ricky and his family emigrated to the United States from Guatemala three years earlier. The North American mediation model I was taught, rooted in individualist cultural assumptions, pointed to Ricky and Joe as parties to the mediation. They were the ones who had had the fight, so they were the ones who had to resolve the conflict. Joe and his parents agreed to this model since its underlying assumptions seemed reasonable to them. Ricky was also willing to use this approach, but Ricky's parents and grandparents objected. From their communitarian starting point, they needed to be part of the process. The fight affected their whole family and it was their responsibility as elders to ensure a fair and proper resolution, so they insisted that they be involved in the mediation.

I was faced with a dilemma. From the perspective of the North-American mediation model, the mediation would have felt unbalanced in favor of Ricky had the mediation included Ricky's family members but not Joe's. I felt the need for balance, so I talked with both families to explore possible options. We finally agreed that only Ricky's grandmother would participate. She would attend the mediation as an observer and only get involved if she thought the process or agreement being reached by the boys was objectionable in some way. Joe and his parents agreed to the arrangement after I explained to them Ricky's family's perspectives.

The mediation went ahead with Joe, Ricky, and Ricky's grandmother. The boys resolved their conflict while the grandmother stayed silent. Everyone was satisfied with the outcome and their role. I learned two lessons from this experience. First, never take anything for granted in trying to resolve a conflict, especially when cultural dynamics are involved. Second, be aware of and explore underlying assumptions and their cultural roots. Discoveries can help in designing a process that fits for everyone.

Developing Approaches to Deal With Differences. In addition to reflecting on what the conflict is about and who is part of the conflict and its resolution, we must think about the best way to approach the situation. In the example above, a North American mediation model was used to deal with Joe and Ricky's fight, but there were other options. Every culture has developed its own norms and ways of dealing with conflict and these approaches can vary greatly. The discussion of cultural starting points in Chapter Three provides us with clues as to some of the possible cultural preferences people may have for dealing with conflicts. The challenge is to find an approach that is comfortable for everyone.

How are approaches to conflict influenced by cultural norms? I posed this question to an Indonesian friend named Rehan. We compared stories of how conflicts between friends are resolved. I told the story of my two friends, Lisa and Kathy, who are both European Americans. One day Lisa came to me in distress. She felt betrayed and extremely angry with Kathy about something Kathy had done and asked for my advice. We both agreed that she should talk with Kathy directly about what happened. Lisa approached Kathy, expressed her distress, and they talked and resolved their differences. They remain friends to this day.

I explained to Rehan that from Lisa's and my individualistic starting points, our expectation was that Lisa needed to talk explicitly with Kathy face-to-face about the situation so they could work together to resolve it. Not confronting the person directly might be interpreted as avoiding the conflict. Talking to others about the conflict, but not the person involved, could be interpreted as "back-stabbing" or spreading rumors. Both accusations are to be avoided. Even though people in conflict may ask other people for advice and assistance, it is still expected that the individuals involved in the conflict will deal with their conflict directly. That is the only way they will be able to understand the situation, resolve differences, build relationship, and know that the conflict is truly resolved. This expectation would be the same between coworkers, employers-employees, family members, groups, and so on.

Rehan's story was completely different from mine. He described a conflict between two of his friends named Sahn and Rey. One Saturday the three friends went out together. Rehan sensed there was tension from Sahn toward Rey. As a trusted friend of both men, Rehan knew it was his responsibility to play the intermediary, determine if there was a problem, and, if so, to help resolve it. The next day Rehan visited Sahn at his home. Rehan hinted that Sahn seemed distracted the previous day. Sahn admitted that he was angry about something Rey had said to him. They talked about what happened until Rehan felt he had reached an understanding about the situation.

Then Rehan visited Rey. Rehan hinted to Rey that Sahn did not seem himself on Saturday. Rey agreed and said that Sahn had seemed upset with him, but he didn't know why. Rehan gently told Rey why Sahn was upset. Rey explained what he had meant to say and expressed regret for upsetting Sahn. Rehan talked again with Sahn and expressed what Rey had meant and that he felt bad about upsetting Sahn. Sahn seemed relieved to hear about Rey's explanation and regret.

The conflict was almost resolved. The next weekend, Rehan invited a group of friends to his home for a party, including Sahn and Rey. They shared food, drinks, and humorous stories. Eventually, Sahn and Rey laughed together at someone's joke and the tension between them melted away. At that point, Rehan, Sahn, and Rey knew their relationship was healed.

Rehan's story reflects the communitarian values of group harmony and face-saving. To discuss a conflict openly and face-to-face would signal disharmony and may cause people to lose face, which would further jeopardize group harmony. Therefore, conflicts are dealt with indirectly, often through an intermediary. Rehan knew that as a trusted friend of Sahn and Rey, it was his responsibility to intervene once he noticed there might be a problem. In other situations, an elder or someone with higher status might intervene. The party Rehan gave for a group of friends created an environment in which Sahn and Rey could interact in a safe and fun setting and bring closure to their conflict. By laughing together, Sahn and Rey signaled that everything was okay; group harmony was preserved. There was no need to say or do anything directly to discuss the conflict or acknowledge its resolution.

While my story and Rehan's story are very different, the result was the same—both sets of friends resolved their differences and remained friends. How could the conflict have been resolved if it had been between my friend Lisa and Rehan's friend Rey, given that they would have very different expectations about conflict resolution? The more Lisa tried to directly confront Rey about what he had said, the more Rey might have avoided the issue, interpreting her behavior as inappropriate and disrespectful. He might resist talking with Lisa about the situation, or try to get outside help from a go-between. If Rey resisted talking with Lisa or involved other people, she might interpret his behavior as cowardly or uncaring. Lisa might become even more upset. The result of their clashing approaches to dealing with the situation might be a worse conflict than was created by the initial event. How could their conflict be addressed given their different cultural starting points?

There are no simple formulas for what to do. Several options are available, each of which requires open-mindedness, flexibility, and creativity. For example, each might begin with their own approach, but if they met resistance, they would need to try another approach. If either of them understood the other's cultural preferences, she or he could try to adapt to the other's preferred approach. They could get together and acknowledge the importance of their friendship, discussing directly or indirectly how it could be handled. They could try to explain their own cultural assumptions about what to do and invite or wait for the other to do the same. They could ask for advice from someone familiar with their friend's culture about how to proceed. They could seek the help of an intermediary. To make face-to-face discussion more indirect, Lisa might frame an exchange as a "what-if" scenario. As discussed in Chapter Six, they could use metaphors, analogies, stories, and other forms of indirect communication to communicate as the Sikh leader and his Euro-Canadian counterpart did. Many options might work for Lisa and Rey's intercultural conflict depending on the issue and their levels of acculturation, including:

- using their preferred approach and hoping the other will adapt;
- adjusting to the other's preferred approach;
- getting together and devising a new approach, directly or indirectly;
- explaining cultural assumptions and inviting the other to do the same;
- seeking advice from someone familiar with the other person and his or her culture;
- involving an intermediary; or
- talking indirectly, in terms of "what-if" scenarios or using metaphors and stories.

✳✳✳

As we can see from these options, there are many possible approaches to addressing intercultural conflicts. These choices may not be appropriate for people in all situations. There is no easy formula for what to do, and the important thing is to realize multiple options. The following questions will help discern which approach to use:

- What or how much do you know and understand about the other's preferred approach for dealing with differences? How do these preferences influence your current conflict?

- ▨ What do you still need or want to know and how can you learn about it? Can you talk directly with people to discover this? Is there someone else you could ask? What can you learn through observation? Are there nonverbal signals or contextual cues that provide help in understanding? What other resources are available to you?

- ▨ If you know the other has a different way of approaching things, how comfortable are you with adjusting to their approach? In what ways would this feel comfortable or uncomfortable? Can you overcome your discomfort and try their approach?

- ▨ Are there ways to perhaps use both of your approaches, or parts of both approaches? Can someone help intervene, directly or indirectly, to help you design an approach that would feel comfortable for everyone?

Preparation helps reveal more choices and options in conflict. It gives a preliminary understanding of what might be happening, a sense of who needs to be involved, and a possible range of approaches. Preparation is an ongoing part of discovery, the focus of the next section.

Discover: Explore and Envision

At the heart of intercultural conflict resolution is relationship: a mutual discovery process through which we learn about others and ourselves, including differences, commonalities, and ways we can build our relationship. Through engagement, we humanize each other and develop mutual understanding and empathy. Positive turning points in relationships are more likely for those who engage with a spirit of inquiry, which facilitates discovery.

In the earlier chapters, we have explored many layers of culture, recognizing that what we see on the surface is only the beginning. It is at the deeper levels that the intersections of culture and conflict can be understood. As we seek intercultural understanding, we discover each other, approaching deeper awareness of concerns, needs, and dreams. To aid us in the discovery process, we *explore* past and present relationships in context and *envision* desired futures to meet people's needs and aspirations.

The discovery process is essentially one of reflection and learning that roots us in past and present explorations juxtaposed with visions of the future. Together, people reflect on what the situation was historically and what it is like right now. In intercultural conflict, this exploration is unlikely to be smooth or even, as those involved will certainly have their own interpretation of the conflict's history and its progression into the present. Rather than trying to develop a neat, linear, and organized timeline, the objective is to give people in conflict the opportunity to voice their perspectives, feelings, thoughts, and memories. This extra time allows people to discover the "other," their experiences, worldviews, and ultimately their connectedness. Similarly, envisioning the future together allows people in conflict to gradually move away from their divided histories and lives to the task of discovering and creating a shared future.

Exploring the Past-Present

How can we explore the past and present to better understand the dynamics of shared histories? We want to understand the past and present in context to give us a glimpse of how to move forward. These questions may help:

- What does the conflict seem to be about?
- What has happened and what is now happening?
- Who has been and who is now involved in the situation?
- What are the dynamics of relationships of the people involved (e.g., family, coworkers, religious or ethnic groups living in the same community or country)? Are these relationships equal or unequal in terms of power and resources?
- What are the different cultural starting points and ways of thinking, being, and doing that are manifest in this situation?
- How are people and groups affected by what has happened or is happening?

Exploring these questions, we begin to understand peoples' thoughts and actions in context. We begin uncovering cultural assumptions and meanings people bring to conflict, both unfamiliar and familiar. We examine cultural differences and commonalities related to our conflict, asking "Why do these differences and commonalities exist and why do they matter?" We explore and create alternative meanings for the differences themselves.

At the heart of the exploration and discovery process is *expressive capacity*. This capacity was described in Chapter Four as the ability to express deeply held assumptions and meaning-making processes in ways that are understandable to others. It is a core capacity for cultural fluency. There are many cultural forms of expressing ourselves that span spectrums from direct to indirect communication and from low-context to high-context communication. Every culture exhibits a variety of approaches that vary with context, but may emphasize some more than others. Lessons learned at Transworld Corporation show us that through dialogue, we can discover approaches that will work for everyone by beginning with the past and working into the present.

At Transworld Corporation, the consultant directly and explicitly explored underlying assumptions of the terms and metaphors used by Alphas and Omegas. For example, she asked the Alpha and Omega groups to explain what they meant by communication problems. They assumed that everyone meant the same thing when using the term *communication* and that the problems were obvious. The consultant asked them to explain what they meant and to give examples. The responses were astonishingly different. Omegas generally used the term *communication* to refer to *who got what information and when*—"He doesn't give me the information I need to do my work. I often have to ask him for it. We need to develop a systematic way to share information in a timely manner." Alphas tended to focus on *how communication was shared* and the relational aspect of communication— "Whenever Phil, our department head, calls a meeting he just sends everyone a memo. Why can't he just come to my office and tell me? There are only twenty of us and his office is near mine. He never stops by to talk." By exploring these different meanings, the task-force members learned more about each other's cultural and personal expectations and were able to identify a more inclusive picture of the communication problems in the organization.

A tool for discovery that is gaining popularity among those who resolve international conflict is to take the adversaries on a "walk through history," as popularized by Joseph Montville (1993), a retired United States career diplomat now working for a think tank in Washington, D.C. The activity usually involves having each party separately draw a historical time-line of all events important to the history of their conflict. After each group draws their time-line or map, they each share the time-lines with the other group. Usually, the groups have very different events on their time-line and different interpretations of the same events. Their subsequent dialogue about events and interpretations—conducted with a spirit of inquiry—enhances their ability to see the world through the other's eyes and develop empathy.

A facilitator who used the "walk through history" with a group of twenty Greek and Turkish Cypriot youth leaders asked the participants to silently view the other side's map and then sit down. She broke the silence by asking the participants to describe what they noticed about the maps and how they were feeling. One young woman stood up and in a profoundly aggrieved voice said, "They lied to us. All our lives, our teachers, our parents, our media, they all lied to us! They never told us there was another way of looking at these events." This profound moment for the young woman and many people in the group opened a deep conversation about their respective histories and the influence of cultural perspectives in their lives. The activity and dialogue marked a turning point in their relationships.

A very creative use of a "walk through history" happened in the city of Richmond, Virginia, the heart of the confederacy during the Civil War. A diverse group of people, organizations, and politicians joined to help city residents deal with the painful legacies of racism to heal wounds and further reconciliation. They sponsored a citywide event including a week-long conference and a "walk through Richmond." The organizers had identified key events and places in the city's history that were important to different cultural groups. Volunteers re-enacted many historic events in period costumes, including slave auctions, Henry Adams' fiery "Give me liberty or give me death" speech calling for freedom from British rule, and an impassioned monologue by an enslaved mother who, after having eight children sold into slavery, killed her ninth baby to rescue him from the same terrible fate. Hundreds of people walked the day-long route together. Those interviewed said they learned history they'd never heard of, felt a new sense of understanding, empathy, and connection with other cultural groups, and felt forever changed by the emotional experience.

Additional tools to support discovery are storytelling, metaphor, and ritual. Chapter Six explores the usefulness of these ways of bringing people together across differences.

Exploring our past and present can help foster understanding and empathy. Sometimes, acknowledgements, apologies, forgiveness, and trust-building activities accompany this discovery process. They helps us let go of anger, resentment, and animosity, and heal damaged relationships. The more mutual and reciprocal the discovery process, the more opportunities we have for transforming relationships.

On a more cautious note, it is also true that walks through history and ways of pursuing discovery can stimulate both positive and negative feelings, reactions, and results. For example, instead of empathy toward someone's painful story, a listener may be angered or "blame the victim" for what happened. In some of the early discussions within the Jewish-Palestinian dialogue groups described earlier, the "other's" stories did not automatically elicit empathy. Some of the listeners tried to explain away or justify the events the storyteller found so hurtful. This minimization of their suffering led to storytellers feeling angry.

Finally, the facilitator intervened and encouraged the participants to shift their focus of attention. Rather than looking for points of disagreement, he asked them to look for germs of truth and common ground. He asked people to listen, reflect on what they heard, and try to understand and feel what the storyteller was describing. He even suggested imagining they were the storyteller. When participants strayed from a spirit of inquiry, the facilitator gently interrupted and redirected them. As a result, the participants were better able to suspend judgment, listen with an open heart and mind, and focus on the other's story. This created a space in which the listeners were moved by what they heard rather than being defensive. Their hearts were touched rather than closed to the suffering of the other. Through these experiences, empathy developed, feelings of connection increased, and participants experienced a positive shift in their relationships. Facilitators need to continually assess the effects and effectiveness of their approaches, and make changes or stop as appropriate.

Envisioning the Future

The discovery process also asks us to consider how dreams and goals for the future are informed by our cultures. Through an envisioning process, we imagine what relationships could look like and co-create ways to proceed. We discover common goals, needs, and values. As we identify obstacles to our visions, we can also explore how to overcome them. The envisioning process flourishes when imagination, creativity, and positive expectations are present.

There are many ways to envision a shared future. Drawing exercises are one way to tap into meaning-making processes. At Transworld Corporation, people drew pictures of how they envisioned the organization three years into the future. Alphas and Omegas worked separately in their groups with chart paper and colored markers. After the activity, the groups came together and discussed their pictures and what they represented. Again, differences emerged between the Alpha and Omega group members. The Omegas envisioned the continuation of the current hierarchical organizational structure, with the executive director as the head, but included more lines of communication, vertically and horizontally, and more input to decision-making by all employees. The Alphas turned the organizational structure upside down.

They depicted the front-line workers, who "got the job done," as the base of the organization. The flow of communication, decision-making, and resources was from front-line workers to managers, department heads and then the executive director. This orientation highlighted the essential function of front-line employees, and the importance of their input into operations and policy at Transworld.

At the outset, these visions seemed too different to bridge. As the Alphas and Omegas explored the underlying assumptions of each other's visions, they realized they had overlapping goals. Everyone recognized that front-line workers served clients and that their work should be supported. Everyone agreed that there needed to be more channels and modes of communication to enhance productivity and relationships. While their pictures looked very different, they were able to agree on many elements of their vision.

Drawing the pictures not only allowed Alphas and Omegas to realize a shared vision for the future of the company, it also provided an opportunity for unspoken cultural assumptions and thoughts to become clear. The pictures helped the groups discover each other's visions including explicit differences and implicit similarities. The consultant could have helped the groups deepen discovery by asking each group to study, interpret, and explain the other's picture, saying "Imagine this is your picture. As well as you can, please explain its underlying assumptions and focus on the strengths of the vision." This would have helped the Alphas and Omegas delve into each others' thought processes and ways of making meaning.

Another technique for envisioning the future as part of discovery is through generating mixed group visions. At Transworld Corporation, the consultant could have created two new groups with Alphas and Omegas in each, trying to keep the groups as balanced in their representation as possible. Each mixed group would be given the task of creating a definitive plan for the future of the company, and the plan would have to include *every* single group member's ideas and thoughts. The two groups would then come together and share their plans with everybody.

Given the different perspectives of the Omegas and Alphas, this would not be an easy task for the mixed group. It is very likely that the final product would not be a realistic or effective plan. Participants might come up with ridiculous scenarios that might help lighten the mood. In their consensus plans, there might be germs of helpful ideas. Overlapping values and shared assumptions might come to light. Ideally, these mixed groups could generate momentum to reconcile their differences and heighten awareness of shared understandings. From this foundation, a workable plan could be developed to integrate their visions as much as possible.

As people in conflict envision a shared future, they begin to uncover shared worldviews. Everyone has hopes and dreams in common no matter how much they believe they are different. A mother in Palestine dreams of a safe and peaceful world for her baby, the same way an Israeli mother does. While these visions for the future may be the same, their thinking about how this should be secured is often different. Even though mothers see different routes to resolution, they can come together over their shared concerns and work from their commonalities. Similarly, both the Alphas and Omegas wanted a better work environment, even though their ideas on how to achieve this seemed worlds apart.

As we have seen, the discovery process can be exciting and rewarding. It can also be fearful, painful, frustrating, and anger-provoking. We may feel uncomfortable or disoriented as our beliefs and expectations are unsettled. Such discovery may call our identity and meaning-making processes into question. There may be cycles of highs and lows as we seem to move forward and backward. This is when the skills of "sitting with discomfort," pausing, and revealing uncertainty described in Chapter Six will serve us well.

The discovery stage can begin with exploring past-present differences or envisioning our future. These approaches are intertwined, complementary, and ongoing, but we may emphasize one or the other at different times. In the end, exploration and envisioning help us discover, acknowledge, and appreciate our commonalities and differences. They also help us become aware of cultural assumptions influencing thoughts, beliefs, and actions. Ideally, they yield empathy among those in conflict, which facilitates turning points in relationships. Gifted with discovery, we now proceed into finding ways to develop a shared plan for moving forward.

The transition to action is not an easy one. People find it less threatening to acknowledge the humanity of their adversary than to act on it. Action—translating our expressed desires for collaboration into reality—can be difficult. This is especially so when people have long histories of conflict. Identities and meanings become fused with maintaining the struggle, and shifting into "doing" is challenging. Members of the Jewish-Palestinian dialogue groups were motivated to action when they discovered their common suffering and shared visions for the future. They felt compelled to act to ease the ongoing suffering of people in the Middle East.

One way to ease into a transition to action is to build slowly toward action planning and implementation. For example, the Transworld Alphas and Omegas could have developed small changes in their communication structure and strategies arising from their pictures. They could have experimented with these small changes in between meetings and reported back. This would have given them an incremental taste of action planning and implementation.

It is essential to remember that the map is a circle, not a straight line. Action and implementation follow from discovery, but new realizations can send people back to discovery and exploration. With this in mind, we consider ways of creating change.

Create: Invent, Implement, Evaluate, and Adjust

Create means many things—to produce through imagination, to bring something into existence by making a new combination of existing materials, to develop something from a latent state. Creating is always relational. Contrary to images of a tortured genius working in a garret, creating involves gathering impulses, inspirations, and insights into an imaginative whole.

Several steps help us create a new reality—*inventing options* for how we can resolve our differences, *implementing* plans to turn visions into concrete reality, and *evaluating and adjusting* where necessary along the way to ensure we are creating the visions we dreamed.

The creation stage is essentially about taking action. We've explored, discussed, and learned about our past and present, and we have envisioned a future. Now, let's *do* something about it! We are ready to develop concrete plans and take concrete steps in establishing and repairing our relationships as we resolve conflicts. Doing something can be as simple as being together in a new way or changing one's behaviors—I used to insult you when I was angry, but in the future I will treat you respectfully as we try to work out our differences. It could be that I need to apologize to you for something I have said or done in order to repair our relationship. Perhaps my group needs to show that we acknowledge and respect your group's identity and meaning-making processes, and that we are committed to building equitable and constructive relationships—and then *do* that. On the other hand, doing something can also be as complex as negotiating a peace treaty between two countries addressing territory, resources, and refugees in mutually agreeable ways.

Through discovery, we learn how others perceived us and how we see things differently. The first step in creating is to invent or imagine action. Through the discovery process, the pro-life and pro-choice groups referred to earlier discovered common ground about several issues. They were united against the feminization of poverty. They agreed that it would be good to reduce the number of unwanted pregnancies. All of them were in favor of better facilities to support women with unplanned pregnancies.

From this common ground, the participants openly discussed whether and how they would continue talking and working together. Did they want to focus all their efforts on advocacy for their side in the conflict, or was there a will to continue some joint activities? As they talked openly about these questions, they agreed that they were interested in continuing to relate to each other, but they had a need to be involved in doing something together that would produce tangible results. The activists decided to continue their engagement and employ their common passions for women and children by working to develop adoption as an option.

The groups talked about a number of different things they could do to improve adoption services, and finally implemented a plan to improve counseling services for pregnant women in their areas. They also took steps to generate educational materials to raise public awareness about adoption. Tasks were divided and materials produced. Pro-life and pro-choice participants spoke together at community forums and gave presentations at high schools. They made sure medical practitioners in their areas had good resources related to adoption. They had moved successfully from invention to implementation.

Their implementation plan designated members from each group to be responsible for monitoring and evaluating progress. They wanted to measure not only the improvement of adoption services, but how their collaboration affected relationships between pro-life and pro-choice advocates. Their evaluation showed them that the experience in their group had wider echoes—people on both sides of the pro-life/pro-choice divide reported improved relationships through exposure to this joint action.

Following the completion of the adoption project and the evaluation, several of the dialogue participants decided to continue working on other issues of shared concern. They joined together to address poverty in their inner cities. Some members went on to write a joint paper about the limits of acceptable activity outside clinics. They adjusted their plans based on what they had learned from their evaluation and where the hotspots in the conflict existed. These men and women had learned that differences need not keep them at loggerheads. They had come full circle, from distrust and misunderstanding, to joint action and relationship.

As we have said, a conflict can be approached from the discovery or creation starting point, depending on circumstances and preferences. Sometimes, the starting point itself is controversial. At Transworld Corporation, one of the differences between groups was that the Alphas wanted to engage in discovery while the Omegas wanted to jump right into creating and action planning. This difference in preferred starting points is common. Some people have large appetites for talking and sharing, and see relationship building as a precondition to action. Others prefer to move quickly into action, and see extended talking as a waste of precious time. They want to find and implement solutions, believing that relationships can be built through the process. Neither is right or wrong; they are just different. In practice, some of each approach may be helpful in deepening relationships and grounding understandings in results. Regardless of where we start in the map, inventing options and plans for action is an invigorating stage of the process.

Inventing Options and Plans

In the parts of the map presented so far, we have explored the past and present and envisioned our future. This future vision is not etched in stone or definitive, but it provides us with an imagined destination as we begin the task of inventing options and plans. For example, two groups in conflict may share a future vision of living in communal harmony, but how do they achieve it? To answer the question, we can generate different possible routes to the vision and ways to travel on those routes.

As earlier chapters have illustrated, conflicts can be resolved in many ways. Engaging in war is perceived by some as a way of resolving conflict, as are other ways of forcing a solution. Our focus here is on constructive resolution of intercultural conflict through *building* relationships, not *destroying* them. Resolutions may range from interpersonal outcomes, such as deciding a menu for a shared meal, to organizational decisions, such as creating a system to ensure equity in hiring and promotion. Whether the focus of the conflict is community or national issues—such as health care, education, employment, food, or shelter—or is international—such as global warming or environmental protection—the steps can be the same. Whether we are working on a very complex issue like the status of Jerusalem or a diffuse one like dismantling racism, there are multiple ways to move from discovery into action.

In South Africa, it was essential to change the country's flag to represent the new democratic country that finally included all people. The question was, "What would this new flag look like?" Given South Africa's past of oppression, lack of voice for the majority, and no transparency and participation in decision-making, it was also important not to echo oppression in the process of choosing a new flag, or in the symbols incorporated in the new flag. It needed to be a symbol of unity. The National Symbols Commission sent out an invitation through the media for all South Africans to participate by submitting drawings of the new flag. South Africans of all ages and races were involved in creating the new symbol so important to representing a united, inclusive, and democratic country.

In some instances like this South African example, it is important to involve the community at large; in other contexts it might be more appropriate to leave option creation to prominent or elected leaders. Some situations might point to having specific people with specialized knowledge generate options. A combination of these approaches could also be helpful. In one organizational conflict where I was asked to help, a conflict over a logo was solved by having a group of consultants talk with everyone involved. They then drafted three options that echoed the things they had heard, and I facilitated a conversation to choose one. Because the options were not generated by anyone inside, it was easier for everyone to choose one. The case of South Africa, on the other hand, cried out for inclusion because of its history of exclusion.

Another example of inventing options also comes from the South African context. In the mid 1990s, the Truth and Reconciliation Commission shone light on the need for reconciliation related to child survivors of violence. Officials knew that children who had been victims of political violence needed holistic services, but they were not sure how to design the program. They wanted to involve grassroots service providers such as teachers, social workers, and community leaders who had direct contact with children and families in inventing the program. Grassroots organizations from all provinces were invited to send representatives to meetings. Together, these representatives designed holistic, caring, and culturally sensitive programs for children in need of help.

Third parties are sometimes helpful in assisting people in conflict to invent options. These third parties may be outsiders who strive for impartiality, or they may be insiders who bring a wealth of knowledge about an organization and its functioning. Sometimes, cultural factors shape the role of the third party. In indigenous cultures, there is often a preference for someone with relational ties to the community and in-depth knowledge of issues. In westernized cultures, outsider neutrals tend to be preferred, though this is not always the case. Whether insider or outsider, the third party can draw on their expertise to help people in conflict imagine options. At Transworld Corporation, the consultant helped the Alphas and Omegas develop this set of recommendations for improving the organization:

- include some front line staff in senior management meetings to improve decision-making;
- develop a mentoring program to match junior workers with senior staff to overcome the barriers erected by the "good old boy" network;
- have a different senior manager host a brown bag lunch every Friday where staff can bring a range of concerns or just stop by to say hello; and
- hold regular social gatherings to build a sense of community.

These options arose from brainstorming a much longer list, and were not definitive ends in and of themselves. The facilitator suggested brainstorming because she thought it might bridge the different starting points of the Alphas and Omegas. Brainstorming is specific, so it appealed to the Omegas who tended to be action-oriented and were drawn to fine-tuning the status quo. At the same time, brainstorming facilitates new ideas, and so it appealed to the Alphas as well. As a result of a productive brainstorming session, everyone agreed to try the recommendations as a way of creating incremental positive changes at Transworld.

Inventing options requires that people put aside preconceptions and judgments, and give themselves to invention and flexibility as discussed in Chapter Six. Option invention can be direct as it was at Transworld, or it can be subtle and indirect through using narratives, drawings, and metaphors. Consider the following story.

A U.S.-based international organization managed a water development project in a small village in Guinea. The organization provided money for the project, which was given to the local village chief and council of elders to manage. It was the chief's responsibility to put the money in the bank. Several months later, the Guinean project manager Mohamed discovered that money was missing from the bank account. Everyone was quite sure the chief had taken the money. The organization pressured Mohamed to confront the chief but it was not culturally appropriate to confront a respected village chief or to directly request that he replace the money.

Mohamed called a meeting with the chief and elders to address the problem. He explained that there was money missing from the account and simply asked, "What are we going to do?" His question was met by fifteen minutes of silence. Finally, the eldest member of the council said, "My five brothers and I are walking down the road. After some time, we suddenly realize that one of our beloved brothers is missing. He is lost. He must have taken a wrong turn in the road by mistake. We must find him. What should we do?" The elder's story was met with more silence. Finally, the chief, believing he would be warmly embraced as the "lost brother," stood up and said, "I have made a mistake. I have the money and will put it in the bank. I apologize for my mistake." The elders and chief were relieved and happy. The money was returned, harmony was restored, and relationships were strengthened as the elders and chief renewed their caring, commitment, and responsibility to ensuring the villagers' well being.

In this example from Guinea, the direct approach expected by the U.S. organization might have backfired. If Mohamed or the council of elders had confronted the chief, they may have heightened tensions and the money might not have been returned. Instead, Mohamed asked the council of elders and the chief to invent options to resolve the problem and the elder, in turn, subtly offered a face-saving option while also tactfully acknowledging the power of the chief. Central to successful option invention is awareness of cultural starting points and capacities and skills, introduced in previous chapters, to ensure that solutions are fitting and workable.

Implementing

With definitive plans in place, we can begin to *implement* the options we have invented to resolve conflict. This is a time of moving from mental and analytic processes that guide preparation, discovery, and option exploration to a more kinesthetic, proactive mode of interaction. It is important here, as it is in earlier stages, to maintain a positive relational climate so that plans are implemented in ways that magnify and support shared goals.

Every dialogue group with whom I've worked has, at some point, decided that they need to move from dialogue to action. Those groups that haven't turned to action have generally withered away. People don't seem to sustain dialogue for the sake of talking and sharing alone. Especially among people committed to advocacy and change, there is a strong drive to act. After discovering concrete ways to bridge differences, not taking the next step is frustrating enough for most people that they drop out of the process.

However, the reverse may also be true—groups that focus solely on action projects, and never take the time to go through mutual discovery, tend to lack depth and durability in their relationships.

In Chapter Two, Figure 2.1 illustrates that material changes are more likely to be meaningful and sustained when supported by relationship-building. When we jump straight to acting on the outward changes that could "fix" our conflict, we risk not dealing with the underlying issues and relationships that feed such problems in the first place. There are too many examples of failed conflict resolution processes where it was believed that merely creating a new border, signing a treaty or agreement, dissolving an oppressive law, or creating a new government was enough to resolve problems. How can any of these material acts stand a chance of success without efforts being made to affect attitudes and mindsets, build relationships, and expand worldviews?

Changed attitudes come from new and changed relationships. Relationships are supported when we realize the influence of culture and are prepared to work across differences. Discovery provides the opportunity to explore our past and present together and open the channels of communication. While working together on action projects can provide opportunities for discovery along the way, an ongoing focus on relationship may also be important. Generally, the deeper and more intractable the conflict, the greater the need for a focused discovery process to achieve real understanding, empathy, and sustainable relationships.

The Jewish-Palestinian Living Room Dialogue Group mentioned earlier felt they were ready to move into action after they had focused on the discovery stage and had been meeting monthly for about a year and a half. When they felt they had "talked long enough," felt good about the relationships they had developed, and saw the benefits of what they were doing, they wanted to share their process with the larger Jewish and Palestinian community. They then focused their dialogues on inventing options to share their process with the larger communities. They brainstormed a number of different ways to do this, but decided to start by holding a community dinner for Jews and Palestinians. After months of planning, they hosted a dinner for 420 guests, including about 150 Palestinians and 270 Jews and "others" (neither Jewish nor Palestinian) who sat and dialogued together at mixed tables. The event included high profile guests, drew people from ten different states, and garnered national media attention. Later, members saw it as a turning point in their process.

While the discovery process had created shifts in interpersonal relationships within the group, the work of organizing the dinner proved people's commitment to making positive changes for the future. The success of the dinner reinforced their belief in the power of dialogue and created momentum for them to take on other action projects to directly benefit people living in Israel and Palestine. One of the things they did was raise money to send hospital equipment to Gaza and western Jerusalem. Another action was to support joint visits of people from the region, especially youth, to the U.S. They also launched a second dialogue group and later developed many more groups across the United States, further increasing the momentum of positive relational change between Jews and Palestinians in the U.S. They put their hope into action—hope for changed relationships that might have positive influences on the situation in the Middle East itself. They also wanted to show people in the region that there are a variety of alternatives to violence.

Another example takes us back to South Africa. During Apartheid, music and song played a huge role among non-white South Africans in facilitating communication, mobilization, support, and hope for the future. With the many bans and restrictions placed on oppressed groups by the white government, these people had to be creative in finding ways to maintain connection and build momentum for the future transition they envisioned. Their music also seeped out to some members of the white community and the international community, carrying their grief, hopes, and needs for a post-Apartheid South Africa. As democratic government came to the country, the songs were central in facilitating the transition. They helped transform people and their system, carrying robust ideas, hope, and inspiration from the years of struggle and fear through the uncertainty of change and into the present day.

The South African example shows us that implementation is not always a neat, distinct stage. It can begin during discovery and option invention, and continue—sometimes in a new or more open form—through a transition to action. Music, like the beautiful new flag of South Africa, became an anchor for a new identity that connected people to their roots and gave them hope for the future at the same time.

In both the Jewish-Palestinian Living Room dialogue group and the nation of South Africa, implementation of changes strengthened relationships and paved the way for further actions to realize the dreams of those involved.

Evaluate and Adjust

As we take action, we also need to continuously monitor, evaluate, and adjust our efforts. Ideally, evaluation is ongoing throughout the stages of discovery, option generation, and implementation. It is essential that it not stop once actions have been taken. Ongoing evaluation can monitor progress, provide clues for self-correction and adjustment, and help us stay on track to achieve shared goals. Evaluation can also help us see obstacles in our path, and point out when we may need to revisit other parts of the map or make adjustments.

At Transworld Corporation, evaluation was a central part of the conflict resolution process. In the earlier stages, the consultant took responsibility for assessing and evaluating the groups' progress. Later on, during the implementation stage, group members themselves assumed more responsibility for evaluation and monitoring. One of the first actions taken during implementation was arranging a new monthly staff meeting including staff and senior executives. Everyone had high hopes for the new arrangement; it seemed as if it would work well.

After a few months, however, it became apparent that the staff was having problems attending these meetings due to other work commitments and scheduling challenges. The group of senior executives and staff met and decided to substitute bimonthly meetings for monthly ones so that attending would be less onerous. They also decided to use email in the intervening month to share information and shape an agenda for the next meeting. Six months later, a quick survey showed that people were pleased with the new approach to meetings and the mixed levels group, and they believed it was helping them achieve their goals of improving information flow. Continuous monitoring, evaluation, and readjustment allowed Transworld to make progress in their quest for constructive change.

Alpha and Omega had also suggested implementing weekly brown bag lunches with senior staff on a drop-in basis. After a couple of months, the experience with these meetings was uneven. Some weeks, especially as the weather got nicer, few or no staff dropped by, leaving the executive in solitude. Presiding at the brown bag lunches was seen by some senior executives as a chore, and they had a hard time with what they termed "gripe sessions." Evaluation and adjustment was needed in this case as well.

Hearing of the unevenness of the brown bag experiences, the vice president for human resources called the Alpha and Omega groups back together. He asked them what they were hearing from coworkers about the brown bag lunches. The response was lukewarm. It seemed that people appreciated the opportunity, but either found that the executive did not listen to their concerns in the way they had hoped, or they didn't get to as many of the lunches as they had intended.

The vice president asked the Alphas and Omegas to go back to option generation. Were there times or forums that would work better for Transworld employees? As they talked, an Omega member observed that Fridays, being casual days at Transworld, were often times people ran out to do errands in advance of the weekend or took walks in nice weather. The Friday brown bag lunches actually conflicted with these established patterns. An Alpha member suggested that it might work better if rotating senior executives had the equivalent of office hours—an open door policy at specific times—that employees knew they could use. This caught the attention of everyone, and they decided to propose it to senior management. Senior management agreed, and a trial period was initiated to last three months.

These examples illustrate the importance of ongoing monitoring and adjustment. How this evaluation takes place will vary. At Transworld, a short survey confirmed anecdotal reports that the monthly meetings were attracting fewer and fewer participants. Attendance served as an indicator of progress, and slowing attendance led the Corporation to readjust its meeting schedule. Attendance was also an indicator that led the Alphas and Omegas to reconsider the brown bag lunch idea. Open-door hours for senior executives were much more successful, as staff stopped by to say hello or share a concern in the course of their work duties. Because senior staff took turns being available, there were more opportunities for staff to get to know management, and vice versa.

Attendance and engagement of people from both communities was an important indicator of progress for those involved in the Palestinian-Jewish Living Room Dialogue group. In South Africa, there were many indicators of improvement in relationships across race including an increase in mixed race relationships and a decrease in interracial violence. The indicators of progress or lack of progress will vary from group to group, as will ways of responding to feedback. Adjustment may mean going back to option generation, or there may be an obvious fix depending on how the initiative is or is not working.

In some cases, it is useful to develop and implement very specific evaluation plans. Transworld Corporation used a longer survey six months into their change process to evaluate the success of the initiatives. Surveys can target a representative sample of affected people to determine if things are on track. They can be as simple as checking verbally with people about changes and their impacts, or as formal as sending out a set of standard, pre-set questions. However monitoring and evaluating are approached, it is important that methods used are culturally sensitive and appropriate. Cultural expectations may influence the identity of the evaluator as well as the evaluation's formality or informality. At Transworld, the people who implemented action plans were also involved in evaluating progress. This was useful because the Alphas and Omegas had viewpoints of several levels of the organization, and could get a pulse of the dynamics of change.

In other contexts including many traditional African cultures, elders or chiefs might be solely responsible for evaluating progress and determining whether and how to adjust strategies. In situations where people are accustomed to large power differences between those at the top and those on the bottom of a structure, elite decision-makers are more likely to have responsibility for evaluation and adjustment. Where people have more egalitarian expectations, they may demand a voice in ongoing monitoring. In many public policy processes in North America, for example, people are requesting and getting ongoing roles in monitoring the implementation and evaluation of commitments by developers and public authorities.

It is important to remember that *progress* and *success* are themselves culturally defined. Evaluating success in intercultural conflict resolution can be quite challenging. Indicators of progress are linked to the cultural starting points introduced in Chapter Three. For example, take the story introduced in that chapter of a South African living in the United States, Venashri, and Michael, her American friend. Together, they attended a meeting to establish a new South African non-governmental organization in the United States whose purpose was to build connections to South African events and issues. The goal of the first meeting was to organize and establish a board. You will recall that Venashri and the other South Africans adopted a more *diffuse* cultural starting point than Michael. From this vantage point, they evaluated the meeting as completely successful—they were jubilant about its transparency, fairness, and relational richness, even though a board was *not* established. Michael was frustrated and disappointed. His evaluation of the meeting was based on his more *specific* starting point. To him, ending the meeting without choosing a board meant that their goals were not reached and the meeting was unsuccessful.

Venashri and Michael had very different assessments of the same event. This suggests that those involved in resolving a conflict are best served when they jointly identify the meaning of progress and the criteria or benchmarks that will be used to measure it. With relationship at the center of our map, we engage at each juncture of the journey. Getting clear about what we mean by evaluation, and how we define progress and success, are important ways to keep the relationships from being undermined by people feeling disillusioned by unwelcome surprises. While action leading to material changes may be indicators of progress, positive shifts in relationships more durably point to ongoing success.

When we find ourselves stuck again in conflict, or we are blocked somehow from implementing our ideas and plans, we might need to go back to another part of the map. Perhaps we have not developed a sufficient sense of our interdependence and connectedness. Or maybe we haven't spent long enough exploring and fully understanding the underlying layers of culture that influence people's thinking, being, and doing. Perhaps we haven't envisioned a future that is inclusive enough or it does not fully meet people's needs and aspirations. Our plans might have too many gaps or weaknesses that fail to support the bridges we are trying to build, or we may not have anticipated obstacles.

Implementation can fail for many different reasons. Sometimes, people do not have enough genuine commitment to work together. They may lack deep empathy and true understanding of each other's core concerns and dreams. Trust is often strained, and there may be residual fear, anger, resentment, and judgment toward the other. Sometimes, events outside a conflict resolution process derail its momentum. Two groups may be making significant progress until an external incident threatens one side, leading to a retrenching of positions and a move away from flexibility. We may think we have built strong foundations, and then something within our community or outside of it shakes it up again, revealing the need for more patient work. We may need to strengthen our relationships further to make change possible.

As we evaluate and adjust, it may become obvious that we need to go back to another part of our process and pick up dropped threads or introduce new colors to our emerging pictures. We may have to go back into a past scar and address its legacy. We may need to change our action plans or link to others who need to be involved for implementation to work. When we return to a previous step in the map, we need not feel stuck or disillusioned. We can actually feel encouraged, knowing that ongoing evaluation has pointed us to ways to sustain progress and anchor constructive relationships.

When people have built strong relationships, they have resilience to navigate storms that threaten them. For example, as the Jewish-Palestinian dialogues are taking place, new rounds of violence and controversial events continue in the Middle East. When the death toll of an event is particularly high or an unpopular political decision is implemented, the participants are challenged not to revert to old tendencies to blame and accuse each other's side of being the "real villain." Relying on their relationships with each other, they have learned to dialogue about current events in ways that invite discovery. They often need to revisit topics and dig deeper into each other's meaning-making processes with a spirit of inquiry. Their groups have developed such strong bonds that occurrences like this only strengthen their resolve to continue their efforts.

Rejuvenate

In spite of challenges and complexity, resolving conflict across cultures can be empowering, energizing, and rewarding. It can also be painful, stressful, and energy-draining. Can you bring to mind a life situation where it felt like the ground was shifting underneath you, the usual rules did not apply, and you saw no way out except through? This uncertainty is typical for people moving through a conflict resolution process. There are no maps that cover the whole territory. The maps we have are still being developed and improved. Maps that work for one group may not work for others. No wonder the process can feel fraught with ambiguity, uncertainty, and distress! Given these challenges, it is very important to maintain motivation and momentum. We need to rejuvenate each other and ourselves along the way because conflict resolution across cultures asks a great deal of us, and refreshment makes it easier to meet ongoing demands.

As we discussed in earlier chapters, complex, multi-layered intercultural conflicts call on us to do something that we may not have practiced a lot in our lives: build significant relationships with people very different from ourselves. There are no shortcuts to doing this, but there are oases along the way. Hopefully, the oasis we find has abundant water, and everyone can pause to rejuvenate.

Rejuvenation gives us a boost—a way of reflecting on where we have been in our finest moments of connection and our times of despair. It is to acknowledge our progress, whether or not we have arrived at our ideal outcome. The capacity for momentum discussed in Chapter Six points toward rejuvenation in its focus on keeping relationships vital through continued engagement. You will recall that the capacity for momentum allows us to keep at it, focusing attention on the heart of our work even in the face of obstacles.

During any long journey, we may get tired, frustrated or stressed, and need to renew our energy along the way. There are many ways we might do this.

Sometimes just changing our environment or approach is rejuvenating. We can take a break, do some stretching, or give ourselves a walk. This might be a good time to review the skill of "pausing," discussed in Chapter Six. Pausing allows us to renew our energies, reducing the intensity of our work for a while to build energy and allow creative ideas to surface. You will recall that Nelson Mandela talks about the importance of pausing on the long road toward conflict resolution. Without pausing, we risk becoming too tired or weak to cross the next hill. It sounds trite, but it is sometimes only pausing that helps us break our pattern of trying more of what is not working to address our conflicts!

It is not always easy to pause and take the time to rejuvenate. There are many conflicts where people do not feel comfortable slowing down because of the serious nature of the situation and possible harm to self and other. Paradoxically, in situations like this, pausing may be even more important because of the potential impact of decisions. Even a short rest—ten minutes, an hour, a day—may be all that is necessary to help regain our energy, refocus our efforts, or just help us survive. In Chapter Six, we learned how pausing triggered the start of relationship building for Venashri and the local people in a township in South Africa. We must find the best ways and times to reinvigorate ourselves so that we expand our capacities and inner spaciousness. From a sense of spaciousness comes constructive energy, and even healthy playfulness—both important to deep and satisfying processes.

Rejuvenation of ourselves, others, and our intercultural conflict resolution process is also facilitated by ongoing reflection. At points along the way, we need to take the time to reflect on and discuss our process and progress as well as our learnings. Reflection is an essential part of learning, and helps us avoid reversals and back-tracking. As we reflect, we notice turning points—both negative and positive. While it is easy to regret reversals, it is also important to notice the places where we made good choices and came together against the odds. Remembering these places gives us a sense of hope for the future, and energizes us to continue.

When possible and appropriate, we can engage in reflection together with our counterparts on the other side. We take the opportunity to acknowledge how far we have come in our relationships. When we are able to do this together, we validate progress and develop a shared sense of rejuvenation for the work still to come. Reflection may be quite informal, or it may be carefully planned and formal. It may be written or drawn; it may be systematic or conversational. However it is done, reflection is a process of discovery, of seeing the whole rather than the minutiae that are unavoidably on our minds when we are in the thick of conflict resolution processes. Reflection is most powerful when done at three levels: internally, with members of our own group, and with members of the other side. Combining all these viewpoints, we are less likely to bask in self-congratulation while missing important parts of the picture.

Rejuvenation came to the members of Transworld Corporation in an unexpected way. As the Alpha and Omega task-force was concluding a meeting where they had reflected on the effectiveness of changes in improving communication, one of the Omegas looked around. "I'm gonna miss you guys," he said, half-jokingly. While their working relationships had improved over the course of their work together, they had kept quite separate outside of formal meetings. An Alpha member seized the moment: "What about a brown bag lunch for *us*?" she asked. They decided to meet the following Friday at a local park near the office.

If you were a passerby that day at the park, you would have been surprised to learn that this group was once deeply divided. As Alphas and Omegas met at the park, they greeted each other with affection and humor. Someone brought out a volleyball, women kicked off their heels, and everyone agreed that Maude's chocolate cake was the best they had ever tasted. Even amidst their play, they took some time for reflection on where they had been. Through joking about their lack of artistic abilities, they reflected on the drawing experience that had shown them their very different visions for the organization. The Alphas teased the Omegas about how much they had relaxed and whether this would have a negative impact on company productivity. The Omegas teased the Alphas about how they had "won," since the cross-sectoral meetings with frontline workers and senior managers seemed to be going well. It was a time to look back and appreciate the progress that had been made, even though it had not always been obvious along the way.

In addition to reflecting on the past and present, we also need to reflect on what is next. Is there more that we need or want to do to bridge differences? How do we continue the process of relationship building and meeting our common goals? Where there are choice-points, which values do we want to keep at the center to guide our decisions? Reflecting in a conscious and systematic manner is important to staying on course.

A very important, but often neglected and forgotten part of the intercultural conflict resolution process, is to mark and celebrate our successes. Giving thanks and acknowledging each other and ourselves for our accomplishments is rejuvenating. We can celebrate major breakthroughs, turning points, momentous occasions, milestones, and smaller stepping-stones that mark our journeys. Often, it is the small acknowledgements or symbolic gestures along the way that are most important for keeping everyone connected, energized, and moving in the same direction.

Celebrations can take many forms. Heads of state use elaborate ceremonies to sign peace agreements and treaties. Historic handshakes between former adversaries publicly symbolize agreements reached and turning points passed and are meant to mark and celebrate success. The director at Transworld Corporation held a company picnic to honor the work of the task-force and celebrate collective progress. In many cultural contexts, shared meals or feasts mark the successful resolution of problems and celebrate achievements. In Chapter Six, for example, Jabu's participation in the cultural ritual of homecoming and reintegration was concluded with a family meal. The festive nature of the meal symbolized and marked the positive turning point in Jabu's relationship with his father and the rest of his family. Youth in gangs may smoke peace pipes to acknowledge and celebrate the resolution of their grievances and transformation of their relationships. Indigenous peoples in North America have many rich ways to celebrate and mark positive shifts in the aftermath of conflict including dancing, sacred ceremonies, and feasts. In many African cultures, successful conflict resolution is marked by ceremonies to honor and give thanks to the ancestors for their guidance and blessings.

Celebrations can be elaborate occasions or as simple as a friendly "thank you," "job well done," or "cheers!" They can be nonverbal—a touch, an acknowledging look, a nod. What is important is setting aside time and space to acknowledge and mark progress and successes. This can be difficult for people focused on results, whose temptation is to dive into the next challenge. But it is important for everyone as a hallmark of reflective practice to integrate insights and consolidate learning. Of course, even as we celebrate achievements, we must ensure that the celebrations are culturally appropriate and relevant. The Palestinian Jewish Living Room Dialogue group feast, for example, would have been significantly undermined if someone had served pork. Celebrating involves hospitality—our focus needs to be on making everyone feel welcome and included.

Celebrating successes marks our achievements and energizes us to keep going. The more contentious the differences and protracted the conflict, the more important celebration becomes. The celebration is not only important for those directly involved in making change, but also for the people that the change affects. It is a way of bringing others into the process and enabling them to feel a part of the shared future.

Transformation

Bridging differences is ultimately a transformational process. When we first recognize and acknowledge our interdependence, we experience a shift in our view of our relationships from "us-them" to "we." Through exploring and envisioning our past-present-future, we transform ourselves, others, and the space that holds us together. We feel surprised and even comforted in our commonalities and begin to appreciate our differences. When we feel empathy with the other's experiences and discover common ground, the meanings we assign to the other and the conflict shift. As we embrace each other's humanity and acknowledge each other's fears, needs, and dreams, we transform fear to openness and animosity to amity. When we create new ways of being together and invent and implement imaginative plans, we strengthen our relationships and co-create our future. Building bridges throughout our work together draws us closer, and this closeness strengthens the bridges we are building. Conflict resolution is a reciprocal, ongoing process. It is seldom linear, just as relationships are never straight lines, but a spiral that can take us to the heights and the depths of human experience.

Not all conflicts resolve in transformative ways. Sometimes, achieving a solution with which we can live is a huge accomplishment. It may be enough to have a glimpse of each other in context and then work on a practical solution that gives people what they need while keeping them moving on parallel lines rather than intersecting ones. Not every situation ends with "win-win"—more than we might think end in "mostly ok-mostly ok."

Let's go back to the dialogue groups on abortion held across North America in the 1990s. Were relationships transformed in those groups? Sometimes. After interviewing dozens of participants in these dialogues, a few things became clear. No one ever changed their mind about abortion. Pro-life advocates emerged from the dialogues as pro-life. Pro-choice advocates left and remained pro-choice. Some participants said they may have moved a bit along the continuum of pro-life and pro-choice positions, but no one abandoned their core beliefs and values. The changes reported related more to attitudes toward the other and new strategies for advocacy than changes in beliefs themselves.

This is a good sign. The purpose of the dialogues was not to change views, but to change the way people with those views related to each other. If deep convictions were changed as a result of the dialogue process, it might be a sign of coercion or negotiation over values—the opposite of a transformative outcome.

Some abortion dialogue groups kept meeting for years following the initial weekend; others met once and chose to end the experience there. Several participants reported being very moved by the experiences they had in dialogue, even transformed; others said it was interesting but not interesting enough to continue. Many reported that they were viewed with suspicion when they returned to their advocacy groups after having met with "the other side." Over a hundred veterans of these dialogues from different cities came together in Madison, Wisconsin in the mid-1990s to celebrate their achievement and reflect on their new culture of "common ground."

It is in the small stories that transformation shines through, diamonds amidst the rough rock of struggle and pain related to the abortion conflict. One of our editors, Michelle LeBaron, remembers well the day she visited a group of clergy involved in ongoing dialogue over abortion in the American West. They were all busy people, impressive for their clarity about their stands on the issue coupled with a fierce commitment to keep meeting. After she had asked them several questions about their dialogues and joint actions that had come from them, she asked them the question that had been building inside her heart for the previous hour. "Why do you keep doing this, keep meeting, even in the face of criticisms from your parishioners and urgency to maximize advocacy?"

There was a long pause. Finally, one of the group spoke. "I come," he said softly, "because I see God in the eyes of the others." There were tears in peoples' eyes. It was a sacred moment. In this moment, everyone glimpsed the transformative power of coming together across differences. He continued, observing that his advocacy remained strong *and* he also cared about the others' feelings. When his side scores a victory in the legislature or the courts, he is glad for the progress *and* concerned about how his partners in dialogue are experiencing their loss. This ability to entertain the complexity of energetic advocacy for a point of view alongside deep caring for those who advocate a different view is the essence of transformation. It is this beacon that keeps people meeting, seeking a place where they do not agree to disagree. Rather, they keep up their disagreement in ways both respectful and generative. They acknowledge their shared humanity, and find new ways to move forward across previously destructive differences.

As we transform, we embody new patterns of relationship characterized by positive attitudes and actions toward each other. These patterns ripple through individual relationships into groups, communities, organizations, and nations. New relationships may eventually be codified in laws, customs, and structures. These new relationships catalyze cultural shifts, making the line between "us" and "them" a little less stark, a little more permeable.

"Little" and "big" transformations take place throughout the process of bridging differences. Sometimes slowly, sometimes suddenly, we change attitudes, perceptions, goals, and ways of relating. As we engage across differences, we change ways of seeing, being, and doing, embracing the other and our common goals, enacting shared futures.

Applying these ideas to ourselves is the litmus test of our work. In the final chapter, we describe our journey in becoming a multicultural team to write this book. Reflecting on our journey, we realize again that conflict resolution is not a straight line and that relationship is at the center of our work. As we will see in Chapter Eight, many unexpected barriers arose as we worked together to combine our individual stories. Applying the ideas of this book to ourselves was not always easy. It was tempting at times to walk away. As M.C. Richards writes: "In the intricate mesh of our mutual involvement, we befall each other constantly." (1998, 244) You will see that we did befall each other. You will also see how we found ways to get up again to re-engage in the exciting process of creating this book.

Full Circle Reflection: Learning from Ourselves

Venashri Pillay and
Michelle LeBaron

We began this book by describing a dream. A group of people from different parts of the world came together to create a series of stories that would hold the keys to deepening their relationships. They brought their multicultural identities, experiences, and studies on the subject of intercultural conflict resolution. It has been four years since we first embarked on that journey. While we are nowhere near final conclusions, we are at a point where we are ready to stop and take a breath, consider our progress, remember the difficult parts, and acknowledge the new questions we have generated.

We have come a long way, and have learned much—and yet much remains to be explored. This we expected given the dynamic and complex nature of our subject. Developing cultural fluency and applying it to resolve conflict must be ongoing because each situation is different. This final chapter summarizes our work and includes reflections on our development as a multicultural team.

Conflict Resolution across Cultures: A Summary

We began by exploring how our individual identities and ways of seeing the world related to our studies of conflict resolution. We had come from around the world to study and teach in the United States. Each of us had a conviction that studying and practicing conflict resolution would help us contribute to the world in a meaningful way. Yet, we wondered: How did the backgrounds and experiences that we each brought shape our understandings of the field? How could rich conceptualizations of culture deepen our understandings? We began with scholarly questions, never dreaming that the journey of writing together would show us as much about ourselves, and about how multicultural teams can come together and thrive, as about our chosen subjects.

As we continued meeting, we realized that it was very difficult to talk about our cultural backgrounds and lenses. They were so much like the air all around us—omnipresent and invisible—that we hardly noticed them. Even as we tried to unpack our cultural ways of being and seeing, we found it difficult not to get tangled in the knots of exceptions and contingent descriptions. Often, we answered each others' questions about our cultural perspectives with "it depends."

We realized early on that to penetrate the layers of deep culture, we would need tools other than ordinary conversation and rational analysis. When we gave ourselves the assignment of identifying and sharing metaphors from our cultures, we experienced a breakthrough. The metaphors made our ways of seeing come alive. We began to sense the textures, nuances, interior structures, and gestalts of the places and people in our home environments. Looking back, if we had not used the metaphors to help us in our exploration, our conversations would have been much thinner. Not only that, but the metaphors probably kept us engaged with each other because they stimulated excitement and energy among us. The dialogues that arose from the metaphors were among the richest of our joint work.

Thinking back to Chapter One, you may find that the metaphors stand out for you, too. Do you remember Venashri's rainbow, stretching out a promise of multicultural harmony in the aftermath of Apartheid? Or perhaps it is Tats' island nation image that is strong in your memory, conjuring the isolation and insularity that is sometimes pursued by cultural groups. Some people will remember Karenjot's image of shifting sands, representing change and struggle experienced by newcomers to Canada. Images seed themselves inside us, and because we can taste, touch, or visualize them, they act as anchors in our memories.

As we developed a deeper sense of ourselves as a group, we began exploring the nature and dynamics of cultures generally. Because metaphors had served us so well in sharing our specific national cultures, we spent many hours examining images that might be rich enough to symbolize culture in general. Culture, it turns out, is very difficult to capture in a metaphor. It is so vast, complex, and dynamic that even the mightiest elements—wind, sea, earth—are inadequate to convey it. Because culture is about humans, we wanted to find a metaphor that conveyed its relational texture. Knowing that culture often moves without being perceived, we searched for a metaphor that would encompass its sometimes hidden nature.

Finally, we settled on the image of the underground river described in Chapter Two. Rivers, after all, are alive, fed by unseen sources. They connect to the seas—vast bodies of water that cover the planet. Rivers are always in relationship: fed by springs, met by tides and silted by banks. They nurture a million forms of plant and animal life, and are nurtured in turn by living things, just as people both shape and are shaped by culture. Rivers have momentum—they carry everything from microscopic amoeba to giant boa constrictors downstream. So cultures are ever-changing carriers of big, important ideas and less visible stories of the past. Rivers can be dammed, their flow stopped or diverted. Similarly, cultures are affected by outside influences and by humans' intentions. But every change, orchestrated or not, has effects far beyond the boundaries of a single culture.

With the underground river metaphor in place, we set our sights on exploring the intersections of culture and conflict. Given that conflict itself is culturally enacted and understood, ways of addressing conflict must take culture into account. And culture, conversely, cannot be understood without conflict. Even the most peaceful society has rituals for preventing or smoothing the differences that could otherwise divide. Chapter Two concludes with an exploration of the relational and symbolic aspects of conflict, emphasizing that conflict cannot be addressed durably unless the meanings people have associated with the issues are shifted. These meanings are communicated through rituals, stories, and metaphors that act as windows into cultural contexts.

Having fixed the boundaries of our ambitious endeavor, we set about describing the workings of culture in more detail. Culture shapes not only behaviors, but identities and meanings. We chose six sets of starting points, outlined in Chapter Three, as touchstones identified by other scholars. These starting points are not definitive, nor is it possible to match any of them with any one of us in direct correspondence. They do not map neatly onto groups of people in general. Yet, they provided a place to begin, and a way of exploring the otherwise opaque complexity of culture.

From these starting points, we sought to present a more dynamic and fluid set of tools for engaging cultural differences. Here again, we encountered challenges. Given the complexity of cultural dynamics and their ever-shifting nature, we argued about which constructs or approaches could be useful. We worried about our tendency to take refuge in stereotypes and neat classifications, sensing that culture is much more unruly and vibrant than any such generalizations.

Traps and distortions abound in generalizations used to describe cultures and cultural differences. We were mindful that some of these generalizations operate to maintain privilege and emphasize difference. Carlos Cortez, in his study of media representations of diverse cultures, points out that adjectives like "quaint" tend to be associated much more often with Mexican villages rather than U.S. or Canadian towns (2004). Contemporary stereotypes about indigenous peoples in North America often relegate them to the romantic images of old daguerreotype photos taken by roving Euro-Americans who brought their own headdresses to make the Indians look "Indian" (King 2005).

We did not want to repeat these errors of romanticization or objectification. We were also concerned about the conflict resolution field itself, and its Western cultural genesis and underpinnings. Our work included examining what we had learned about conflict resolution with attention to cultural valences and root understandings.

These early discussions were enriched by those who had grown up outside the United States. Al Fuertes, an original member of our group from the Philippines, was particularly helpful in helping us understand the effect of U.S.-based scholarship on conflict resolution initiatives in the Philippines. Venashri spoke of her early life in which she learned powerful lessons about the superiority of whites, and what a long and challenging journey it had been to come to graduate school in the United States, living and working alongside Euro-Americans and others in diverse settings. Tats spoke of his life in Japan and the surprises he had encountered in Rwanda, surprises that displaced his old images of African society with dynamic questions and respectful relationships.

As we listened to each others' stories, we were drawn to the idea of cultural fluency, an idea developed by Michelle LeBaron in her earlier book *Bridging Cultural Conflicts* (2003). We recognized that there were no checklists or sets of rules that would help people work effectively across cultures. But, just as learning a language is an incremental process that gives increasing insight into the dynamics of an unfamiliar group, we wanted to uncover how fluency could extend beyond language to an understanding of the hidden grammar of values, norms, and identities. We set about exploring cultural fluency in Chapter Four.

We came to realize again the truism that cultural fluency is not about coming to know another group. Cultural fluency arises from knowing something about the lenses that *we* look through, and then learning from the surprises we encounter as we come to glimpse the world through others' lenses. In this way, we begin to anticipate, internalize, express, and navigate in unfamiliar systems. Cultural fluency encourages us to:

- *anticipate* a range of possible scenarios about how our future relationships will evolve in unfamiliar cultural contexts;
- remain conscious of unfamiliar cultural influences that come to be *embedded* in meaning-making processes;
- *express* deep cultural assumptions in a way that is understandable to others who are unfamiliar with our meaning-making patterns; and
- *navigate* cross-cultural dynamics to co-create a constructive future together with cultural others.

As we deepen these capacities, we experience the same delightful surprises a new language learner finds when he understands and is understood for the first time. We discover that progress in bridging cultural understandings and misunderstandings is possible through self and other awareness.

To bring the capacities of cultural fluency alive, we are introduced to a group of desert travelers arriving at an oasis in Chapter Five. As the travelers come to know each other and to address the apparent shortage of water, their different ways of seeing the world come to the surface. At the oasis, we see how identity and ways of making meaning shape what seems like natural behavior when conflict arises. We also clearly see how conflict cannot be understood fully without considering the cultural dynamics that inform and express it. Finally, we encounter the possibility of violence that attends a lack of cross-cultural understanding as it escalates in times of stress.

Clearly, something needs to be done at the oasis. Survival is at stake, and people feel threatened and afraid. Water, not creativity, is the resource on which they are most focused. Yet, to find ways to use the water to sustain life, the travelers need to summon the creativity to collaborate. Given their building enmity, collaboration does not come naturally. Chapter Six presents capacities and skills needed by the travelers if they are to interrupt their negative trajectories of relationship.

Capacities are those deep resources within us that we reach into in times of creation and conflict alike. They are often innate, yet they can be deepened through practice and application. The capacities of flexibility, creative engagement, and momentum are explored in Chapter Six. How often have we been counseled to "be flexible?" This edict shows us something about capacities: they have to do with states of *being* more than *doing*. Skills take over at the intersection of being and doing. We need both capacities and skills to successfully engage intercultural conflict—capacities to imagine different choices (flexibility), invent new paths (creative engagement), and maintain progress (momentum). We also need associated skills that help us realize the potential of these capacities.

The skills described in Chapter Six will not make solving intercultural conflicts easy, but they will increase our odds, and almost certainly improve our relationships. Engaged conscientiously, they may also change our habits of relating, and even our views about conflict itself. The skills of flexibility—interrupting patterns, sitting with discomfort, and dancing with surprise—are all useful in helping us move on when we are stuck and helping us avoid stasis in the first place. Conflict can send us heading for the hills where we feel at least marginally more safe and secure. Using the skills related to flexibility will help us counter this impulse and find ways of engaging change in the midst of difficult or stressful times.

The skills associated with flexibility can be understood by imagining conflict as a dance involving two or more people. In the process of learning the dance, someone's toes may get stepped on. The skill of interrupting patterns helps us make different choices when we come again to a challenging part of the dance. Patterns of frustration leading to anger and defensiveness can be shifted when one person recognizes "the dance" and resists blame. Sometimes, stopping the practice can be helpful when the alternative is escalation or frustration. Then, sitting with discomfort can help both people get perspective and come to the learning with new energy. As they return to practicing, they will probably encounter surprises—perhaps the music changes, or someone loses track of the rhythm. Continuing to dance through the surprises can help them develop their facility to learn new dances in the future.

Creative engagement is the capacity to relate with genuineness and spontaneity to others. It is to use the raw materials of who we are individually and collectively to yield new possibilities and outcomes. It arises from a spirit of inquiry, a sincere desire to at least broaden the angle of our blinders to admit another's reality. Metaphor, story, and ritual are skills that help us engage creatively. Metaphors, as Chapter One illustrates, are powerful sensory anchors that convey textured and holistic understandings of cultural dynamics. Stories, universally used and appreciated, provide us with ways of building relational bridges as rational analysis never can. Rituals mark progress and smooth transitions to ease our ongoing progress.

Momentum is the third capacity described in Chapter Six. Momentum is important because navigating intercultural conflict can be discouraging and fraught with many challenges, both unforeseen and anticipated. The skills associated with momentum are revealing uncertainty, pausing, and intuition. Revealing uncertainty may arouse feelings of vulnerability. We prefer to believe that we know what to do. We like to believe that our data is authoritative. But there are limits to data, and sometimes revealing uncertainty can be the space where light gets into an otherwise dark situation. Revealing uncertainty can operate like an invitation for others to collaborate because our vulnerability makes us less threatening.

Pausing, another skill related to momentum, is to stop—even if momentarily—and get perspective. It may involve a contemplative practice, or simply quieting the mind. In the action-oriented worlds where many people live and work, it is too often neglected. And after a pause, intuition can arise. Intuition, knowing something without knowing how we know, is an invaluable asset for intercultural conflict resolution. All of these skills are explored in Chapter Six, as you recall. You probably remember the stories that illustrated the skills more easily than the skills themselves. Stories are powerful ways to anchor understandings.

With these skills and capacities, the travelers at the oasis are still not fully prepared to navigate their conflict. They need an idea of how to proceed, a frame or structure in which to magnify their capacities and apply their skills. Chapter Seven presents a suggested map through conflict that might have been useful to the people at the oasis. It is a suggested map because there are many routes—not one route—to collaboration. This map serves as a navigational guide to making sense of differences in a variety of contexts. It outlines four aspects of a relational process designed to support collaboration: preparation, discovery, creativity, and rejuvenation.

In this process map, relational connections are at the center, reminding us that our wisdom for relating to others is never more needed than in times of conflict. The identities, meanings, and passions that move us can connect as well as divide us. This map provides one way to make constructive connections more likely. Users of the map, like any travelers on a long journey, are first urged to prepare before acting. Stopping to consider who is involved and what they care about can go a long way to preventing missteps.

The second aspect of the map is discovery. No journey can be anticipated in all its aspects. There are always layers of discovery within ourselves and between us and others that can richly inform our attempts to bridge differences. As we discover ways to engage, the map helps us to cultivate creativity.

We cannot solve intercultural conflicts using tired or worn tools. As much as possible, each conflict calls for custom-design. We invent creative options and plans, and evaluate progress, making adjustments as necessary.

Just as preparation should not be neglected, so rejuvenation is an important part of the map. It may be tempting to come to closure in a conflict and move on, relieved at no longer engaging "the other." Not all conflicts end in transformations, and many one-time adversaries remain among those we would rather not see. Yet it is important to mark milestones in our journeys, individually and together. Sometimes, pausing to acknowledge incremental progress and celebrating achievements helps anchor our progress. Rejuvenation is also important because rest gives us energy and perspective to continue engaging quests to build communities and healthy workplaces.

These ideas inform the synthesis of cultural fluency depicted in Figure 8.1. They can be taken together as in this figure, or used as singular nuggets to spark inspiration.

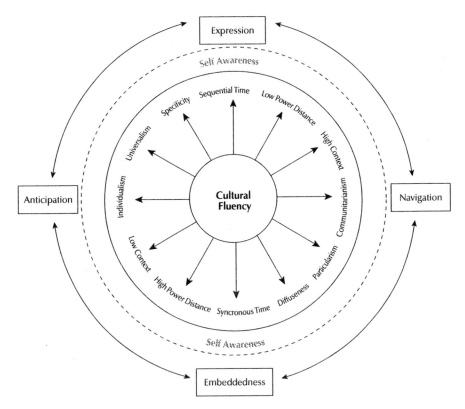

Figure 8.1 Conflict Resolution across Cultures

Trials and Triumphs: Becoming a Multicultural Team

When the five of us came together to write this book, we faced many choices. Originally, there were twelve of us who met several times to talk about writing a book about culture and conflict. At that time, we were doctoral students and a faculty member who shared similar questions as well as frustrations with the many unacknowledged cultural assumptions embedded in the things we read and quoted back to each other in papers, exams and dissertations. We wanted to draw on our diverse experience to give future colleagues and students a sense that their experiences matter and that cultural fluency is both attainable and useful in conflict resolution. All twelve of us were initially committed to the process of dialogue and relationship that we hoped would yield a joint book.

Being scholars and practitioners of conflict resolution meant that we had a number of things in common. We valued process, and knew that we would most likely get somewhere we wanted to go if we agreed in advance on a route and a destination. Early on, we talked about the challenges of doing collaborative work, especially across cultural boundaries. We tried to anticipate obstacles, and identified several, including possible differences over content, questions of credit for authorship, and the pull of commitments outside our process that might derail our efforts. Writing a book, we knew even then, was not for the faint of heart.

We all remember the first meeting distinctly. Spring was just beginning outside the window of our conference room where we assembled around a long rectangular table. Michelle had just finished her book *Bridging Cultural Conflicts* and was excited about collaborating on a related subject with colleagues from different cultures and backgrounds. We were a mixture of curious, enthusiastic, deeply committed scholar-practitioners who started from a foundation of mutual respect and a shared body of theory. Some of us knew each other very well; others had only heard of each other. But everyone in the group was connected to at least one other person, and everyone knew Michelle.

The idea of a culturally diverse group writing a book about cross-cultural conflict was exciting to all of us. At one of our first meetings, we talked about who was not there but should be invited. We began to do a survey of world regions. With Venashri, Africa was represented; with Tatsushi, Asia; with Karenjot, rural Canada and the South Asian diaspora were present; Nike, raised in Texas but born in Europe, gave us a thin claim to Europe and the unique culture that is Texas; and Michelle, a Canadian who had come to the United States to teach, led the conversation.

We wondered about South America being unrepresented. And what of African Americans, indigenous Americans, Eastern Europeans, Middle Easterners, Australians/New Zealanders, and Africans from outside South Africa? What about religious diversity, linguistic diversity, generational differences? Many different groups were named in our sincere quest to think about representativeness. We then invited people to join us in subsequent meetings from several of these regions and identities. We learned huge amounts from their contributions to our ongoing conversations.

Interestingly, only one of those whom we invited after the initial conversation stayed with the project through the writing, even though we extended ongoing invitations to several people. Had we developed some cohesion very early on, an unwitting sense of insiders and outsiders? Surely, we were unaware of that, and had not intended to do so. But looking back, we wonder whether inviting people into the journey who were not present for the take-off was a factor in their choice not to stay with the group for the landing. Perhaps groups begin to take on their unique textures and ethos before any members are aware of it.

We also realize the fallacy in our early thinking. Of course, none of us are representative of our cultures or national origins, and none of those we invited from various regions were, either. In our attempt to invite more diversity, we had focused on specific facets of identity and place, and set for ourselves an impossible task of representativeness. Later, we realized that we were each multicultural ourselves, and that the project of writing together would only surface many of these differences.

Looking back on that first meeting, the choice of a conference room at our university as a venue was significant. It seemed a natural enough place to meet for a group of scholars all affiliated with the university. We continued to meet in that same room out of convenience. It seemed hard enough for us to get to meetings at the campus; if we had tried to hold them offsite, logistical challenges of schedules and transportation may have derailed our efforts. Yet now, at the end of the project, we wonder whether holding some of those early conversations in a different setting might have been important. This question arose during a conversation between two group members after the manuscript was complete.

Michelle and Tatsushi were together to present material from this book at an international conference away from their homes. Because the conference site was a long drive from their hotel, they shared a car. As they chatted in the car, they learned things about each other's lives. Tatsushi learned that Michelle was a single parent with four children and that she was good at navigating in strange cities. Michelle learned that Tatsushi's wife was an expert at baking cheesecakes, and that she and Tatsushi shared a dream of opening a peace café together. Tatsushi had just finished his dissertation on creativity, and they shared excited conversations about his discoveries and their related experiences.

The things they talked about were mostly simple. There was laughter and the fondness that arises from work done well together and separately. The conversations were passionate with their excitement at what they were learning in their work, and how their lives were unfolding. They talked of their future dreams and the stories that led them to the dreams in the first place. In those few hours, they learned more about each other than they had over the previous three years. At the airport before running to their respective flights, they hugged.

Michelle and Tatsushi had never hugged before. But before they parted, they wondered whether their group might have bonded more easily and deeply if they had gone on more walks together, shared picnics, or taken car journeys. They had been so task-focused that their relationships had developed in the interstices of their collaborative work. The joy of playfulness and sharing other aspects of their lives that might have made the whole process easier and more enjoyable was only beginning to show itself.

This observation was echoed by the whole group when we met to reflect and celebrate the book's completion. This meeting was difficult to arrange and involved expenditures of significant time and money for authors coming to Vancouver, Canada. Venashri's visa for Canada did not arrive until the day before she was to leave Durban, South Africa. Karenjot had just returned to Canada from India. Nike was on her way to Bolivia, and Tatsushi was in the midst of final preparations for his dissertation defense in Washington, DC. Yet we were committed to coming together again to savor and celebrate our relationships.

What had happened that made these relationships so important? The book had happened, and so had much learning. One of the most powerful things we learned is the importance of valuing time together and having intentional conversations about things outside of work tasks. During those precious months in Virginia when we were able to meet personally, we sandwiched meetings between other commitments, and let values of efficiency and closure direct us. In retrospect, we wished that play, beauty, family, and our creative selves had been given places at the table of our collaborative work.

None of us anticipated that we would be completing the book from places around the world three or four years from when we began it. Of course, we knew that we might not always live in the same place and that it could become difficult to meet regularly, or at all. We never dreamed that before the book was finished Nike would be living in Barcelona, Venashri in Durban, Michelle in Vancouver, and Karenjot in Surrey (near Vancouver.) Only Tats remained in Virginia near Washington, DC when the manuscript was completed. Conference calls spanned multiple time zones, and computers became our virtual conversational space.

In the midst of these challenges, the relationships we had formed when we were together sustained us. Our common work kept drawing us back to this project as we saw more and more instances in our practices with communities and organizations that cried out for new thinking. In this last part of Chapter Eight, we reflect once more on our journey – how we got from twelve people exploring ideas to five close friends. We draw out lessons from our process that may be helpful to others.

Twelve people are too many to write a book unless the book is to be written as a series of articles loosely constellated around a theme. Thankfully, we never had to play a "survival game" like a lifeboat simulation where we had to collectively decide who would be able to stay and who had to go. Rather, life itself called members of our group in different directions. Most left very early in the process. One colleague's wife had a multiple birth that defined his priorities differently. Another left to do research abroad. Three or four people just drifted away, coming to meetings less and less frequently as the group receded in their priorities.

We had identified at the outset that we wanted not only to write about resolving intercultural conflict, but become a functional multicultural team ourselves. When people left the group, we pursued them, asking for their reflections on our process and their reasons for leaving. Sometimes people had felt overwhelmed by the enormity of what we were trying to do. Most often, other priorities intervened. There were a few times when someone was not a good fit for our group, and both they and we realized it. These latter instances caught our attention: Didn't we want to embrace diverse ways of approaching our subject?

As we reflected then and reflect now, our answer is a qualified yes. We definitely sought to bring a group as richly diverse as possible together. At the same time, some ways of communicating or approaching our subject were less generative given our chosen focus. Generally, people who were comfortable with prescriptions, attached to specific or narrow methodologies or ranges of theories, and those who were either didactic or withdrawn were not a good fit for our group. This realization only crystallized as we looked back, though our ideas about *fit* dawned organically and incrementally as we went along, and people self-eliminated.

We did not know who would see the project through to its conclusion when we sat together as a dozen or more people at initial meetings. We acknowledged that the group would have to shrink to make our writing feasible. After a few months, a core group of five members remained and undertook the task of writing this book. This smaller number facilitated more in-depth and meaningful interaction between the remaining members and we gradually became a cohesive unit as we worked toward our shared goal.

Even when our group had shrunk to a manageable number, we encountered challenges. After several initial writing exercises and conversations conceptualizing the book, we began to write in duos. For some duos, like Michelle and Venashri, the writing process worked relatively easily. We had written together before and worked together for a couple of years. This relational foundation combined with similar writing styles and previously established roles facilitated our collaboration.

For others in the group, collaborative writing was very new. Karenjot and Tatsushi wrote an early version of Chapter Five, but found their styles and experiences so divergent that it was difficult to make a "whole" out of it. Their writing styles were different, too. Tats wrote in lyric pictures, while Karenjot wrote more factually and sequentially. Each of them had learned English as a second language, and though both are completely fluent, their original languages may have had some role in their different ways of expressing themselves. Eventually, the group decided in conversation with Karenjot and Tatsushi to assign each of them separate chapters, even as all of us continued giving feedback on everyone's work.

Nike was in a unique position in the group because she was part of an earlier cohort at the university. She did not know Tatsushi, Venashri, or Karenjot before joining the group. Her writing style was probably the most information-centered of any of us. Because of her extensive background in cross-cultural conflict resolution, the group asked her to write Chapter Seven, a key part of the book. Nike's facility with complex material made her synthesis a strong one, but she frequently expressed a desire for additional input from other members to check any ethnocentrism that had written itself into her chapter.

There were also challenges related to roles. Michelle had taught every group member at some point during their programs, except for Tatsushi. She was a dissertation supervisor to two members. Especially for group members like Tatsushi and Venashri, whose early educations had featured deference to teachers and minimal back-and-forth engagement, there was reticence to counter Michelle's suggestions. When dealing with ideas on which Michelle had previously published, there was a reluctance to deviate from the way these ideas had been framed, even as Michelle invited creative departures. For example, Tatsushi took on the challenge of writing about cultural fluency, originally staying close to Michelle's original conception. Only after much feedback and encouragement from the group did he develop new dimensions of this idea, dimensions that Michelle and the group agreed enriched the concept.

As is clear from these examples, the journey was not without trials and tribulations. There were many challenges as well as moments of discouragement and celebration. Essential to moving through these challenges was our commitment to taking time to reflect on our processes, relationships, and products. Reflection allowed us to remain true to our original goal of deepening our understandings of culture and conflict through applying our ideas to ourselves. Each of us has been changed in positive ways through the experience. In the next section, we present the elements important to building a multicultural team illustrated through our interactions.

Learning from Ourselves: Elements of Multicultural Teams

A common desire to contribute to scholarship and practice about resolving intercultural conflicts brought us together. Interestingly, it was our very diversity that provided the sparks to keep us writing and engaged even when we did not understand each other. Sometimes, our collaboration also yielded the opposite of sparks: *skraps* (sparks spelled backwards)—those forgotten or buried remnants of ourselves where hurt or pain is lodged until triggered by someone's comment or action (LeBaron 2002). In addressing the sparks and skraps among us, we came closer to each other even as our life-paths diverged.

In reflecting on our work, we identified three elements essential to our multicultural teamwork—process, relationship, and outcome (PRO). Figure 8.2 provides a visual image of these aspects.

Process refers to how we did what we did. It is how we worked together to become a multicultural team, how we structured ourselves as a working group, and the means by which we completed our collaboration.

Relationship refers to how we interacted with each other. It includes our patterns of relating, group dynamics, and shared commitment. It includes how we developed our identity as a team.

Outcome refers to our achievements. Outcomes arose from goals established at the very beginning of coming together, and include our progress in understanding how to "do" intercultural conflict resolution. It also refers to outcomes we wished for but could not be sure would result, including strong working relationships and personal growth.

Process, relationship, and outcome (PRO) imply investments of time and energy; they are ongoing parts of establishing a successful multicultural team. These three elements are interdependent and mutually reinforcing factors that create synergy for effective multicultural teamwork. Relationship building is itself a *process,* and engaging in a quest for *outcomes* with others facilitates the deepening of *relationships* and learning about useful processes. Good working relationships among team members increases the likelihood of goal attainment (*outcome*), while achievement of goals together fosters team-building (*relationship*).

Our experience shows us that when process, relationship, and outcome reinforce each other, a multicultural team can be empowered to develop its own cohesive identity and culture. Team members begin to develop shared patterns of meaning as they work and become comfortable with each other. Rituals develop that have meaning only for the group, like shared humor and patterns of work.

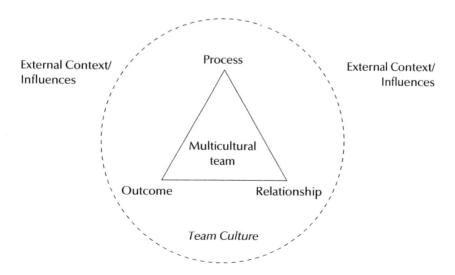

Figure 8.2 PRO Multicultural Team Elements

As much as the development of team culture facilitates progress, the permeable circle boundary in Figure 8.2 reminds us that external context and influences infiltrate and impact a team. For example, even as we evolved our unique team culture, values, and norms, we were always influenced by external cultures. Even as we strove to make our ideas accessible and clear, we were mindful that we came from a shared academic culture. Recognizing this, we questioned each other often about the assumptions and shared understandings within our group that might be opaque or not shared by others.

How do these PRO elements apply in practice? The following section discusses how processes, relationships, and outcomes played out through our group experiences. Readers will notice that as we sought to become a well-functioning multicultural team, we became a test of the very ideas and suggestions presented in this book. These tests had to be met for two important reasons: first, if we failed, we would not complete the book; and at least as important, if we were unable to apply these ideas to ourselves, they would not have been robust enough to share them.

Process: Reflections on Becoming a Team

We began with the objective of writing a book, but we had no fixed approach or process. We all agreed that relationship was central to what we were doing. We were less aware of the significant influence of the academic culture surrounding us that tended to proscribe relationship to functional categories rather than letting it spill out more seamlessly across our lives and work.

We wonder, for example, what our coming together would have been like if we were not a group of scholars, but artists, gardeners, or birdwatchers. Would our delight at aesthetic beauty have surfaced even more freely than it did through our metaphors for culture? Would our playfulness in pursuing elusive birds have bonded us in experiential ways that the discussion of ideas did not? Would the resolution of paradox inherent in art have brought us to a more complex awareness sooner, and held us closer in the bosom of our own whole selves—the light and the shadow parts?

We can not know these things, but it is fair to say that we started with only a slim awareness of the profound effects of the academic culture where we worked. We were aware of its influences on our ideas, but less cognizant of its effects on our relationships. With PRO in mind, we realize that the process of coming into relationship is always influenced by the cultural milieu surrounding the players. When, as for us, the cultural milieu seems positive or at least benign, we may not look to ways it shapes or excludes understandings.

For example, we were well aware that we wanted our product to reflect multicultural realities and sensibilities. We knew, too, that Western academic culture privileged particular ways of gaining and expressing knowledge. Yet we did not realize until we were in the thick of writing the book how difficult it was to step outside the academic frames within which we worked. We wrote in stories, but our academic culture influenced our need to anchor the stories in concrete theories, even when the theories were unarticulated. Our conversations were often about theoretical ideas and how to translate them into accessible language. This movement back and forth between stories and theories helped us feel more comfortable, but sometimes took our attention away from the stories' inherent, holistic wisdom.

Of course, relating to each other through discussing theories seemed natural to all of us. We were a group of scholars, and theories were our currency. At the same time, we realized from the outset that our relationships were important. We extended this understanding directly into our writing, realizing that relationship development is essential for effective cross-cultural conflict resolution.

Figure 2.1 shows relationship-building as the centerpiece of our approach. This image was congruent with our awareness that multicultural collaboration would mean ongoing efforts and investments in relationship-building. We understood that a strong team foundation based in trust and respect would facilitate our work together and make success more likely. Both dialogue and debate filled our initial meetings, as we shared general thoughts and ideas about culture, conflict resolution, and the state of the world.

Flexibility and openness to various ideas and ways of doing things was a hallmark of our evolving process. Early on, it became clear that agreeing on definitions and meanings was our first challenge. A sustained process of joint exploration evolved as we engaged each other in discussions of conflict and culture, and traced ways these themes played out in our lives. These meetings were filled with dialogue and debates as we grappled with understanding ourselves and each other better and developing a base of shared understanding.

While early meetings were energizing with their mix of stories and explorations, there were also challenges. Michelle's suggestions of writing about metaphors came more easily to some group members than others. For example, for Venashri, living through the transition from Apartheid yielded an immediate connection with metaphor. She explained that the image of the rainbow was ubiquitous for South Africans. Karenjot found it more difficult to identify a metaphor that conveyed her experiences of culture in a coastal Canadian community where Sikhs were unevenly welcome—there were no obvious symbols or images that suggested themselves. Eventually, she settled on shifting sands as a way of communicating the cultural flux that characterized her childhood. When the group discussed these and other metaphors, it became clear that every metaphor—whether intuitively obvious or the product of considerable reflection—had a reference to the environment where the writer grew up.

After several months of engaging each other regularly and undertaking short writing exercises like the metaphor explorations, we had the pieces in place to support the collaborative writing process. It helped a great deal that we spent time initially devising a process for working together, as the first step in cultural fluency suggests (see Chapter Four). We embraced flexibility, not wanting to pigeonhole ourselves into a preset way of doing things. At the same time, we needed ways of monitoring progress and continuity. Initial time spent anticipating how we would manage logistics, interactions, and decisions of group members to opt out of the project proved very beneficial.

Six months into the project, our process took a different turn. We were now ready to begin the writing process. We quickly realized that five people could not sit down and write a chapter together, so we proceeded to divide up work, tasks, and responsibilities based on members' interests, time availability, and strengths. At this point, the feeling of collaboration decreased slightly. We all contributed our feedback to each chapter's author, but collaboration became a lot more difficult as some members moved across seas and continents, and life in general intervened.

Still, we met for long sessions whenever we could. When face-to-face dialogues were not possible, we relied on telephone conferences and e-mails. Our foundation of connections and experience collaborating enabled us to continue despite overwhelming distances. Our larger shared commitment to conflict resolution scholarship and practice certainly helped us sustain our relationships despite the many twists and turns we encountered along the way.

Writing and Work

Our writing at the beginning of this project reflected the flexible nature of our process. Meetings and conversations energized us to begin putting our ideas to paper but we struggled with where and how to begin. We went back to what was known and familiar: ourselves. Our very first exercise in written dialogue was to describe our diverse worlds using metaphors. Our second writing exercise was a narrative on self-awareness. There were many exercises, some more similar and others quite different that followed and, after each exercise, we would meet and discuss each member's piece.

These exercises were very revealing. As mentioned earlier, the metaphors were very different, but all were evocative. Discussing them together showed us things we had not realized about our home contexts, as well as opening windows into each other. The pieces on self-awareness were also revealing. Venashri's piece painted a self inextricably bound up with the momentous events of her life through the transition from Apartheid, a self whose identity is inseparable from the liberation and ongoing struggle of South African people. Nike's description of self-awareness was precise, thorough, and abstract, conveying an autonomous individual with choices as its locus of awareness. Tatsushi's contribution was a poetic picture of external and internal landscapes, revealing a felt connection between awareness and nature, time, and season. Karenjot's writing showed a self interconnected with others as she recounted how her earliest memories were of a shared identity affected by ongoing tensions between her community and Euro-Canadian neighbors. And Michelle's exploration was internal, ranging through the secret spaces where sense is made but not articulated and intuition glints in an emerging life story.

Much of this early work has fallen into the background, but engaging in the seemingly long and laborious writing processes was both important and beneficial. These incremental steps allowed us to experience small accomplishments and achievements, while learning about each other's ways of making meaning. They helped develop our relationships and bolstered our confidence that this project was possible, and that we could do it together. As our conversations became more focused, we were able to transition from metaphors and images to more specific ideas.

Giving voice to our thoughts and ideas, both individually and jointly, was certainly a challenge. We were accustomed to studying culture, but less accustomed to investigating our own. Sometimes, the things we discussed were emotional and triggered old hurts. At other times, we disagreed about the nature of the things about which we were talking. Culture and conflict are both human phenomena. They are complex and quite diffuse. In our struggle to write about them specifically in our book, there were many choices. We did not always agree on which fork in the road to take.

As we differed with each other, we had to make choices about how much our writing should reflect our diversity, and how much convergence we should seek (Brown, Griggs, and Louw 1995). We wanted our product to be a book—a cohesive, flowing piece of writing that would make sense to our readers. At the same time, we were committed to honoring our differences and distinct voices.

In the end, our various cultural lenses remain distinct within the book. We realize that it cannot be otherwise; we would not be true to our message about the richness of diversity if we suppressed individual voices for the sake of the whole. Each of us, and every reader, uses cultural lenses to filter information. Just as we became more aware of the powerful effect of these lenses, we hope that readers have become more aware of their lenses while reading our book.

At the same time as we tried to remain true to our distinctness, we sought a coherent flow of ideas and a common language. We imagined that we were having conversations with readers, and as we wrote we held a picture of people coming together for conversation in mind. Recognizing that different storytelling styles can make conversations richer, we drew on experiences from our lives to illustrate our commonalities and differences.

Still, tensions arose among and between us. Some group members wrote colloquially, others more formally. Sometimes, we differed over what was relevant, and whether a straight line or a spiral was the best route to make a point. We learned to welcome the tensions even as they felt confusing and overwhelming, recognizing that as we moved through them, we developed a stronger team and a better product.

One of the key reasons we were able to move through these challenges was the self-awareness of individual members and the shared commitment of all group members to valuing others' perspectives. For example, Nike was always aware of her preference for straight lines, clearly connecting one point to another. Michelle was aware of the ways her previous work may have shaped her and others' notions of the boundaries around ideas. She frequently invited members to step outside previous work to try new concepts, aware of the need for creativity in the conflict resolution field.

In later stages of our collaboration, our early spirit of open flexibility had to be tempered with the need to complete our project. We examined draft chapters for flow and connection, within and among themselves. Even as we believed we were close to finishing, the voices sometimes seemed too distinct and different from each other. In the end, the editors went through the entire manuscript, massaging sections and chapters into congruence with each other. We realized that collaboration works best when leadership is exercised in ways that group members trust.

Relationship: Reflections on Group Dynamics and Interactions

We started our conversations with each other in rather loose ways, focusing on relationship building rather than roles and role definitions. Initial conversations and interactions were tentative as we each tried to determine how we could fit into this group and the project. We were en route to developing a group identity and also assessing ourselves in light of the proposed group purpose. Becoming a multicultural team meant making way for a new team identity incorporating diversity and productivity.

Later, many of us reflected that we were in awe of each other during those first meetings. We saw enormous richness in each other's experiences as conflict resolution thinkers and practitioners, and as cultural beings. Many of us questioned ourselves internally, asking "Do I really have anything to contribute here given others' tremendous expertise and experience?" We stayed because we were intrigued by the possibility of doing something unique and different: producing a collaborative book reflecting the collected wisdom of a culturally diverse group of people who have thought about and practiced conflict resolution.

Relationship building is facilitated in multicultural teams when members begin sharing their life experiences with each other (Solow 2004). As we shared our individual and collective stories about conflict and resolution, we became aware that we had a wealth of information on the subject. We could not help but be inspired, motivated, and energized by each other. Chapters Six and Seven highlight storytelling as a powerful tool that breathes clarity and understanding into the unknown with the potential to positively influence interactions. Stories were very powerful for us. They gathered us together, creating windows into our home contexts and avenues for dialogue. They also generated questions for us, and our curiosity about these questions kept us working together with an ongoing spirit of inquiry. True to our initial, collective vision, we always maintained an atmosphere of respect, mutual regard, and humility, even during times of disagreement.

To understand our group formation and the challenges of building relationships, it is important to return to the way we came together initially. As previously mentioned, Michelle LeBaron had been a professor at the Institute for Conflict Analysis and Resolution at George Mason University for over ten years. When she invited a dozen doctoral students to explore the challenge of writing a book collaboratively, she imagined moving into a mutual, collaborative role as the project evolved. As mentioned earlier, this process of changing roles and sharing leadership was more difficult than any of us anticipated. As many of us had hierarchical cultural expectations about relationships with teachers, Michelle continued to be seen as the leader.

Balancing a leadership role with being a team player can be quite challenging. Michelle tried to even out roles, encouraging group members to adopt increasingly more autonomy. In turn, we also gradually learned to adjust our cultural lenses to facilitate developing less formal relationships of interdependence with Michelle. Later, we discussed this in detail and recognized that it would have been better to name this challenge overtly earlier and find ways to work with it. We also realized that even when seemingly opposing and contradictory views are given voice with a spirit of inquiry, it is possible to embrace multiple ways of knowing and doing.

One of the challenges related to leadership and the flat structure into which Michelle invited us into arose from our varying levels of experience. Michelle had published two books in the two years previous to beginning this one. She had clear ideas of what constituted strong writing, and what needed revision. As we began to write sections of the book, Michelle took primary responsibility for providing feedback on writing style and appropriateness, while the whole group gave feedback on substance. This meant that Michelle remained a de facto leader, even as many aspects of our work were shared. Reflecting back, it would have been good to clarify this aspect of her role as editor, as well.

By the time we began writing, we had already developed a sense of group accountability for the work we were doing. Parceling out individual responsibility was not as easy. Sometimes, group members did not meet deadlines. Other times, they came back with work that went in a different direction than others had envisioned. For example, one group member's writing about a cultural incident caused some consternation among us. The writing was colloquial and personal, and other members had difficulty seeing its connection to our themes. For the writer, the connections were obvious and did not need elaboration. The writer also had other pressing commitments, and did not have time to elaborate in the way group members requested. When pressed, this author suggested that another group member could freely adapt the work to meet our criteria, but no one was up to the task. We could not fill in the gaps in the story because we did not understand enough of the context.

That particular story was left out of the final manuscript. Gradually, we evolved clearer criteria about writing contributions, so authors were able to operate within these parameters. We also came to more easily balance group and individual responsibilities, working back and forth between them like an accordion.

Throughout the earlier parts of the project, we had frequent meetings when we would discuss each chapter and the evolving ideas in the book. As our comfort level with each other deepened, our ability to provide constructive criticism and feedback increased. We became less concerned with preserving each other's feelings and more able to be respectfully candid. We understood and accepted that there would not always be consensus, but difference and lack of consensus did not need to detract from working together.

Tensions

Conflict was unusual among us, perhaps because of our deep respect for each other and our proactive work on relationship building. But tensions did arise, sometimes threatening to derail the project. There were places where we stumbled; times when we were lost and unsure of which path to follow; when we felt alone or overwhelmed by the daunting nature of what the group was trying to do.

Balancing individual perspectives with group identity and voice became harder during the writing phase. Chapter authors found balancing individual, independent thoughts and views with group ideas particularly difficult. Nike was quite uncomfortable at many points during the writing process because she was acutely aware of her Western biases and the ways they had influenced a great deal of accepted conflict resolution theory and practice. If we were to write a book that truly reflected our multicultural make-up, she reminded us, then it was essential that we not simply adapt the Western concepts so much a part of the doctoral program where we were students and faculty.

Yet, these concepts influenced us in many ways. Each of us had chosen to be affiliated with a Western academic program, and it was hard to trace our ideas back to cultural origins. Nike reflected later that she frequently held back from contributing because she did not want to impose Western frames on conversations. She hoped for something more organic to grow from our diverse backgrounds. For the same reason, writing an important chapter in the book was difficult for Nike because—even to the extent we could tease out perspectives that predated our involvement at the university—it was a mammoth job synthesizing our worldviews into a coherent whole.

The group responded to Nike's reluctance in a number of ways. We encouraged her to reference personal experiences, even as she sought to move away from Western-centered ideas. Her willingness to question assumptions and rethink accepted approaches made her a very valuable member of the group.

Though we wrote the book collaboratively, everyone could not hold the same pen. We took turns taking the lead on draft chapters. Sometimes, the lead shifted from one person to another as the collaboration unfolded. Questions of voice and credit then surfaced, as we struggled with whose voice was most central to specific chapters. One team member wrote about the challenges this way:

> I needed courage and boldness to present an initial image of what this chapter should look like and contain—because I know that one person's view is often drastically different from others. . . . I appreciated everybody's willingness to suspend judgment and place himself/herself in my shoes, trying to work within my worldview first while providing candid feedback that was outside my worldview.

This observation has implications for the process of multicultural team-building. A multicultural team is a single unit made strong by individual members' diversity. Effective cross-cultural work calls for a delicate dance between group and individual voices, and frequent open communication. In multicultural teams, it is important to balance self and group expectations so that they are not competing orientations but complementary (Watson, Johnson, and Merritt 1998). In mixing our voices we sought to honor individual meaning-making, while distilling such expression in ways that speak to diverse audiences.

Another tension experienced in the group related to attrition. As mentioned, our initial numbers went from twelve to six over the first several months. Many members left as other life priorities intervened and they realized that they could not maintain the commitment the book would require. All of these departures were amicable, with those leaving offering to be ongoing sounding boards and resources. Although this initial attrition was a disappointment because we were losing their experiences and voices, it was early enough that the work was not derailed. With time, the remaining core group realized that a smaller number also facilitated stronger cohesion and easier working relationships.

The withdrawal of a core member at a much later stage in the process was more difficult. This particular departure brought into focus yet again the tenuous balance between group identity and individual identity mentioned earlier. It is possible that in an effort to create a strong group identity and engage in teamwork, individual needs and ways of engaging were sacrificed or insufficiently addressed. It is also possible that the group process did not provide enough recognition for the member who left. We all did our best, individually and collectively, to remain in dialogue with the member who left, and remain friends despite our diverging paths.

Reflecting later, we realized that events unrelated to the book project had probably influenced the sixth person's departure. The person had requested academic mentoring from Michelle that she could not provide. Michelle had asked the person to take on tasks related to promoting the book and developing training materials related to the book; this had been interpreted as less serious than the roles of some other members. Hurt feelings were buried rather than surfaced—this is not infrequently part of multicultural team experiences. But its frequency in other settings did not make the experience any easier for the remaining group members. Each time we met, the subject of our sixth author would eventually surface, and we extracted as much learning from it as we could.

Intrapersonal tension was not uncommon during our writing process. We all carried personal guilt about our inability to meet deadlines and attend all meetings. No one was unique in this sense—each one of us failed to meet a deadline at some point. This tension was minimized by our group goodwill and the shared recognition that we would all have times when unexpected things happened. Not only were we able to be patient with each other, but we frequently met together to address issues like writer's block and overscheduling. Group synergy was realized through a context of co-operation in which we provided help and assistance to each other (Watson et al. 1998).

The hardest period related to time and deadlines that came after we had projected the book would be complete. Everyone had taken on new commitments, and our editors had moved worlds away from each other—Venashri in South Africa where she works for ACCORD (African Centre for the Constructive Resolution of Disputes) and Michelle to a new position at a Canadian university. Finding time in between other projects to go back over our ideas was very challenging, and both Venashri and Michelle noticed that email response times from other group members grew longer as the book was no longer front and center.

At times, logistics and changes affected group morale and caused us to question the sustainability of this project. Significant life transitions happened for all of us as we moved to other countries, took doctoral exams, and defended dissertations. Meeting together as a team became all but impossible. Work seemed to come to a standstill as we all dealt with other priorities. However, our strong ongoing commitment to each other and the book got us over these hurdles, and we found that meeting in person helped rekindle our enthusiasm for the project. Any diverse team of people with numerous commitments who work over a lengthy period will likely face such challenges. If the group is initially formed with flexible norms, it is more likely that such periods of stagnation will not result in the team's demise.

Reflections and Debriefs

This chapter was written after we spent much time reflecting individually and together. Each group member answered a questionnaire about the writing process. The group then set aside two reflection periods to meet and talk about our process, relationships, and outcomes in greater detail. While these were the longest times set aside for reflection on our process, monitoring our dynamics was a constant focus.

During our group reflections, we provided feedback to each other about work and responsibilities, in the form of constructive criticism, alternatives, positive affirmations, and encouragement. Feedback was given and accepted in a team-spirit which reflected respect and goodwill. Such periodic process feedback is important for the effective performance of multicultural task groups. Taking regular time-outs to examine how the diverse team can work in a synergistic manner and to examine individuals' expectations and their changing perspectives is important (Watson et al. 1998).

Reflecting on our trials and triumphs provided us with the big picture and more depth of understanding about our group experiences. Coming together and talking about the journey gave us an opportunity to express our thoughts, feelings, and opinions about our strengths and weaknesses as a team and individually. We gave voice to questions and sensitive topics, we analyzed and shared, we laughed and were sad—but above all, we learned tremendously from this time of reflection. As we talked, we witnessed the power of greater openness taking root and grounding our team in a bond much stronger than we had had at any previous point.

Interestingly, it was not during these planned reflection sessions that the hardest challenges arose. For many groups, transitioning from vision to reality is a point of tension. When we signed a contract to publish this book, one group member was unhappy with some of the terms of the contract and with the way authorship had been handled. Despite earlier efforts to be sure we understood how we were proceeding, a misunderstanding had arisen. The misunderstanding did not seem like it would derail the project, but it certainly had a cooling effect on some relationships within the group.

People in the group were aware of different aspects of the problem, but everyone knew there was a problem. Because we were scattered across the globe at this point, we scheduled a conference call. During the call, Tats facilitated an informal conflict resolution process, reminding all of us of our shared values and deep convictions about the importance of this work. He helped us apply our methodology to ourselves by inviting a spirit of dialogue and reminding us of our potential for creative problem solving. Everyone engaged constructively, and eventually a resolution was found that brought closure for everyone.

As we reflected on group dynamics, we could identify patterns and roles that emerged over time. Nike kept us focused and asked hard questions; Tats helped us stay congruent with what we espoused; Ven acknowledged everyone's efforts and provided ongoing encouragement; Karenjot noticed when someone's feelings were hurt and took personal initiative to connect; and Michelle was the glue, keeping us all together even as we spread around the world.

In the end, the flat organizational structure to which we had aspired was partly realized. It came to fruition as we stepped into our roles as colleagues and professionals, bringing a rich array of experiences back to our group. Group members saw through repeated experiences that everyone had a great deal to contribute, and no one's contributions were superior to others'. At the same time, because of Venashri's and Michelle's roles as editors, and their task of making changes to the final manuscript, they remained leaders of the group. Venashri and Michelle initiated meetings and calls, sent reminders when feedback was needed, and generally kept the project on track. From the vantage point of the book's completion, it would have been helpful if we could have articulated these role distinctions early on. Doing so was probably impossible, however, because these roles emerged and changed over the course of our work together.

Outcome: Reflections on Achievements

The book you have read is, for us, another beginning. It not only informs our ongoing practice and scholarship, but it generates questions and leaves us with valuable lessons about multicultural teams. We share some of our reflections about the unique dynamics and gifts of multicultural teams here.

The Value of Multicultural Teams for Conflict Resolution

It is one thing to write about intercultural conflict and multicultural team-building, and quite another to apply ideas to ourselves. While this was the litmus test of our work, it was also the hardest part of following through. Even in our final debriefs, we found it easier to talk about the conflicts relating to the departure of our sixth member than the conflicts that arose amongst the five of us who remained. This was because not everyone was party to each conflict, and we did not want to violate confidentiality. Also, there was a sense that issues between us had been resolved, and there was an unspoken desire not to let old tensions resurface.

Reflecting on our experiences, we recognize that intercultural conflicts are frequently generated or escalated through miscommunication, as with one group conflict we had about the publishing contract. Sometimes, meanings and identities collide, and they collide more forcefully when power imbalances complicate dynamics. Who would be better equipped to meet these challenges but practitioners who have experienced cultural clashes themselves, and found ways to address them? Who understands the potency of stories to bridge differences better than those who have needed stories to explain themselves to each other and who have created new stories together? An effective multicultural team models the importance and potential of relationship-building across differences. There is no substitute for self and shared-awareness when we walk into the fires of conflict.

Several practices, summarized below, help groups to meet these challenges.

Key Lessons about Multicultural Team Development and Functioning

Reflecting on our collaborative writing process, team dynamics, and growth over a three year period yielded significant lessons about multicultural team development and functioning. These lessons have been presented in the preceding discussions of process and relationships, but they are summarized here as key points:

- **Balance voices**—Adopt communication norms that honor individual stories and collective learning;
- **Monitor process**—Ensure that process, relationship, and outcome (PRO) needs are met over time;
- **Value yin and yang**—Balance emphasis on achievement and exploration, being and doing, creativity and standardization, leadership and team collaboration, and uncertainty and closure;

- **Monitor core assumptions**—Engage in ongoing dialogue about assumptions informing collaborative work, especially hidden or privileged assumptions;
- **Expand cultural fluency**—Encourage each other to anticipate, express, and navigate differences with a spirit of inquiry;
- **Deepen collaboration**—Involve group members in ongoing attention to process dynamics, relationships, roles, and outcomes;
- **Cultivate flexibility**—Attend to tensions between assimilation and diversity;
- **Utilize sparks and skraps**—Use moments of uncertainty, tension, and "ah-hah" as cues for reflection and dialogue;
- **Invite reflection**—Foster honest reflection on processes, relationships, and outcomes.

Personal Growth

Not only did we grow in our capacities as a multicultural team, we grew as individuals during this project. As we reflected, we recognized several ways the project augmented or jump-started members' personal growth. The richness of our diversity, our charged and passionate conversations, and the creation of new ways of thinking and working together all contributed to a powerful learning experience.

Thinking back, we see that it was the risk of sharing personal stories that contributed most to our learning. It wasn't easy for Tats to write about his wedding, or Karenjot to write about painful experiences in her community. Yet writing about these times not only gave the writers perspective on themselves and their choices, it stimulated new stories and perspective-taking for each of us. Not all these experiences were shared—sometimes skraps unearthed through one member's story were processed with spouses or close friends because of their delicate or private nature.

Another aspect of personal learning relates to generosity. Especially with stories "close to the bone" like Tats' story of Rwandan family members who lost a brother, or Venashri's story of her struggles as a new social worker in a South African township, we learned to tread gently, acknowledging the risk the storyteller was taking. We learned to be generous in sharing stories and as listeners, understanding each other in context without judgment as much as possible.

Finally, we also learned that not everyone has the same appetite or aptitude for monitoring processes, relationships, and outcomes. In our group, Tats and Venashri were often the most aware of relational concerns in an ongoing way. During times when they were absorbed in other work, relational work was neglected, and tensions arose. When they re-engaged, it helped us address our collective relationships. Nike and Michelle were more attentive to outcome, encouraging the group onwards when our work floundered. And Karenjot was most aware of the overall process—how it was developing and where weak links threatened to derail progress.

Interestingly, we did not assume each other's roles about process, relationship, and outcome very readily. These roles were quite beneath our conscious awareness for most of the project, but it may have been useful to explore them earlier so that we could switch-hit for each other when needed.

In Chapter Four, we make the case for cultural fluency grounded in self-awareness. Working with others on our team ultimately meant seeing more about ourselves; our cultural identities, cultural biases, worldviews, and the lenses through which we experienced the world and each other. Our learning community became a powerful mirror for us, revealing more than we had previously known about ourselves. Before we can help others, we need to know ourselves and come to understand the assumptions and frames that influence our thoughts and behaviors, and which will ultimately influence the conflict resolution processes we manage.

What did we learn about ourselves and conflict? First, we learned, again, that conflict happens. As careful as we were to make intentional choices about communication and process, we came into conflict in more than one instance. Second, we learned that we—a group of committed, educated individuals from around the world—can experience conflict as learning and choose to renew our relationships as we engage it. Finally, we learned that engaging conflict, whether in a team or community, is an ongoing process, never complete. As we work together over time, we will surely encounter new issues that cry out for the application of the ideas in this book.

Remaining Questions

Books, when complete, are finite in their reach. Their promise is only realized if readers use them, engaging with the ideas in communities of practice. Any book, focused on a specific area, will be limited in its applicability to other areas. This book is no exception.

Because we chose to focus primarily on interpersonal and group conflict, our work may have less application to larger scale issues. These issues are some of the most pressing of our day, including genocide, terrorism, and ethnic cleansing. Whether ideas here are useful in these contexts is a matter for exploration. We share the conviction that work at all levels of conflict is essential to the ongoing development of our communities.

The approaches outlined here take time to implement, and require attention to developing relationships. Not everyone can or is willing to invest this kind of time. We recognize that this may limit the effectiveness of our work, yet we can find no substitute for a caring connection as a basis for responding to and preventing conflict. In our world of increasing alienation and disengagement, we come back to relationships as the lifeblood of all systems— political, organizational, familial. When relationships cannot be developed, or the will does not exist to further them, conflicts will escalate and may be destructive. Future work that focuses on how systems and conflict resolution processes can foster relationship development would be helpful.

Another question is how these ideas apply to multicultural settings when there are multiple levels of identity, languages spoken, and complex dynamics. We limited our examples and stories for purposes of simplicity. The real world is not always so amenable to simplification, and we acknowledge that more complex situations cannot be addressed without exploring the effects of history, old wounds, and unsalved hurts.

Even as we hail from five world regions, we recognize that it is impossible to capture multiple cultural perspectives in one book. The ideas we present here reflect our cultural and personal identities and we do not suggest universal transferability to other cultural groups, or even to others in our cultural groups. While we believe that our ideas about how cultural dynamics and conflict can be understood are transferable and valuable, questions remain about how to discern groups' and individuals' starting points in time to prevent conflicts from escalating.

Finally, we invoke intuition as an area that needs further exploration. People around the world regularly handle conflict constructively. They create and maintain functional organizations and peaceful families. Many of them have no formal training. How do intuition and the cultural glue that comes from relationships help them achieve peaceful outcomes? When are cultural traditions an asset in preventing and resolving conflict, and when a hindrance? While there are no definitive answers to these questions, they are all fruitful ground for future inquiry.

This Book—and a Way Forward

We began this project with the goal of understanding how to "do" intercultural conflict resolution, documenting our experiences and learning. This book marks the achievement of this goal. While much of our learning is contained within these pages, our most important lesson on intercultural conflict resolution is that our work must be ongoing and continuous given the changing dynamics of culture and conflict.

In the end, we leave our stories, carriers for our hopes and dreams of a better world. Because hope, like trust, can take a long time to build and be dashed in an instant, we have aspired to engender hope. If our story of emerging as a team of not only colleagues but lifelong friends inspires you, we have met an important objective. We end with many questions, but with more certainty than when we began about this: even when conflict is characterized by vast differences, building relationships is not only possible—it is essential to create positive change.

For each of us, welcoming diversity in our communities and workplaces is a renewed commitment. Embracing diversity, we ultimately enrich ourselves, our families, and our world.

References

Preface

Arnold, Matthew. 1851. *Dover Beach*. Edited by J. Middlebrook. Columbus, Ohio: Merrill.

Chapter One

Gandhi, Mahatma K. "Co-Mingling of Cultures." In *Mahatma—A Golden Treasury of Wisdom: Thoughts and Glimpses of Life,* edited by M. T. Ajgaonkar. 1995. Bombay, India: Mani Bhavan Gandhi Sangrahalaya.

Chapter Two

Bennett, Milton J. 1979. "Overcoming the golden rule. Sympathy and empathy". In *Communication Yearbook,* edited by D. Nimmo. Washington DC: International Communication Association.

Lederach, John Paul. 1995. *Preparing for Peace: Conflict Transformation Across Cultures.* Syracuse, NY: Syracuse University Press.

Mbamara, Oliver O. 2004. *Why Are We Here? Soul-Searching Stories, Parables, Essays and Poems.* Bookman Publishing and Marketing.

Volkan, Vamik. 1997. *Bloodlines: From Ethnic Pride to Ethnic Terrorism.* Colorado: Westview Press.

Chapter Three

Fuertes, Al. 2002. *Personal Communication.* Fairfax, Virginia: Institute for Conflict Analysis and Resolution.

Geertz, Clifford. 1973. *The Interpretation of Cultures.* New York: Basic Books.

Hall, Edward T. 1976. *Beyond Culture.* Garden City, New York: Doubleday.

Hampden-Turner, Charles and Trompenaars, Fons. 2000. *Building Cross Cultural Competence: How to Create Wealth from Conflicting Values.* New Haven and London: Yale University Press.

Hofstede, Geert. 1984. *Culture's Consequences: International Differences in Work-Related Values.* Beverly Hills, California: Sage Publications.

Horatio Alger Society. www.ihot.com/~has/. Accessed January 23, 2005.

LeBaron, Michelle. 2003. *Bridging Cultural Conflicts: A New Approach for a Changing World.* San Francisco: Jossey-Bass.

LeBaron, Michelle and Nike Carstarphen. 1999. "Finding Common Ground on Abortion." In *Consensus Building Handbook, A Comprehensive Guide to Reaching Agreement,* edited by Lawrence Susskind, Sarah McKearnan and Jennifer Thomas-Larmer (Eds.) San Francisco: Sage Publications.

Novinger, Tracy. 2001. *Intercultural Communication.* Austin, Texas: University of Texas Press.

Russikov, Karen, Liliane Fucaloro and Dalia Salkauskiene. 2003. "Plagiarism as a Cross-Cultural Phenomenon." *The Cal Poly Pomona Journal of Interdisciplinary Studies,* no.16.

Sandercock, Leonie. 2003. *Cosmopolis II: Mongrel Cities in the 21st Century.* New York: Continuum.

Saxe, John Godfrey. 1882. *The Blind Men and the Elephant: The Poetical Works of John Godfrey Saxe.* Boston: Houghton Mifflin.

Whiting, Robert. 1989. *You Gotta Have Wa.* New York: Macmillan.

Chapter Four

Krishnamurti, J. 1998. "Listening to the Silence." In *Inner Knowing: Consciousness, Creativity, Insight and Intuition,* edited by Helen Palmer (Ed.) New York: Jeremy P.Tarcher/Putnam.

Chapter Five

Fadiman, Anne. 1997. *The Spirit Catches You and You Fall Down.* New York: Farrar, Straus and Giroux.

Hirsh, Lee. 2002. *Amandla: Revolution in Four-Part Harmony.* Vancouver: Lion's Gate Films.

Huntington, Samuel P. 1997. *The Clash of Civilizations and the Remaking of World Order.* New York: Touchstone.

Chapter Six

LeBaron, Michelle. 2003. *Bridging Cultural Conflicts: A New Approach for a Changing World.* San Francisco: Jossey-Bass.
Mandela, R. Nelson. 1994. *Long Walk to Freedom: The Autobiography of Nelson Mandela.* Randburg, South Africa: Macdonal Purnell (PTY) Ltd,.

Chapter Seven

Montville, Joseph V. 1993. "The Healing Function in Political Conflict Resolution." In *Conflict Resolution Theory and Practice: Integration and Application,* edited by Dennis J.D. Sandole and Hugo van der Merwe. Manchester, England: Manchester University Press.
Richards, M.C. 1998. "Separating and Connecting: The Vessel and the Fire." In *The Fabric of the Future,* edited by Mary Jane Ryan. Berkeley, CA: Conari Press.

Chapter Eight

Brown Griggs, Lewis and Louw, Lente-Louise. 1995. "Diverse Teams: Breakdown or Breakthrough?" *Training and Development* 49, no.10.
Cortez, Carlos. 2004. "How the Media Teach about Diversity." Presentation at the Summer Institute for Intercultural Communication. Forest Grove, Oregon. August 2, 2004.
King, Thomas. 2005. *The Truth About Stories.* Minneapolis, University of Minnesota Press.
LeBaron, Michelle. 2003. *Bridging Cultural Conflicts: A New Approach for a Changing World.* San Francisco: Jossey-Bass.
LeBaron, Michelle. 2002. *Bridging Troubled Waters: Conflict Resolution from the Heart.* San Francisco: Jossey-Bass.
Solow, Larry. 2004. "Multicultural Team Building." *www.frankallen.com/Executive_Reports/Diversity_In_the_Workplace/Multicultural.* Accessed August 2004. Frank E. Allen & Associates, Inc.
Watson, Warren E., Lynn Johnson, and Deanna Merritt. 1998. "Team Orientation, Self-Orientation, and Diversity in Task Groups: Their Connection to Team Performance over Time." *Group & Organization Management* 23, no.2.

Index

CROSSING CULTURES

from **Nicholas Brealey Publishing**

and **Intercultural Press**

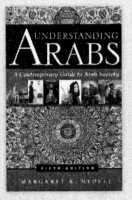

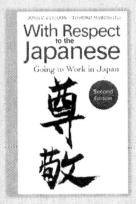

AMONG THE
IRANIANS
A Guide to Iran's
Culture and Customs
by Sofia A. Koutlaki
ISBN: 9781931930901
E-ISBN: 9780984247134
US Price: $24.95
UK Price: £14.99

AU CONTRAIRE!
SECOND ED.
Figuring Out the French
by Gilles Asselin and
Ruth Mastron
ISBN: 9781931930925
E-ISBN: 9780984247189
US Price: $29.95
UK Price: £16.99

ENCOUNTERING
THE CHINESE,
THIRD ED.
A Modern Country, An
Ancient Culture
by Hu Wenzhong,
Cornelius N. Grove, and
Zhuang Enping
ISBN: 9781931930994
E-ISBN: 9780984247196
US Price: $24.95
UK Price: £14.99

FROM NYET TO DA,
FOURTH ED.
Understanding the New
Russia
by Yale Richmond
ISBN: 9781931930598
E-ISBN: 9781931930727
US Price: $27.95
UK Price: £14.99

GERMANY
Unraveling An Enigma
by Greg Nees
ISBN: 9781877864759
E-ISBN: 9781931930420
US Price: $27.50
UK Price: £12.99

LEARNING TO
THINK KOREAN
A Guide to Living and
Working in Korea
by L. Robert Kohls
ISBN: 9781877864872
E-ISBN: 9781931930437
US Price: $35.00
UK Price: £16.99

MODERN-DAY
VIKINGS
A Practical Guide to
Interacting with the Swedes
by Christina Johansson
Robinowitz and Lisa
Werner Carr
ISBN: 9781877864889
E-ISBN: 9780585434414
US Price: $25.95
UK Price: £16.99

SPAIN IS DIFFERENT,
SECOND ED.
by Helen Wattley-Ames
ISBN: 9781877864711
E-ISBN: 9781931930819
US Price: $19.95
UK Price: £10.99